Dam Greed

Frances Brown Dorward

Dam Greed

Frances Brown Dorward

To order additional copies of this book, contact:
Xlibris Corporation
1-888-795-4274
www.Xlibris.com
Orders@Xlibris.com
50199

Contents

Prologue

The Political and Socioeconomic Context

The threat of the Tellico Dam loomed over the valleys of Little Tennessee River and Tellico River from 1937 when brass markers were placed by the Tennessee Valley Authority (TVA) to mark the flooding line. A second stirring to flood the valleys began in 1942 but was stopped by the building restrictions caused by World War II.[1] In October 1964, the Tennessee Valley Authority again threatened to dam the rivers.[2]

The project would involve a six hundred foot-long, one hundred foot-high concrete dam; a 2,500-foot-long earthen dam; and an 850-foot-long, 500-foot-wide canal connecting the new reservoir with Fort Loudoun Reservoir.[3]

There were several drivers for the proposed dam. These included industrial sites,[4] navigable channel for barges,[5] and stopping out-migration of the age bracket twenty—forty from the area.[6] The area designated as prime industrial land is in the vicinity of Vonore where the L & N Railroad tracks and the U.S. Highway 411 cross the new lake. The Tennessee Valley Authority proposed to buy about five thousand acres of the prime industrial sites and sell them to selected developers to control the land use.[7]

The Tellico Reservoir extended commercial navigation almost all the way up the Little Tennessee River to Chilhowee Dam but stopped about four miles short of the dam. The channel, suitable for barge shipping, would also extend fourteen miles up the impounded Tellico River, which emptied into the Little Tennessee at Niles Ferry.[8]

In a speech to a joint meeting of the Kiwanis Club of Maryville and the Maryville-Alcoa Optimist Club on December 8, 1964, Mr. Aubrey Wagner, chairman of the Tennessee Valley Authority, cited economic reasons for the Tellico Project. Mr. Wagner pointed to the out-migration of the age bracket twenty to forty from the area as proof that there are not enough job opportunities in Blount, Monroe, and Loudon counties. In the decade of 1950, there was an actual loss of more than 15 percent in this highly productive group.[9] Young men in the valley had a tradition of leaving their native counties and traveling north to find work in industry. In season, many returned and later migrated north again. The promise to stop this custom was a strong reason to support Tellico Dam.[10]

National politics pointed an accusing finger at the Appalachian Mountain region. The eleven-state Appalachian Mountain region was chosen by Washington as needing fixing and bringing up to a national standard of living.[11]

Lyndon Baines Johnson became the thirty-sixth president following the assassination of John F. Kennedy. President Johnson had served many years in the Senate, and his understanding of how bills and appropriations were passed served him in good stead. He proposed War on Poverty to create new jobs and to build up areas where the economy had faltered. The program to accomplish this was called the Great Society; and a separate piece of legislation, the Appalachia bill, singled out Appalachia for attention.[12]

A critique of economic development reported at the time on television, radio, newspapers, and magazines is beyond the scope of this book. However, Ray H. Jenkins, prominent and nationally known lawyer who grew up in Tellico Plains, summarized the Tennessee Valley Authority's reasons for flooding the valley and buying land above the flood line for resale in his 1978 book.[13] Jenkins wrote it in 1978, so some of the TVA arguments supporting to "flood the valley" are now disproved. However, it is interesting to note the figures he cites from the *Statistical Abstract of the United States*, 1978, and the *Tennessee Statistical Abstract*, 1977. The average per capita income of the United States is reported as $4, 572, and the average per capita incomes for several relevant East Tennessee counties are reported as follows:

Monroe County	$3,009 (behind $1,563)
Loudon County	$3,976 (behind $596)
Blount County	$4,196 (behind $360)[14]

The statistics Mr. Jenkins cites mark the area with less cash but do not reflect the full extent of the resources of residents of the Little Tennessee Valley of that time. Could the area's wealth be found in land, animals, and an independent lifestyle rather than solely in cash income?[15]

This book seeks to document, primarily through eyewitness accounts of those who were present, what actually happened from 1964 until the time water began to cover homesites and cultural artifacts in 1980. Most of these stories are positive and uplifting on a personal level, reflecting the spirit and stamina of the East Tennessee people. However, there are bigger questions raised here that deserve to be more systematically explored. These include the abuse of the law of eminent domain, the arrogant and illegal behavior of a government agency, the failure of the political system to protect the rights of the individual, and the long-term rights of future generations.

The lessons to be learned here, while relevant to environmental protection, cut much more broadly across the expectations of individuals and the obligations of the government. It is only by learning from the lessons of the past that we can prevent their recurrence.

Part One

The Early Fighters, Landowners, Fishermen, and a Historian

Introduction

The Local Response

In the autumn of 1964, a small group of men gathered on the bank of the Little Tennessee River at Rose Island near Vonore. These men knew their counties well and understood politics but lacked the ability of the Tennessee Valley Authority and their employees to get speaking engagements in the small towns or stories in the newspapers. Nevertheless, they stood in the twilight and resolved to ferret out the facts and to try to talk sense about the flooding of the valley and the buying of land to resell.

A bright yellow leaf floated in the October twilight, reminding the men that life and communities are never always the same. The men stood between the children's sandbox and swings, watched the clear white water race along, and thought about how life was always to be reformed. Across the river, green beds of pine seedlings grew in orderly beds of millions of tiny trees.

The men left their vigil by the Little Tennessee River, entered the house, and resolved to organize to preserve the Little Tennessee River valley. John Mowdy Lackey was elected chairman, and C. Griffin Martin, secretary-treasurer. Others present agreed to serve as board of directors: Claude Hammontree, Philip Appleby, Wendell Perry, Clayton Curtis, William Kilpatrick, Judge Sue K. Hicks, Judge Bennie Simpson, and Robert E. Dorward. Judges Hicks and Simpson and Robert Dorward agreed to prepare a constitution, charter, and the bylaws for the new organization, which the group named the Association for the Preservation of the Little Tennessee River.[16]

A meeting was set for the following Wednesday at Rose Island Nursery. Some two hundred attended the organizational meeting—historians, archaeologists, landowners, farmers, and public servants like Judges Sue K. Hicks and Bennie Simpson.[17]

These opponents, and even those who came later, were unable to effectively attack the cost-benefit ratio TVA proposed, largely due to the lack of data and the opacity of the projected financial assumptions. On an emotional level, they knew the project was phony and the destruction of the valley unjustified. TVA proposed to buy 16,500 acres above flooded land to resell for profit. The powerful agency forced the farmers to sell to them at the price set by TVA. TVA later resold the land at a significant profit.[18] How much money was returned to the U.S. Treasury by the Tennessee Valley Authority is unknown.

The law of eminent domain allows the government to buy land in order to help the greater number of people.[19] It is doubtful that this purpose was served in this case. Justice and fairness for the ordinary citizens and the environment were clearly not served. At a minimum, it is questionable practice, and certainly appears to be unethical practice, when a government agency such as TVA resells a homeplace and farm so that a private land developer can build houses and golf courses. Other practices, such as allowing TVA to choose the judges to determine land payments, also are questionable.[20]

The personal stories that follow are evidence of the greed, treachery, and lies that dammed the last thirty-three miles of the Little Tennessee River, covered 14,400 acres of farm and pasture as well as a trout fishery, and abused the use of the law of eminent domain. Justice was denied the poor in order to make work for a government agency in danger of losing its former political luster, to provide cheap land for foreign investors, and to build housing developments and golf courses for out-of-state wealthy.

The stories of faith, hope, and courage of the people who lived in the area will alert all citizens that vigilance is required to protect land, water, fish, and powerless people.

John Lackey Jr. Says Daddy Was Outraged

Evil is for good men to do nothing.
John M. Lackey Sr. paraphrased Edmund Burke (1729-1797)

John Lackey Jr. starts, "My daddy lit the fuse to fight the Tennessee Valley Authority to prevent the destruction of the Little Tennessee River and some of the Tellico River area. He loved farms and valued the assets of the area. My parents never saw their community as needing fixing by the government although they were active Democrats in the local elections. Daddy was six feet tall, muscular with broad shoulders, and civic-minded.[21]

"Dad was born in South Carolina and had worked several places before my mama captured his heart, and they eloped. Dad had a broader, longer-term view of land use than the 'use it, pave it, build it, discard it, and throw it away' attitude of developers today. His friends of like mind were Dr. Bill Kilpatrick, the druggist; Dr. Troy Bagwell, a surgeon and medical doctor; local politician and farmer Claude "Tubby" Hammontree; Beryl Moser, the rural mail carrier; and Bob Dorward and Bill Keithley, the tree farmers. I guess that I could say they were the country capitalists against the city socialists.[22]

"Dad agreed to serve as president of the organization[23] to fight the Tennessee Valley Authority (TVA), who had said the dam would be built only if the people wanted it.[24] Dad worked building Fontana Dam, 1943-1945, so he respected TVA. Like Bill Kilpatrick, Troy Bagwell, Bob Dorward, Judge Simpson, Judge Sue K. Hicks, and others, Dad was a factual-minded man. True, it was an emotional issue, and feelings ran high. But facts about the benefits and the costs were unattainable.[25]

"Dad and Bob Dorward tried to get facts on the cost-benefit ratio TVA was using.[26] Today, I know the numbers were skewed and would not stand up before the scrutiny of minds that understand numbers and can spot sneaky thinking. After the fight was over, Daddy had a book by Professors Wheeler and McDonald that reported about Mr. Aubrey Wagner before a House committee. Mr. Wagner testifies that the Tennessee Valley Authority already owned 3,607 acres of prime industrial land elsewhere in the Tennessee River systems and that another 23,740 acres of prime frontage was in private hands and clearly developable."[27]

John Jr.'s mind floats back to the supper table lectures and defenses made at the Vonore Drug Store. "The Little Tennessee is impounded already by four dams: Fontana, Cheoah, Calderwood, and Chilhowee. The Tellico Dam would impound the last remaining thirty-three miles of the clear, cold river, which heads in North Carolina and flows into Tennessee between the Great Smoky Mountains National Park and the Cherokee National Forest."[28]

Lackey Jr. closes his eyes and recalls the way Dr. Troy Bagwell protected the Indian mounds on his river bottoms and says, "The valley was a treasure trove of archaeology and history. Now archaeology sites are underwater, flooded.[29]

"After I graduated from Tennessee Wesleyan College, Burlington Mills sent me to La Follette, Tennessee, to run a textile factory. A lot of weekends, Bob Dorward, Price Wilkins, and I would float the river and fish. The scenic beauty was unique to the eastern United States, but I am told the White River in Arkansas compares to what was destroyed here." [30]

Lackey Jr. recalls, "I loved the fishing. The brown trout was a native species, but the Tennessee Game and Fish Commission would stock rainbow trout. After they fed in that forty-five- to sixty-six-degree water on the various aquatic flies and bugs for weeks they would be good eating. Bob Dorward was an expert fish fryer, so we ended our float trips at Rose Island picnic area.[31]

"Now so far as I know, my daddy never floated the Little T, but we did go fishing once. Daddy's plan was to throw out a trotline from the bank of the Tellico River on our farm and get some fish from the spring run (spawning). Dad threw out the line from the bank but forgot to tie it to the tree. My daddy hated to make a mistake, so we walked back to the barn and drove back to the house in Vonore."[32]

Lackey Jr. remembers, "At the beginning of the talk about building a dam, my daddy thought arguments against flooding the 14,400 acres would be heard. Dad respected TVA for the progress achieved in bringing electricity to rural Tennessee, so he was unprepared for the struggle to tell the opposition's point of view. Dad quickly learned newspapers, radio stations, and TV stations feared to criticize TVA.[33]

"My daddy and the farmers worked for about sixteen years to try to stop the dam. The Association for the Preservation of the Little Tennessee was organized with Dad as president, Griffin Martin as secretary, and Mrs. Alice Milton as chief pusher. A lot of the 1,200 dues-paying members came from the information she supplied to garden clubs and historians wherever she had a contact.[34]

"Daddy was the front man for the organization in that he was the man who went to testify in Washington before the Committee on Ways and Means and other committees. No, matter how stressful the confrontation, Dad was always the epitome of a Southern gentleman. I think he was the best man to speak for the exploited people."[35]

Lackey Jr. recalls, "Many times, I've heard Daddy and Bob Dorward study facts to bolster their arguments. The Johnson administration and the national press pictured Appalachia barefoot, idle, and hungry. The truth I experienced was busy men, feet shod in work boots, and enough to eat. The school was not a prep school for Harvard, but all children were transported by bus to high school. Hiwassee College in Madisonville could prepare folks for varied work or advanced college work.[36]

"Another thing I want to say," Lackey Jr. continued, "is that I never knew anyone who married their cousin or had a baby with their father. I am sure that such unfortunate stuff might have happened, but it was not common. Monroe County was known nationwide for the finest corn whiskey (white lightning) and home brew (a sort of beer or ale).[37]

"Daddy would fume at TVA's claim that a TVA lake would solve economic problems. He would cite the December 1963 Tennessee Department of Employment Security figures. Monroe County, where 70 percent of the lake would be, had a 4.8 percent unemployment rate. However, Meigs County, where Watts Bar Lake is located, had an unemployment rate of 10.5 percent. Rhea County, where Watts Bar Lake is on the east side of the county, had a 9.4 percent rate of unemployment. Loudon County, where Fort Loudoun Lake is, was 6.6 percent. The overall Tennessee rate was 5.7 percent, and the national, 4.9 percent. Daddy could go on and on with the numbers but didn't know how to get media attention.[38]

"Another argument Dad made was that Monroe County, while poor with 4 percent receiving public assistance, two counties with lakes, Meigs and Rhea, had 6 percent and 5 percent on public assistance. Dad was proud to point out that Monroe County increased in population between 1950 and 1960. However, the two countries with lakes had a 3 percent decrease during the decade.[39]

"My daddy wanted the best for his country and was a strong leader before he worn down, but he was doomed to fail against the vast bureaucracy and a society's disregard for natural resources, like pure water, rich soil, and fishery protection and development. The promises for high-paying jobs[40] persuaded many to want to get rid of the farmers and landowners in favor of forced industrial development.[41]

"A weaker man than my daddy might not have protested, but I'm glad that he tried to help his country and the folks who lived in the Little Tennessee River and Tellico River valleys although I think his failure to save the Little T pushed his death."[42]

Frances Brown Dorward
Remembers Growing Pine Trees

The first time I saw Vonore and Rose Island was a Sunday afternoon in January 1957. We traveled a narrow dirt road and stopped at a weathered farmhouse with a hand-lifting pump in the yard. We drank some cold, sweet well water from our hands and walked to the ford on the slack side of the Little Tennessee River. A steel cable hung from a huge sycamore to a sturdy oak. We climbed into a wooden boat, and Bob worked hand over hand along the cable to the island.

Bob Edgar, president of Hiwassee Land Company,[43] and Louis Camisa, forest manager, hired men looking for a first job. Bob drew maps and worked in the land-management offices for several months. The company's plan was to buy idle farmland and rough mountains suitable for growing pine. The investment in a nursery was vital to keeping the Bowater paper industry working without interruptions. The vision was to work with North Carolina State University in an experimental program to develop pine trees that grew to paper or pulpwood size in less time and are made into superior paper.[44]

The opportunity excited Bob Dorward, who had completed his military obligation as a lieutenant commander in the U.S. Navy. A gentle-teaching grandfather introduced him to growing and nurturing plants in the Green Swamp of Columbus County, North Carolina. His father and mother practiced composing before gardening magazines recommended building up the organic matter in the soil.

The first season the trees were ferried across the river to the farmhouse for packing. That year (1957), nearly six million seedlings were grown. Hiwassee engineer Tom Walbridge with construction superintendent Gene Pendegraph erected a two-hundred-foot bridge to the island out of West coast Douglas fir. Employing only six men, a crane, and a bulldozer, they built the thirty-ton capacity Little Golden Gate Bridge in six weeks. Rose Island was then ready to supply seedlings to the South. A bridge and building for sorting and wrapping the pine seedlings provided large refrigeration rooms, so the seedlings could be kept dormant until the districts in five states were ready to plant. The nursery family and Rose Island Nursery settled into the community. Underemployed farmers from nearby provided the crews. By 1960, one hundred million seedlings were grown; and the next year, twenty-four million.[45]

In order to replace the organic matter in the soil, Dorward planted corn on the resting beds. Some stalks produced five or six ears, so all the workers and their families and even Bowater folks from McMinn and Bradley counties came to pick the corn. Even a public relations professional could not have figured out a better way to make friends.

After the seedlings were grown and weeded, the crews built a picnic area on the north side of the island. Rock from the river made a control wall so that the river could not rush through the sandy beach during spring high water. Picnic tables, a fireplace for fish frying, and a tenting area made it perfect for overnight camping or for putting a boat in after a day's float from Hoss Holt's place near Chilhowee Dam.

Neighbor Kenneth Lane chose the serene beauty of the shady area for his wedding. Boy Scout troops camped on the island, but the Vonore Scouts sometimes wanted a primitive spot and camped on their leader Griffin Martin's farm.[46]

Bob served as treasurer of the Fort Loudoun Association, a private nonprofit organization devoted to preserving the location of the English fort built to protect the East from the French and to make friends with the Cherokee clans by opening trading with South Carolina. He organized and was president of the Vonore Lions Club.[47]

The community welcomed the new family. Both Bob and I shared the sense of soil that planting and growing entail. One of the fond memories was the invitations to Ben and Frances Clark's on New Year's Day to see the Rose Bowl parade. We did not have a television, so the children appreciated the treat of color television. I was awed by the history of the Foute mansion. The Clarks' working farm was profitable at a time when financial success required careful management. Several families lived on the property and worked tending to dairy and beef cattle and growing crops.

Our special friends were John and Patsy Carson, who had backgrounds similar to Bob and mine. The Carson's farm ownership went back four generations; however, Johnny was ready to leave the grueling, marginally profitable dairy business. Therefore, he worked to get the Tennessee Valley

Authority to build the Tellico Dam. As a college-educated couple, they wanted to pay off long-standing banknotes on the land and go on to other work. The debt helped them get a better price from the Tennessee Valley Authority land buyer because they had proof of value.[48]

Before the land-use conflict, the Carsons introduced the newcomers to the county's social life. Bridge dinner parties for couples rotated to different homes; and regularly, I played bridge with Ruth Williams, Rachel Carson, and Patsy Carson. Vonore folks entertained in their homes.

The churches welcomed us also. Mr. Evans from the Vonore Missionary Baptist Church called and insisted he was in dire need of help teaching the teenage class at the vacation Bible school. Bruce was a toddler and, to my horror, took his blanket. To ease my embarrassment, Margaret Evelyn Sheets assured me she thought it cute, just precious. Vonore was a community where children were accepted; even the babies had a place at Bible school.

Since I was a cradle Methodist, at some point Cheryl Carter, who was in my Cadet Girl Scout troop, put her mama up to recruiting me to teach her junior high class at the Vonore United Methodist Church. The remarkable thing was that the two boys and two girls were never absent. Delano and Sharon Frase, another young man, and Cheryl, who was the preacher's daughter, gave me lots of joy that has lingered for over forty years.

At Christmas, a live Santa visited. Missy, my baby, sat on his lap; and Elaine and Bruce stared in awe. John Lackey Sr. was the superintendent of Sunday school at the Vonore United Methodist Church. John Jr. says, "Dad would slip away from the party and appear in his Santa suit. Most of the people couldn't figure out who he was."

Ricky Maynard claims, "My little sisters and brother hadn't a clue it was Lackey."[49]

About 1962, news reached the area that the Tennessee Valley Authority planned to build a dam near Loudon (the town) and flood the valley clear to Citico Creek, about thirty-three miles and fourteen thousand acres underwater. The crowning blow was that land above the waterline would be purchased for resale for industrial development.[50]

Bob Dorward explained the maps to many people and pleaded with the Tennessee Valley Authority for facts concerning the cost-benefit ratio. Even the lawyers at the Bowater's mill at Calhoun couldn't get the information to question the project with facts. Farmers, fishermen, folks who lived in the valley, the Native Americans who cared about the ancient landmarks, and the soil and free-flowing rivers were ignored concerning the benefits. Persons directly involved fought rumor and half-truths.[51]

The county governing body known as the county court, the town mayors, and civic clubs were courted by swarms of Tennessee Valley Authority employees as speakers. City folks were promised prosperity by flooding the valley and moving the landowners out of the three county areas.[52]

In 2008, it is forty-six years since the threat of destruction of the valley in the sixties, or seventy-two years since the first survey of the valley (1937). The threat of being moved out influenced business in a negative way.[53] Since the closing of the dam twenty-seven years ago, changes race to move the former farming and recreational areas to a distribution and manufacturing area. Today, buildings worth millions occupy the former farmland that folks were forced to sell at TVA's price. Thousands drive to Vonore to work. Many of the businesses have tax-exempt privileges, so land taxes of the folks in Monroe County have soared. You might think the immigrants would spend money locally, but some homes are for vacations. Local businessmen complain that some newcomers buy little locally.[54]

By about 1967, the seed orchards and the seedling production were established; and Dorward worked with the community to prevent the flooding of the valley, especially the Rose Island Nursery. I had completed the master's degree program at the University of Tennessee and hoped to work in the local Monroe County School. At this time, the Hiwassee Land Company moved Bob to the central office at Calhoun, Tennessee, to supervise the planting and land preparation for Tennessee, Georgia, Alabama, and Mississippi. Our family of Elaine, ten; Bruce, eight; and Missy, six, moved to Athens, Tennessee.

Our new jobs and location took us from the thick of the controversy. Each spring and summer, we packed up and built a primitive camp on an island in the Little T. When the fish weren't biting, we walked the bottoms of Chota; and after a rain, the arrow points glistened for us to find.

The dam closed in 1980, and Bob packed his clippings and books into boxes and put them in the attic of the farmhouse at the foot of Starr Mountain where I now live alone. My granddaughter Susannah brought them to my attention in 2002 with a phone call from Maryville College. She complained, "My interim ecology class doesn't know anything about the destruction of the Little Tennessee River and the government land grab. My professor wants to invite you to come and tell the class about the struggle to prevent the flooding. This class doesn't even know where Vonore is."

I pulled out fact sheets about the objections to flooding the valley and made some overhead projection slides. The weather turned sour, and the interim classes were cancelled due to ice and snow on two Fridays, and the term ended without hearing my story. My interest was further peaked at the

Vonore library when I read a history of Vonore prepared by Violet Wolfe. The book ended with a statement to the effect, 'A time of turmoil and struggle gripped the area for years due to the building of the Tellico Lake by the Tennessee Valley Authority.' No names, no facts."

A visit to Fort Loudoun State Park revealed that Mrs. Alice Milton's name was nowhere to be seen. The state park and relocated fort would not be there except for the indignation and tireless work of Mrs. Alice Milton, Judge Sue K. Hicks, Bill Selden, Ms. Suzie Williams, Bob Dorward, and others.

I felt this period in the history of the area should be remembered, especially the people whose land was grabbed by the law of eminent domain and resold for housing development instead of the promised factories. I was ignorant of the work required to compile the stories and lacking in boldness to talk to people, but nevertheless, I plodded on collecting first the stories of people that I knew but whom I had not talked to in thirty years or so. Each person sent me to another person, and throughout the years, the personal stories of this book unfolded.

The book is not a proper history, sociological work, or economic comment: it is true as told to and as remembered by persons who were directly involved. The societal change in the area is reflected in the personal stories, and the reader may judge the losses or the advantages.

David Dale Dickey Recollects the Early Fight against Tellico Dam

It seems to me that Bob Burch, a longtime outdoorsman, was the first person to express alarm about the little-known plan of the Tennessee Valley Authority to build Tellico Dam on the Little Tennessee River.[55]

Burch, who was information and education officer for the Tennessee Game and Fish Commission in its Knoxville office, had some inside contacts at TVA who early in the sixties told him that the long-dormant plans for constructing the dam were quietly being resurrected.[56]

Burch and Price Wilkins, cold-water fisheries biologist for the commission, approached Floyd Watson, who was manager of the Knoxville Tourist Bureau, and me (I was industrial director for the Greater Knoxville Chamber of Commerce), asking for our help in opposing the plan.[57] The four of us drove to the White River in Arkansas, a stream similar to the Little Tennessee, to visit Al Gaston's Resort, a prime example of the beneficial use of a free-flowing stream for recreation as opposed to industrial development on a reservoir behind a dam. Burch, Wilkins, and I began a campaign to showcase the assets of the Little Tennessee as a free-flowing stream, which we believed far outweighed the benefits from the proposed dam and reservoir. I believed the Little Tennessee River was a major trout fishery and had industrial-development potential, which a reservoir would not have.[58]

In addition, the thirty-three miles to be drowned by the Tellico Project had irreplaceable scenic beauty and significant archaeological value, was prime farmland, and was the site of a unique tree research facility at Rose Island—all of which would be inundated and lost forever.[59]

Further study showed that TVA's justifications for the dam were tenuous at best. They touted industrial site development while thousands of acres on their mainstream reservoirs were available and unused. Electric power production from the impoundment would be infinitesimal compared with that from the mainstream dams and the coal-fired steam plants, which already provided some 85 percent of TVA's power.[60]

In a meeting of the Knoxville Chamber's industrial committee, Aubrey "Red" G. Wagner, TVA's chairman, stated that the Tellico Dam was merely being considered and that there was "no compelling need" to build it for power or flood control or electric power production. At later meetings elsewhere, Wagner stated publicly that the dam would not be built if people in the affected area did not want it.[61]

However, it was obvious to many this was little more than bureaucratic propaganda. Many persons in the Little Tennessee River valley began to marshal defenses against the project. Meetings were held at Vonore, the principal town along the river, and at Fort Loudoun.[62]

Residents understood TVA could condemn their property and, in effect, confiscate it at a price of its own choosing. The landowners had no legal recourse, even though many families had lived on the river for generations.[63]

My personal role in the effort to preserve the river was to compile information showing the negative effects of the dam and to distribute those facts to legislators and to the press. At the time, I was working on an advanced degree at the Industrial Development Institute at the University of Oklahoma in summer sessions. My thesis project was entitled "The Little Tennessee River as an Economic Resource: A Study of Its Potential Best Use," which demonstrated the immense value of preserving the river. The Tennessee Game and Fish Commission, in its Nashville main office, published the thesis in abbreviated form and made copies available to the public.[64]

Meanwhile, Burch, Wilkins, Bob Dorward of the Rose Island Nursery, Alice Milton of Fort Loudoun, and others jointly developed information sheets and brochures defending the river. A region-wide coalition known as the Association for the Preservation of the Little Tennessee River was formed by citizens opposed to the Tellico Project. Substantial numbers of persons influenced by TVA's promises of economic benefits supported damming the river.[65]

I sent copies of my thesis and many supporting fact sheets to every member of the U.S. House and Senate, with personal letters asking for help in stopping the dam. I was not alone in contacting these legislators. Concerned citizens mailed letters, many handwritten on tablet paper.[66] Eventually an Association for the Preservation of the Little Tennessee River delegation went to Washington to make a direct appeal.[67]

I also sent letters and documents to every major environmental organization in the country—among them the Nature Conservancy, National Wildlife Federation, Izaak Walton League, and other well-known conservation agencies—asking for their endorsement and support. Most of them readily assented. My press campaign needed this support. The Tennessee Outdoor Writers Association had joined our efforts and sent weekly news releases to the media throughout the country.[68]

The *Knoxville News Sentinel,* a longtime major booster of TVA, used none of the facts we provided despite personal visits by Burch, Wilkins, and me to present our case. *News Sentinel* writers were prohibited from writing stories in opposition to the dam, a sad day in that newspaper's otherwise illustrious history.[69]

On the other hand, Guy Smith, editor of the *Knoxville Journal,* told us that he would publish any legitimate news we could provide. He did. The *Journal* was a longtime opponent of TVA projects; but Smith warned us, with bitterness, "You can't beat the bastards." Ultimately, he was right, but we gave him lots of good ammunition. A stalwart in our fight was the *Journal's* outdoor columnist, Walter Amann, who hammered away ceaselessly at TVA's arrogance.[70]

It was Amann and Bob Burch who enlisted the help of the Cherokee Indians in opposing the dam project. They drove to the Quall Reservation at Cherokee, North Carolina, and prevailed on the tribe to send representatives in full costume to a major meeting planned at Fort Loudoun to demonstrate opposition to the destruction of river and ancient village sites.[71]

Although the Cherokees had shown little interest, they knew the Little Tennessee was the site of Chota, the sacred capital city of their ancestral Overhill Cherokees, along with other Indian villages, including the birthplace of Sequoyah, inventor of the Cherokee alphabet.[72]

Harvey Broome,[73] a past president of the Wilderness Society and a hiking companion and personal friend of Supreme Court Justice William O. Douglas, arranged for Justice Douglas to come to the river to receive a written appeal from the Cherokees to save the river and their ancient homelands. Justice Douglas presented their document to Congress.[74]

Justice Douglas received an assignment from *National Geographic* magazine to write an article about the Little Tennessee River and the efforts to preserve it. Photographers from the magazine documented its natural assets and beauty. Ultimately, *National Geographic* canceled the article. It is rumored that political pressure caused the rejection because the magazine, a nonprofit, benefits from government grants.[75]

My personal involvement nearly cost me my job with the Knoxville Chamber of Commerce where I was employed for ten years. TVA chairman Wagner went so far as to summon the entire chamber board of directors to meet with him at TVA headquarters where he insisted I be fired. Fortunately, there were members of the chamber board who did not agree with Mr. Wagner, and I survived.[76]

My direct efforts in opposition to the dam ended in about 1970 when I moved from Knoxville to a new job. By that time, many organizations and individuals had joined the battle; and soon, the famous "snail darter" controversy arose. I must leave that story to others.[77]

November 29, 2003

Alice Warner Milton was a Little Thorn by Frances Brown Dorward and assisted by Bill Selden

A little thorn moved the Tennessee Valley Authority to preserve a relic of the French and Indian War. Fort Loudoun was built in the classic English style on the Little Tennessee River near the mouth of the Tellico River. The purpose of the fort was to stop the French from uniting with the Indians and making all the area west of the Appalachian Mountains French. Fort Loudoun, built by the colony of South Carolina from 1756 to 1757, was located by the request of the Cherokee Indians on the Little Tennessee River in the midst of the Overhill Cherokee towns and near their principal town of Chota.[78]

Alice Warner Milton came to Vonore to direct the Fort Loudoun Association, a private group who owned the land and preserved the site. She was a tiny woman but a thorn to TVA. Like a creeping sharp vine, she knew people all over the state of Tennessee and in Washington DC. If not known to her personally, she knew who to contact them in order to get support. Her devotion to history earned respect and an audience who listened to her point of view.[79]

When she learned of TVA's plan to flood the Little Tennessee Valley, she organized committees within the Fort Loudoun Historical Association. Individuals tried to get information from TVA. No compromises could be reached. The site of the English fort against the French and Indians would be underwater like the Cherokee Indian villages of Toqua, Little Toqua, Chota, Rose, or Mialaque Island—landmarks and farms for thirty-three miles. The dam would back up water from the mouth of the Little Tennessee River at Fort Loudoun Dam near Loudon to near Calderwood Dam, covering fourteen thousand acres. The Tennessee Valley Authority proposed to buy five thousand acres near Vonore exclusively for industrial development.[80]

Educated and intelligent, Mrs. Milton worked and never let up. She enlisted the aid of farmer and community leader John Lackey, forester Bob Dorward at Rose Island Nursery, Toqua farmer Griffin Martin, Judges Sue K. Hicks and Bennie Simpson, and hundreds more. With the help of Judges Hicks and Simpson, she urged the organization of a local group to fight TVA. When the senators, Albert Gore and Howard Baker, and representatives, Bill Brock and John Duncan Sr. asked for letters of support or opposition to the dam: Mrs. Milton made certain letters were sent from all over the state to Washington, DC. At the beginning of the protest, the local people believed their problem with TVA was personal and local. Her experiences let her know it would be settled on a national level.[81]

The rumors were that Alice Milton was a rich widow who owned a house on Signal Mountain, Chattanooga. It is true she knew all the people interested in historical preservation and garden clubs and also people in the Democratic Party organization. Boldly, she asked for their letters to Washington.[82]

One example will show how she endeared herself to her friends. When former senator Carey Estes Kefauver died, Miss Alice was at the Kefauver mansion in Madisonville with punch and refreshments. She was a close friend of Miss Lottie, Estes's sister, and she had worked in the senator's office in Washington DC. Mrs. Milton was a friend of people in the Republican Party. Her friends secured the help of Representative Bill Brock. Her organizational skills helped select the people to appear before the congressional committees. She was not shy in reminding organizations the Association for the Preservation of the Little Tennessee River needed funds to send their president, farmer John M. Lackey, to Washington for his presentations before congressional committees.[83]

When Justice William O. Douglas indicated his plan to prepare an article for the *National Geographic* magazine, Mrs. Milton planned the route for the photographer and for Mrs. Douglas's interviews. Miss Alice knew the history of all the families and farms. At one old mansion, Mrs. Douglas admired an old brown Coke bottle used as a vase for daisies on a round cherry table. The young man insisted she take it as a remembrance.[84]

It was a cool spring day, and Mrs. Milton had grabbed a ragged and worn sweater. She met the guide, Fran Dorward, and the visitors at Johnnie Bell Kirkland's restaurant at Chota. Later, Johnnie Bell wondered how she got past Mrs. Grace McCammon in that sweater with the elbows out. Alice lived with Miss Grace, a widow, who farmed a large tract on the river near the fort. Mrs. Milton concentrated on the important issues but could appear in a worsted wool suit with bound buttonholes.[85]

The struggle to stop the TVA moved on for years. One by one, the landowners settled with TVA, moved away, and stopped coming to the "Save the Little T" meetings. Sarah Simpson Bivens remembers how Mrs. Milton encouraged her magazine, *Southline.* By this time, Mrs. Milton had moved to Chattanooga, but her heart continued in the battle carried by the snail darter environmentalists and the Cherokee Indians. The struggle to save the Little Tennessee River valley and Fort Loudoun moved to the federal government.[86]

The outcries and protests eventually caused TVA to raise the entire fort area seventeen feet to form a peninsula near the original site of the fort. From pictures, a replica of the fort was built and is now Fort Loudoun State Park. After TVA condemned the property, they gave it to the State of Tennessee for use as a park, and TVA built a modern visitors' center at its expense.[87]

Bill Selden of Athens was a member of the Fort Loudoun Association and is a well-known regional historian. His contribution to Mrs. Milton's story is appreciated.

No plaques or the film at the new park mention the little thorn that caused such a sting. However, all who lived though the defeat know the replica would not tell the story about Fort Loudoun, the English, and the Cherokee Indian if it had not been for the pain the little thorn caused.[88]

Roy and Burma Kennedy Fret No More

Rest in the Lord, and wait patiently for Him;
Do not fret because of him who prospers in his way,
Because of the man who brings wicked schemes to pass.
Cease from anger and forsake wrath;
Do not fret—it only causes harm.
—Psalm 37:7-8, NKJV

Roy and Burma Kennedy's beautiful spacious house looks toward the Smoky Mountains and down the hill at cattle grazing in lush pasture. It is January 29, 2003, and they are the first neighbors that I asked about their memories of the fight to save the Little T. Burma is a petite, beautiful, professionally coifed lady. Roy stands straight and looks toned. He announced that he is eighty-one years old, and he is farming fifty-two acres in Blount County near Greenback, Tennessee. They built this house thirty-two years ago after having been forced to move by the use of the law of eminent domain in order to flood the valley for redevelopment. Roy is retired from Rittenbach Engineering of Knoxville, and Burma from the Greenback Merchant and Farmers Bank.

They built their first home from scratch. They bought fifty acres from Burma's parents, the Att Millsaps, and enjoyed their hilltop for six years. They looked down on Rose Island in the Little Tennessee River. The beauty of the fog rolling down the river remains a treasured memory. In season, they watched the beds of pine seedlings planted, nurtured, and taken up to replant the southeastern United States.

Roy and Burma believed they had the best home and community that God could provide anyone. They heard rumors. Then news releases from the Tennessee Valley Authority confirmed the fears. Burma recalls, "I was angry and fretted and worried."

Roy explains, "TVA strung it out. It was talked about before World War II.[89] The dam talk died down, so we built our house. I wanted to breed purebred cattle, so I went to Senator Albert Gore's cattle auctions and bought the best. TVA kept it quiet and surprised everybody when the dam was proposed again in 1962 or so.[90] After years of efforts to preserve the river, the water rose quickly and again surprised everybody. I thought it was still before Congress. It was done so quickly that the land up Citico was not cleared of brush. That was thirty years ago, but I remember all the meetings and letters people wrote."

Roy recalls that the river had many places where the trout grew large and sweet. He frowned. "Fish don't do good in that lake. The TVA stocked it and stocked it with bass, but it is hard for me to catch a fish there. When the water can't flow, the trout can't grow and reproduce. Most of the boats that I see on Sunday when Burma and I go back to the Vonore Baptist Church go up and down the river, making waves for the few who try to fish."

Burma put in her opinion, saying, "The lakeshore is about at the old county road, so our place was not covered by the lake. Thirty years has brought vast changes to the area. On some of the twenty-two thousand acres adjacent to the shoreline that TVA purchased to regulate development and maximize their project, there are some huge businesses at Vonore. Of course, only 5,000 acres are near Vonore, and the lake covers 16,500 acres. It surprised me that the impoundment goes more than twenty miles up the Tellico River.[91] Every time I hear the name of the lake, I burn hot. Not an acre near Tellico Plains was grabbed for development or flooding. I guess that Mr. Charles Hall, the telephone man, protected his town."

The Kennedys appreciate their life and the government of their county. Roy warns, and Burma nods in agreement. "People got to watch what goes on in Washington. When Albert Gore got to the Senate, he forgot the people like us. Gore wanted federal money and didn't care about the farmers and the people whose land TVA bought to make a profit. No barges come up that lake, and I don't know a soul who works at the businesses at Vonore, but thousands drive there every day. It was a wicked scheme of lying and greed, but I say, 'No use being mad about it from this distance in time.'"[92]

Milred Lane Enjoys the Company
of the Righteous

The fool has said in his heart, "There is no God."
They are corrupt. They have done abominable works:
God is with the generation of the righteous
You evildoers frustrate the plans of the poor,
But the Lord is their refuge.
—Psalm 14:1, 5, 6 NKJV, verse 6 paraphrased

Mildred Williams Lane called the children who lived nearby to help her tell her story. She points to the large photograph over the sofa. My great-grandmother was half Cherokee but was married to a white man. They hid out on Jake Best Creek and escaped the removal between the years 1830 and 1838.[93]

"I think I look a bit like my grandmother. She was tall and thin. I grew up on a farm in Loudon County. My husband, Ralph, grew up at Morganton Ferry where Rarity Bay is now. We farmed there until we went to Junior Pugh's place. Ralph and I and the children farmed the east end of Rose Island until TVA bought it. My children are Richard, Kenneth, Judy, and Debbie. Except for Ken, they live near.

"We made a family party of planting tobacco and handing it in the fall. Ralph grew corn and soybeans, and my boys worked hard. The children roamed the woods near the house on the mainland. Hunting for rabbits and quail on the island gave us many good suppers. The children and I grew a garden and had chickens. We had a slow, good life. The seasons and the weather dictated it.

"I worked at a sewing factory in Madisonville. Twice a year, the company let us buy dresses for our family. My girls always looked pretty. That was before girls wore pants out in public. Britches were for driving the tractor or getting in hay.

"When TVA bought the farm, Ralph was beside himself. He and Junior Pugh could not find good farmland to buy. Ralph and I had farmed since childhood, but Ralph made friends with one of the TVA land buyers. He complained that TVA was taking away the only way that he had to make a living for his four children and wife. Ralph kept asking the man to get him a job. 'TVA is taking my livelihood. TVA should give me a job,' he kept arguing.

"The man helped us. Ralph went to his first hired-out job. Ralph never wasted anything on the farm. The way TVA burned good leftover material made him sick. He worked until the dam was finished, but he was thankful to get that job. We fought to save the river every way we knew, but after we lost, I am glad that Ralph could work for TVA.

"The sewing factory closed about a year after the union came in. It was moved to Central America, so I got a job at Loudon making boat covers for the Great Lakes Boat Top. When GLBT opened a factory at the TVA industrial park, I moved to that job.

"We bought a house at Vonore so Debbie, our youngest, could graduate from Vonore High School. After the families were moved out, the county closed the high school. The period of shock when nothing was happening lasted for years, but now the Vonore Elementary has seven hundred or more children.

"Thank goodness, the county is healing. People are moving in, and the factories are busy. I don't know anyone working at Vonore right now, but people drive in from miles around.

"After Ralph died, the house at Vonore was lonely. So when Richard learned the house next to him was for sale, I moved here. I'm happy up on my hill with only one acre. Our neighbors are helpful and friendly. Judy's boys are twenty-one and twenty-four now and come by often. Richard's boys come over every day. I like it here. I belong to the hiking club, and I enjoy the mountain trails.

"Here comes my oldest son, Richard, and his wife, Sandra. They have been married about seven years. Richard has two sons, fourteen and eighteen. And Sandra has a daughter, seventeen. The teenagers keep us busy. I try not to miss one of their games."

Richard looks like his dad. He is six feet and has very broad shoulders. He begins, "Vonore and Rose Island were the best places to grow up. I played football. I took off the football uniform and put on my basketball uniform.

Then I played baseball in the spring. The high school years were good for Kenny and me and prepared us for Hiwassee College.

"Now I sell real estate and pastor the Friends Church at Rafter. I started off in the Methodist Church as a child. I was a Baptist for a while. I tell the people at Rafter that I'm just a country farm boy. I didn't come to change their church but to help them have church their way. The Quakers are good to me and our children.

"This fall, I took my boys on the juvenile deer hunt on TVA land. Some of our old farm is above water, also the Att Millsaps', the Carters', and the Kennedys' farms. The land has grown up in trees and brambles. The road is gone, but we walked back to the old woods where Kenny and I played as children. I showed my boys where Kenny and I carved our initials on a sycamore tree and the year '1961.'

"When we were growing up, we rented boats at Hoss Holt's near Chilhowee Dam and floated the river many times. Hoss would pick up the boats at the picnic area on Rose Island."

"Did you know that Kenny got married at the Rose Island picnic area? Mama, please show us the picture. It is the only picture we have of the river."

Richard grinned. "Mama could always catch the most fish. Daddy liked to take Mama and his children fishing. It was $3 a day to rent an aluminum johnboat. We floated three to a boat.

"I really hated to lose the fight to save the Little Tennessee River. We went to all the meetings and did all that we could. The bitterness and feeling is still strong in the community. I remember the day Mr. Harrison came to the house to tell Daddy that he had sold out to TVA. He just cried and cried. In six months, he was dead.

"My daddy was lucky to get a job building the dam. Daddy and Junior Pugh, who owned the land we worked, looked everywhere. But they could not find land to buy that was fit to farm. The soil on Rose Island was twenty inches deep and so rich that Daddy made a profit for us and Mr. Pugh. Folks who haven't planted beans and corn and watched them grow can't appreciate that we considered working the soil a sacred trust from God. When such rich soil is covered by water, it is gone forever.[94] Maybe I need to let Judy talk before I sound like I'm in the pulpit. Mr. Pugh worked at Oak Ridge ever since it was a secret place, but he hated to let the family land go. When the weather was right for planting or combining, he was taking his turn on the tractor or planter. Some men play cards or go to movies, but he felt happy seeing the soybeans and corn growing."

Judy has listened to her mother and brother and waited her turn. Judy lives with her two sons near the old Morganton Ferry where her parents started married life. She is in the Lakeside community about three miles from the new lake through Rarity Bay development.

Her life as a divorced registered nurse is full and happy. She enjoyed tours of work in the Caribbean as a labor and delivery room nurse. After 9/11, she returned home to work at Sweetwater Hospital, caring for newborn babies and in the labor and delivery room. She has worked all night and cut her sleep short to tell her story.

"I remember what good times we had growing up. We felt safe. I rode my bicycle about four miles on our dirt road and along the river on the other side of Highway 411 to visit my friend. Playing basketball in high school kept me busy, but all the teachers pushed us to learn all we could."

Debbie Lane encouraged me to write this book. She changed from spin fishing to fly-fishing. She said, "Folks did not know what they had until it was gone."

The writer remembers the night Judy worked as a babysitter for my three children. Bowater employees had a Christmas party at the Springbrook County Club in Athens, so Mildred let her come to spend the night even though she was only thirteen.

In the sixties, weather happened, and no announcements warned folks. When we left the party, the road had several inches of ice. The forty-minute trip from Athens took three hours. The ice and snow piled on the windshield, but we were almost the only car on Highway 411. We kept moving because we feared Judy would wake up and learn we had not returned. It was a blessing to have neighbors like the Ralph Lane family.

Richard Lane and The Hunt

Crunch, crunch, crackle, crunch
The dry leaves sound an alarm.
My sons with fresh hunter-training certificates
voice excitement.
Their first deer hunt starts.

Deep red locust and sweet gum catch the early-morning light.
The overgrown farm, once fertile and productive, is now wasted land
except for TVA's once yearly
juvenile hunt.
Blackberry briars give evidence of deer hair.
Their worn, eroded path is smooth.
Deep red leaves of honeysuckle catch the sunlight.

Shoo, shoo,
I put my finger to my lips.
A cheerleader's voice asks
Can the deer hear us?
My lips push tight.
The questioner repeats.
Can the deer hear us?
His brother answers
and smells us too.
Shut up.

I walk back into my childhood.
The bramble wasteland is Att Millsaps' old farm,
once the living for a family.
The Tennessee Valley Authority
decided to take the farmer's land.
The authority decreed the river must go.
Floating the Little Tennessee River enriched my youth.
It is no more.

Where is the farm where I labored as a youth?
I guide my sons to mature woodland.
A poor place to find deer
I look for landmarks.
The sycamore tree stands,
tall scaly bark
beside the spring.
I reach out,
touch my initials
RL and Kenny's, KL, 1961
We were twelve and fourteen
roamed the woods,
fished the river,
hunted quail, rabbits, and squirrels.
All recleaned and cooked
by our indulgent mother.
It was a slow childhood.
No one hurried us to grow up.

Life taught us.
Day by day with our parents and sisters
We plowed.
We planted.
We gathered.

I show my initials.
My boys are unimpressed.
Didn't you have anything else to do?
I'm sweatin'. Let's go home.
My TV show will be on.

I place each one
at a likely place,
instruct them to wait.
Let the deer come near.

I go sit,
and stare
at the evidence
of a time.
The time before my family
was rescued from poverty
by TVA,
and I was forced to be a city man.

Richard Lane's thoughts as captured by Fran Dorward

JD and Elizabeth Galyon Say
Life Is Like a Ladder

For He [God] will deliver the needy when he cries,
The poor also, and him who has no helper.
He will spare the poor and needy,
And will save the souls of the needy.
—Psalm 72:12-13, NKJV

No one should be shaken by these afflictions.
—First Thessalonians 3:3, NKJV

Elizabeth and J. D. Galyon welcomed me to their home on Sinking Creek Road near Greenback, Tennessee. Elizabeth telephoned her daughter, Gail, who lives near her parents. The Galyons have lived there thirty-two years, but health problems scaled down their farming. They moved into a one-story house, selling some of their farm and their large house.

They are at peace about their removal by TVA and hope their hill is high enough this time. Elizabeth remembers losing their farm in Harden Valley for Center Hill Dam. JD laughs. "We are double-displaced persons. We are not mobile people. I like my roots, and I want to know my neighbors.

"We had 230 acres on the Little Tennessee River. TVA promised to help us find a place to move but never did." Elizabeth recalls, "You had to put the money they paid back into land. One of the most humiliating times was the Internal Revenue Service. They treated us like crooks. They didn't even offer us a chair. They acted like it was their money, and we were thieves. That was the IRA, not Tennessee Valley Authority."

Gail reminds her daddy how hard he worked on the farm. He worked in Oak Ridge all day. Before daylight, he would ready the mower for Johnny to mow hay. Johnny could drive the tractor after the mower was in place. JD would bale the hay after the nearly two-hundred-mile commute.

JD agreed with Gail that he worked hard on his cattle farm. "I always told you kids, life is like a ladder. Every time you get to the top rung, somebody knocks you in the head. You start over again."

JD explains that he has put bathrooms in five houses. "Every time I move, I have to fix up," he said.

JD has powerful opinions on education. His granddaughter, who listened to the conversation, attends an innovative year-around school in Maryville, Tennessee. JD recommends education. "I served in the navy and went to every school I could," he said.

Gail, his daughter, is a registered nurse. When questioned about what she did, she said, "I work in a GI lab."

JD laughed and explained, "That means butts and guts." Gail nodded and said that she had done these exams for about ten years. Immediately, after high school, Gail joined the air force. During this time, she received her nursing training, married, and had children. After a divorce, she returned to East Tennessee.

JD summed up his life. "I'm in good shape for the shape I'm in. My heart doctor says so." Elizabeth and Gail agreed the family is strong and showed me pictures of Johnny who also lives in the area.

When Elizabeth lived on the farm next to the nursery, we spent time watching our preschool daughters play. I think neither of us realized how young we were or how outside events would separate our friendships. My box of newspaper clippings has a letter to the editor that she wrote protesting the flooding of the valley, but her family was swept along by the societal changes decreed by socialist's planners without regard to her opinion. As JD might say, "We got knocked off the ladder of life, but we stood up as soon as we got our breath back."

January 30, 2003

Sarah Simpson Bivens Used a Ballpoint Pen as Her Weapon

Sarah Ann Simpson Bivens lives on the original land grant made to her great-great-grandfather, Benjamin Talbert Simpson. The ridge overlooks the bottoms that reach to Harrison Bend on the Tennessee River and now pasture her beloved horses. Harrison was a maternal ancestor, and the Harrison Bend Road ends at the Simpson antebellum mansion.[95]

Her great-great-grandmother was a Blair. The Blair farm was on the north side of the Tennessee River. Captain John Blair fought in the Revolutionary War and is known for his part in the Battle of King's Mountain in North Carolina.[96]

Judge Bennie or Benjamin Bailes Simpson, Sarah Ann's father, was famous for his values and idealism. He loved nature, the soil, and respected all that God created. He may be labeled a transcendentalist. Before the environmentalist movement was popular, he insisted on sorting the trash. All that could return to the soil made compost. All that would not rot went to the dump. He defined the environment as how all of life worked together.[97]

Judge Bennie Simpson was a stanch conservative Republican. On December 18, 1973, Richard Nixon signed the Environmental Protection Act into law. "The Democrats try to take loud credit as being the environment party, but the Republicans started protecting the environment," Sarah Simpson Bivens has heard her daddy proclaim.[98]

Bennie Simpson worked in the U.S. State Department as an economic attaché. He served in the Foreign Service before returning to Loudon to work as an attorney. Later, he served as county judge for many years. As judge, Bennie Simpson believed an individual had the right to own land. He was convinced the Association for the Preservation of the Little Tennessee River had a strong case to take to the Supreme Court. He was outraged that a government agency could condemn land and resell it for a profit. As an educated economist and lawyer, he saw the Tellico Project as a land grab. The Tennessee Valley Authority forced the landowners to sell at TVA's price, and the landowner had to appeal to a three-judge court controlled by TVA. Simpson argued it was a misuse of the law of eminent domain, which permits a government agency to take land for the good of all the people.[99]

Tennessee Valley Authority workers made presentations to civic groups, governing bodies, and clubs.[100] As an economist, Simpson suspected the cost-benefit ratio.[101] He boldly explained the cause and effects of the destruction of the valley by the narrow lake that proposed to make no power, provide no flood control, but would move people away. Land was taken from the tax base.[102] Unfortunately, many government and community leaders heard TVA lies and half-truths and hopped on the bandwagon to build the Tellico Dam.[103] The first action of TVA after buying the farmland was to sell it for housing. Tellico Village brought new homeowners to Loudon County. Rarity Bay, Harbor Place, Foothills Points, and other developments were later established: and debate continued concerning the economic controversy.[104]

Bennie Simpson urged the farmers to stick together, but TVA used the divide-and-conquer method to demoralize the affected citizens. First, they bought out prominent absentee landowners, such as Ray Jenkins's farm near where the dam was built.[105]

TVA ignored the court order (Sixth Circuit Court of Appeals) to stop building the dam while the snail darter[106] controversy was argued in court by continuing to buy out the small farmers.[107] Sarah S. Bivens said, "Proposals to save the land and free-flowing river were ignored by the Tennessee Valley Authority because the agency needed to keep their employees working. Landowners were told that condemnation was certain and that the buyer's price must be accepted. Daddy knew that the dam was first proposed in 1937 and how the threat of the flooding had worn out the fight in the landowners. The average price paid was $380 per acre, but persons with high debt on their land got more. A few people went to the courthouse and raised the appraised value for taxes on their land, and that helped them get more.[108]

"My daddy was a tall strong man who sincerely believed the Tellico Dam project lacked merit. He was recognized in Loudon County by his snow-white hair, strong back, and erect carriage. But in his last year, he became blind and ill and could not continue his protest.[109]

"I graduated from the University of Tennessee at Knoxville with a bachelor degree in journalism and went on to Ringling School of Art in Sarasota, Florida, to refine my art. For a time, I taught horseback riding and art at Hiwassee College, Madisonville. I worked with editor Dan Hicks on the *Tri-County Observer*. I found Hicks in TVA's pocket and listening to his advertisers, who expected the dam to make them wealthy. Editor Dan Hicks pushed hard for the building of Tellico Dam. Occasionally, I was allowed to write a feature story opposing the dam. After a time, I became disgusted with the bias and false slant to Hick's editorials.[110]

"I left the *Tri-County Observer* to start a magazine, *Southline: A Magazine of the Country South*. Every issue pointed out reasons to stop building the dam, which was nearly completed. I recall that the greatest number of subscriptions came from Oklahoma because of the Cherokee Indians' interest in the sacred tribal sites, such as Chota and Toqua. The magazine had readers in all fifty states; however, it was money in and money out. After three years of showing no profit, I ceased publication. That was my proudest contribution to the fight, but it proved to be too little too late.[111]

"Mrs. Alice Milton, curator of Fort Loudoun, encouraged me. Mrs. Milton had fought long and hard to influence the Tennessee Valley Authority to spare the historic British fort of the French and Indian War. Even after she was removed, her frequent factual and helpful letters continued. She lost her struggle, and the original fort is underwater today. However, she is remembered for her spunk and courage. I suspect Mrs. Milton enrolled subscribers for the *Southline* magazine.[112]

"Alfred David was president of a landowner's association, and he sent an article or a letter that I wrote and was published in the *Knoxville Journal* to the CBS *60 Minutes* show. *60 Minutes* sent a film crew. And David Smiley, the photographer for *Southline*, and I led the crew to Ms. Nellie McCall's home. I remember the event differently from the report by historians Wheeler and McDonald in their book *TVA and the Tellico Dam Project 1936-1979*.[113]

"Big orange barrels and tape blocked the road to the McCall farm, but I remember leading the crew through the woods. We lay on our bellies for a long time watching, but they got excellent pictures of the wrecking ball destroying Miss Nellie's home. She was one of three who held out until the federal marshals served papers on them. The loss of the homeplace broke the valiant old woman, and she did not live too long after her failure to keep her home, which was not under the water of the new lake.[114]

"The CBS *60 Minutes* program was well received. I'm still glad I could serve as their guide. I was the activist and hippie that every parent cringes to have in the family.[115]

"Beryl Moser invited David Smiley and me into his home to photograph the federal marshal serving him papers. I knew we were recording the ordinary citizen being overridden by the determined bureaucracy of Tennessee Valley Authority. David got an excellent picture of the face of the federal marshal. It was a perfect example of the misuse of the law of eminent domain. Beryl Moser got $12,000 for his house, outbuildings, and land. He is a poor man in worldly goods, but rich in integrity and courage.[116]

"Another way I tried to stop the dam was by working with the Cherokee Indians from Oklahoma. I am an activist who slept on the ground at Chota with the Oklahoma Cherokee Indians who came to register their protest at the flooding of their sacred lands. Vice Chief Hair of the Oklahoma Cherokees adopted me and made me an honorary member of the tribe. This framed certificate is kept with other mementos of my fighting days."[117]

In January 2004, Sarah Ann lives with her husband in a very old and modest cottage on the original land grant left to her and her brother, Benjamin. Benjamin lives in the mansion that was originally built by great-great-grandfather Benjamin Talbert Simpson. The cottage is decorated with the Bivens' art, and more work is in process.

She complains, "My husband never wants to proclaim his paintings finished."[118] Sarah Ann loves the quiet and serenity of her woodland trails where she rides her horses and goes for long walks with her collie mix. The last few years were spent nursing her frail mother, who died in October 2003 at age ninety. She remembers the boxes tucked away with a historical novel that needs editing and an agent. Her hippie years as a street artist and her time as a political activist seem part of a long-gone past as she enjoys each beautiful day on her ridgetop.[119]

Mabel and Charles Niles Felt
the Price of Progress

Charles and Mabel Niles live down a narrow but paved lane, Ingram Road, or County Road 350. It is off Oak Grove Road about a mile from Oak Grove Church. The fair May day highlighted tulip poplar flowers. Below the tree, strawberry blossoms flourished. A huge bed of yellow trillium and wild iris show the tender nurture of the botanist.[120]

Mabel Cannon Niles says, "I came to Blount County after the damming of the Clinch River for Norris Dam. Charles Niles and I married over fifty years ago, and I taught second grade, and he high school science. In our seventh decade, Charles is my caregiver now. He suffered a major stroke twelve years ago and limps but can write, read, and speak clearly and with ease. Our farming is limited to mowing our hayfields."[121]

Charles Niles says, "I grew up near Vonore. My great-great-grandfather had a fifteen-thousand-acre land grant following the removal of the Cherokees about 1830. My great-great-grandmother was a McGhee, a family with extensive holdings in the Little Tennessee River valley. Both families were slave owners. Later, the land was rented and then sold, except for my father's small farm.[122]

"In the late twenties when I was born, my father farmed thirty-two acres near Vonore. Tobacco, milk, and soybeans were the cash crops. I bought three acres of the original land grant near Fort Loudoun to build my home. My grandfather John Niles was noted for his twenty teams of mules and extensive farming business. He owned Rose Island and had rental families on several farms."[123]

Charles Niles states, "My plan was to move my house to this land when I determined the fight to save the valley was lost. The Tennessee Valley Authority (TVA) refused to let me do that. The house still stands on Fort Loudoun State

Park. For a time, a park ranger lived there, but the state has let it run down. The property isn't kept up, and the area is now a game preserve.[124]

"I carried my daddy all over McMinn and Monroe counties looking for a farm he could buy. TVA only paid him $16,000 for the land, house, and barns. I would drive, and Daddy would cry. I was able to get this farm for him to work as long as he was able. It really broke him to lose his farm. That land is above water. And TVA has let it grow up into brambles, weeds, and native hardwoods.[125]

"There was no fairness to the land buying. I tried to talk to Mr. Woodward, the TVA land buyer. He told me to take his offer or go to court. He said, 'You can't win an appeal. TVA picks the judges, a three-person commission.'[126]

"An example of unfairness was Lon Stamey, who was paid $16,000 for one acre. Lon Stamey worked for TVA. My daddy worked for himself, and his little farm was his only living. It was a sad time for the farmers.[127]

"This place is an ideal garden spot. Since Mabel bumped her head and lost her short-term memory, I've cut down the size of my vegetable garden, but I've found the ideal tomato. It can grow to two or three pounds. Instead of my gardening, I spend my days with the cooking and cleaning and being with Mabel.[128]

"My mama liked to tell the story of my birth. When her time came, Dr. McCollum came to the house to wait on her. When he delivered me, Mama said that he said it is another Tom Hughes. Tom Hughes was my cousin who was seven feet tall. I was a long thin baby, but I'm only six feet, seven inches tall.[129]

"When I was in third grade, I got shot in the eye with an arrow. A cataract developed, and by the time I was in high school, the doctors removed the eye. I taught biology and chemistry for forty years: seventeen years at Vonore High School, thirteen years at Madisonville High School, and ten years at Hiwassee College. I have excellent peripheral vision. Some of the students swore I had an eye in the back of my head.[130]

"I graduated second in my class from Vonore High School, but Betty Moser Black beat me by one-half point for valediction. We both went to Maryville College. The tuition was $75 a semester, and the room and board was $225. I had a scholarship and trapped to earn some cash. A mink hide sold for $50, and a muskrat brought $4 or $5. It was easier to trap muskrat. I could see from the boat where to put the trap. My brother loved to hunt quail, but I loved to fish.[131]

"One time, I caught a forty-pound catfish. I tied it to the boat and got my daddy to help me get it into the boat. Now we are told not to eat a fish from the lake if it is over fifteen pounds. The PVCs get in the fatty fish. I've always enjoyed fishing and walking, but the impoundment of the Little Tennessee River killed the river species. TVA keeps stocking it with bass, but they don't seem to thrive.[132]

"I have a bed of Tennessee wild iris shaped like a heart in the yard here. It is about five feet in diameter now. The wild iris is the Tennessee state flower. I moved them from my favorite place for fishing from the bank. I also moved a bed of yellow trillium from under the railroad bridge. The Little Tennessee Valley was rich in hundreds of wildflowers. I'm glad I saved a few before the water covered the land.[133]

"I remember when Johnson grass came to the Little Tennessee River valley. In 1933, a terrible drought ruined the hay crop. Hay was shipped in from Texas by railroad cars. We scattered it on Rose Island for the cows. That's how that pest got here. I was six years old that winter and helped my daddy and Grandpa Niles. Cane grew on the east end of the island. The cows could get fat on that most winters, but that year, the folks bought hay.[134]

"I can remember twice that the spring rains almost covered the 360 acres of the island. All the rabbits gathered in about a five-acre dry space. The boys from Vonore came with sticks and slingshots and killed rabbits. Everyone ate rabbits for weeks, and we sold the skins. A big haystack floated down the river with a great red rooster perched on top. It was such a funny sight that no one can forget seeing it.[135]

"Rose Island grew beautiful holly. Every Christmas, I gathered some for church and for my mama to decorate. I rooted a sip of the *Ilex opaca*, or American holly, from the bush near the old farmhouse near the ford. I remember a weeping willow tree and a hand-crank pump in the yard. I liked the water at the spring near the ford better though. It was so sweet and pure.[136]

"I remember when Wintz Keller and Kenneth Wolfe, that's Robert Estel Wolfe's brother, tried to build a swinging bridge over the river to Rose Island. They picked a spot on the slack side of the island near the ford where there are high banks. They used green oak lumber and anchored it at each end by a half-inch cable. That cable broke. Wintz got tangled up in the cable and drowned. We had a cistern at the barn and a stick with three prongs on it. I used it to hold the bail of the bucket to lower it into the cistern to water the cattle. I used that stick to drag for the body. When he was brought up, I could see where I had had him by the arm. Kenneth almost drowned too. A huge crowd gathered to try to find the body, but it was way into the night before we got him out of the river. That would have been in the forties, I guess.[137]

"My parents always took their children, all five of us, to church. We walked the railroad tracks to the Vonore Missionary Baptist Church. I started teaching Sunday school when I was seventeen years old. I have taught Sunday school for fifty-five years now. Herbert Millsaps, Melvin Sheets, and George Kidd are the only ones still living of the original group. Those three are there every Sunday. Once at a revival, the preacher said he visited the class once and found out you got promoted from it to the graveyard. I reckon most of my bunch will see the Pearly Gates. Many of my former students are in my Sunday school class now.[138]

"I knew John Mowdy and Johnnie Bell Lackey well. Miss Johnnie was my first-grade teacher. Mowdy came to Vonore to build the Highway 411 and bridge. At that time, a woman teacher could not be married. If she married, she was immediately fired. Miss Johnnie and Mowdy slipped off at Christmas, married, and kept it a secret until school was out. In later years, married women were allowed to teach, and she went back to first grade. She inherited their farm from her daddy, Dr. McCollum. My grandfather Williams, my mama's father, had the farm rented when Dr. McCollum bought it. Mowdy loved that land and his cattle. I was not surprised when he put all his energy and money into trying to save the Little Tennessee Valley. TVA is so big and rich and such a political force, no group has ever opposed them successfully.[139]

"I remember the first meeting of the Association for the Preservation of the Little Tennessee River. About three hundred of us met in the Vonore school lunchroom/auditorium. Bob Dorward had the maps, but few believed the TVA would grab so much land above the flooded valley.[140]

"The land developers have made fortunes by reselling the land. The taxpayers have not benefited because TVA leases the land. The developers get the profit, not the citizens of the United States or Monroe, Loudon, or Blount counties. I wonder if there ought to be limits on the use of the law of eminent domain. The intent of the original law is valid. It forces people to sell and lets the government and public utilities do projects for the common good. The way it is now, TVA can force the sale of land that has been in a family for generations and then let it be used for a golf course or a rich person's mansion. The controversy boiled up again in 2003 when TVA sold 116 publicly owned acres that were protected for public recreation and green space to luxury-home developer Mike Ross of Maryville, Tennessee.[141]

"The times keep us changing. When I started teaching, the students called me Mr. Niles. The younger ones call me Charles today. They mean no disrespect. The times and customs have changed. This year, the Vonore High

School class of 1953 has their fiftieth reunion. Back then, a teacher stayed with a class for four years as sponsor and homeroom teacher. The children were together for all twelve grades. I started teaching in 1950.[142]

"One of the funny things I remember is Jim Lowe's answer to my question, what holds atoms together? He said atomic glue.[143]

"One of my teaching experiences' biggest kicks was at Madisonville High School. One of the black students was called Spook—I don't recall his real name. That day, we had delicious white beans with ham. Everyone ate all they could hold. I was lecturing about the compounds benzene, ethane, and ethylene. About that time, three little black males raced to the front of the room as if one person.

"'What is the trouble?' I asked.

"'It is Spook. He is smoothing us to death.'

"'It is the Beanzene,' they declared as they fanned.

"My black students knew how to make me laugh. Beanzene was the class joke that year.[144]

"Around here, the men like to go to the higher elevations like North River, Jake Best Creek, or Strawberry Gap and gather a bait of ramps in the early spring. Ramps are a garlic-type herb and can be found on the north slopes in the early spring. Then the tops die down, and the bulbs grow, and the ramps spread. One spring day, Herbie Bowers came to chemistry class after eating a bait of ramps. I got a chair and put it in the hall. He was expelled from the company of the righteous. I told him to listen from the hall as his breath was a stench in the nostrils of Mr. Niles. In a closed schoolroom, a few boys' breath and sweat after eating ramps can make the class sick.[145]

"Not much ever happened in Vonore or out where I grew up. I roamed the woods and the river. I can identify a bird by its nest or their eggs. I thought of a career as an ornithologist, but I settled on biology. I was not afraid of the water or the dark. One night, I went to a program at school and was walking down the railroad tracks. Men were searching for the pieces of a man who had been run over by the train. I found his arm and some bones.[146]

"Like I said, I was not afraid of the dark. But that night, when I got to the gate, two tomcats were in dispute. The noise was like a scream. The gate barred a run to the house, and my hair stood up on the back of my neck.[147]

"My mother had several proverbs or maxims that she said often. One was 'If a task great or small is worth doing, it is worth doing well or not at all.' Another was 'If at first you don't succeed, try and try again.' Those thoughts sum up Mabel and my life. Teaching children biology and chemistry was my excitement, and second grade for Mabel. I'm proud to have lived in the

Little Tennessee Valley for my seventy-six years. It was a beautiful river and productive farmland.[148]

"The socialists of the TVA did major surgery on this country. The TVA took the best farmland and the beautiful river and put rich people's homes on the farmland, made golf courses for the idle and windowless buildings in which men can labor. The land, the water, and the people paid the price for TVA's fast progress and bureaucratic planning. As a scientist, I know an independent study and analysis of the cost and benefits can prove the flooding of the Little Tennessee Valley did not result in the progress and change the past thirtysome years have brought. Our country needs development that allows us to use the natural resources and use them again."[149]

Gail Galyon Tells a Child's Memory of the Little Tennessee River

The weeping willow stood as a sentinel
near the school bus stop.
It is a special day.
I am invited to play.
The clean, fresh green limbs hang to the ground.

My friend's mother met the bus.
Baby sister and brother jump for joy.
A picnic under the weeping willow
hidden from view of all.
We had a magic place.

Upon a blanket we sat
eating our after-school fill.
Jonquils and pink flowering quince
Added to our first-grade joy
of spring

To the ford we explored.
A cable strung from tree to tree.
Holding the stout steel
Strong hands could move a boat
over fast water to Rose Island.

Childhood memories stay.
Families lose their land.
It is the law of eminent domain.
TVA has the rights.
Years pass. Thirty or more.

Now I am in my adult years.
From our boat, I walk to the picnic place.
The road is no more.
Community displaced.
The river flows pure and clean no more.

The weeping willow stands.
Nude, stark.
Lightning has finished the tall tree.
I walk barefoot now
in the mud of Politic Lake.

The river flows no more.
Neighbors are dispersed.
The land is lost.
It is the law of eminent domain.
TVA has the rights and power.

Bitterness abates.
The Little T flows pure and free no more.
A child's memories last forever.
My first-grade joy of spring
Stirs my respect for God's creation.
Even today, years later.

Gail Galyon's thoughts as captured by Fran Dorward

Beryl Moser Judges Forgive

Forgive, and you will be forgiven. Give and it will be given to you:
a good measure, pressed down, shaken together, running over,
will be put back into your bosom. For the measure you use,
it will be measured back to you.
                                                          —Luke 6:37b-38 NKJV

Beryl Moser tells me, "I'm a retired rural mail carrier. For the last thirty-four years, I have served as city judge for Vonore and as a juvenile court judge in Blount County when called. I've experienced injustice and lies, so I respect justice and truth and always try to be fair. When a kid comes before me for stupid driving, I send him to driving school and let him keep his transportation to college or work."[150]

He remembers, "I was one of three whose property was condemned. Everybody else moves as quickly as they could find a place. I had five acres, a house, barn, and sheds. I was paid $12,000 for everything. It cost me $5,500 to dig a well on the property I bought. The government requires that the money paid for the land be put back into land somewhere. I am lucky to have a place in Vonore.[151]

"The community was stripped of leadership, Fizz Tallent—he's the mayor. Margie Swafford, Blanche Farnsworth, and Louise and Qualls Kennedy, a group of us, we've tried to do what seems best for Vonore. Often, we feel quite powerless.[152]

"TVA forced the sale of about forty thousand acres. Water covers six thousand acres. They paid an average of $358 an acre. The highest price was $850 for a farm that had a large debt. One man got $800 an acre. He attended the Association for the Preservation of the Little Tennessee River and went home and phoned the TVA concerning what was said and done. TVA paid their debt to him.[153]

"TVA brought in an out-of-state developer, Cooper, from Arkansas. The agency let them lease the land near Loudon known as Tellico Village. The company sold ninety-nine-year leases to individuals to build mansions. That's all leased, so now Rarity Bay is being developed by Ross with acreage from the Tellico Reservoir Development Agency (TRDA).[154]

"A man named Wallace from Maryville has the lease, but he doesn't have to pay $10,000 an acre until he sells a lease. Last year, two acres went for a million dollars. The taxpayers didn't benefit. The land developer company got the profit. TVA has not managed the land to benefit the county government or the taxpayers of the USA.[155]

"I fought in Korea with the army. I love my country. But some lawmakers, like Albert Gore Sr., Howard Baker Sr., and John Duncan Sr. made mistakes. They had to because TVA has enough employees to defeat any candidate who fails to support any socialistic scheme they want to cram down citizens' throats. You can't win against TVA. They have the power. Nothing can hurt them.[156]

"As I stand in front of city hall and look at that sign on my old property, I get mad. I can wake up mad at them and go to bed mad at them. Families were divided over the building of Tellico Dam and the land grab. Brothers and sisters and neighbors had different opinions. The wounds in this community are deep.[157]

"As the city court judge for thirty-four years, I take no salary. The budgeted item is put into the police department. I love my community and all the people, even those who work for TVA, Cooper Land Development, and Rarity Realty. Stan DeLosier of Blount County put it in the *News Sentinel* that I said I wish the Yankees would go home, but I try to cooperate with them.[158]

"Yes, I can visit the cemeteries in Rarity Bay property and think how the people cared for the land and the river. The free-flowing water is gone forever, and the wealthy have taken the poor farmers' means of production. As the rural mail carrier for years, I knew the people. As far as I know, no one went hungry. No one had wealth, except the land. I believe change would have come without TVA flooding the valley and buying the sixteen thousand acres that were not flooded. No farmer is stupid, and working in a factory is not the only way of life.[159]

"I have found peace with TVA and its supporters. I work hard, keep busy, and refuse to dwell on being taken advantage of by the bureaucrats. I watch and listen and do what I can for my community. I remember the first time I voted. It was by absentee ballot. They sent it to Korea where I was in the army. I voted for Adlai Ewing Stevenson and Estes Kefauver. I knew the

Kefauvers from Madisonville. Eisenhower won. I always voted democrat until Albert Gore Sr., Howard Baker Sr., and John Duncan Sr. let the TVA grab the land. Now I think about the candidate.[160]

"TVA has brought in several Japanese and German companies and American-owned Lowe's. Lowe's has warehouses here for the stores in this area. All this land development needs is to be looked at by somebody who can understand the cost and benefits ratio. TVA employees are too smart to break a law in such a way that charges can be brought against them. There is one plastic company that keeps changing its name in order to get government grants that don't have to be paid back and that give them tax breaks. The employees stay the same. It is a paper thing. A building was built by a government agency to study nuclear waste. They brought it in from other places, but they only operated for about six months. It was finally sold at auction for half of what they asked for it, and that was half the cost to put it up. If TVA doesn't like a law, they lobby to get it changed. They got Howard Baker Sr. to change the law so the road over the Tellico Dam could be lower than the law in place required. There are other examples, but I talk too much.[161]

"Someday, the Lord God will reveal the truth about how the bureaucrats have served us. Many unemotional and educated people could prove the power of TVA should be contained. It will take an act of God, but maybe a new generation will speak out. I have served and serve in my way. I speak the truth as I see it and express my pain.[162]

"My advice is from the Good Book. 'Be strong and courageous. Do not be terrified; do not be discouraged, for the Lord your God will be with you wherever you go. (Joshua 1:9, NIV).'[163]

"For the people who still get spells of bitterness and anger, I suggest they learn this prayer. God, grant me the serenity to accept the things that I cannot change, the courage to change the things I can, and the wisdom to know the difference."[164]

Alfred Davis Knows the Davis Family Struggle

For I am the LORD, your God,
who takes hold of your right hand
and says to you, Do not fear;
I will help you.

—Isaiah 41:13, NIV

Alfred Davis sank into his recliner to tell me his story. "My shop is busy servicing and repairing tractors I've sold. This year (January 2004) the manufacturers failed to make enough to meet the demand, so I move tractors out as soon as delivered. I remember my customers and can tell you the year, model, and power of the tractor they bought, even twenty or thirty years ago.[165]

"My great-grandfather got 118 acres at Wears Bend (pronounced 'Weir') in 1863. Later, my father, Robert Greenway Davis, bought sixty acres more. The farm adjoining my daddy's belonged to my uncle Wilson. Both men had three children, and Uncle Wilson's sister farmed an adjoining tract.[166]

"My father and mother believed if you treated people good, they will treat you good. The neighbors along the Little T River got along well and watched out for each other. I was already in the machinery business when one night, I got home about nine PM and found the TVA land buyer, Mr. Woodward. He had offered $43,000 for 188 acres, house, barns, and sheds. At first, my daddy thought Mr. Woodward meant the sixty-acre farm. But no, that was the total offer. We were outraged. Mr. Woodward told us he could not tell us what a nearby farmer accepted. Then in five minutes, he told us $250 an acre.[167]

"Great-uncle Wilson Davis had the center part of the original land grant. He was born and never moved out of his father's house until TVA bought him out at $250 an acre. His great niece, who was a schoolteacher, lived with him. After the TVA man left, he sent her to Loudon to hire a lawyer. Uncle Wilson was heartbroken to receive so little for his life's work and his means of making a living from his father's inheritance.[168]

"My cousin went to three lawyers. None would take a case against TVA. All advised that the price was a pitiful disgrace but could not be won in court. Uncle Wilson had never been out of the state of Tennessee, and the thought of going to federal court scared him. He was so embarrassed about his disgraceful treatment and that he had signed under pressure that he never told his two sons the price he accepted.[169]

"TVA's deceitful practice was to buy a farm here or there and brag to a neighbor about how cheap they got it. When this happened to us, I had one brother in business with me and a sister with the brains in the family. She was a college English teacher. She went to researching people who had gone to court against TVA. She found one lawyer who would go to court against TVA, J. Randal Clarke of Russellville, Kentucky. She sent him a summary of the case. Only thirty-five acres would be flooded on the homeplace at Morganton Bend, and they took the sixty-acre farm for real estate development. That is where Tellico Village is now. Mr. Clarke said no one has ever sued TVA on the right to take land that is not needed for the dam or is not flooded. He advised that we had a good case. Daddy asked, 'How much to file our suit?' Daddy wrote him a check for $500.[170]

"TVA almost stopped harassing us after the suit was filed. They didn't clear our riverbank or cut our trees. It was five or six years before we went to court before Federal Judge Taylor. He ruled that previously ten years ago, land prices must be used. We lost a lot of money right there.[171]

"The second appraisal was by three independent witnesses hired by TVA and the state. They came in March wearing sneakers and sports coats. They walked the fifty-acre tract to the river. But then, they said, 'We're going to lunch and will meet you at the Morganton property.' The day started with pleasant early-spring weather, but by afternoon, the wind chill felt like fifteen degrees. The three men did not walk fifty feet from their car before one said, 'We have seen enough. Yes, I think so.' In five minutes, 118 acres was appraised. The land lays in two levels with the barns on the higher level and the bottomland along the river. I told Daddy on the way home they will offer less in a month.[172]

"In a month, there was a phone call saying the independent appraisal was that two men said exactly the same as TVA and one man $50 less. Of course, we did not take it. It rocked along for two or three years, and we planned how to go to court. We found several parcels that had sold about the same year as our appraisal. The owner had pictures of the run-down house and broom sedge grass in the field. He offered to help us any way he could. Mr. Clarke, our lawyer, told him that 'If anyone comes to your door, don't talk to them. I don't ever want you to meet a TVA appraiser.'[173]

"I figured they would use Bobby's farm. Bobby Wagner was his name. When we got to federal court, Mr. Clarke asked if he could call a rebuttal witness. We got Bobby into the courthouse basement early, so no one knew he was ready to testify. Mr. Hill was the TVA appraiser, and he had big pictures of Bobby's farm and other land. They had pictures of Holstein cows, but they were of the neighbor's cows.[174]

"Mr. Clarke asked if Mr. Hill knew this property. Mr. Hill said, 'Yes, I've driven by it many times in the past ten years. I know Mr. Bobby Wagner paid $250 an acre ten years ago.' Mr. Clarke asked if he had met the landowner, and he replied, 'Yes.'

"Mr. Clarke called Bobby. TVA lawyer Beverly Burbage raised objections, but Federal Judge Taylor let him testify. Mr. Clarke explained that he only wanted to prove what liars TVA were.

"Our lawyer, Mr. Clarke, asked Bobby, 'Have you ever met Mr. Hill there?'

"'No, never in my life.'

"'Did the house and land look like this when you bought it?'

"'No, but I brought my scrapbook with my pictures. I have my tax records on how much I have spent.'

"On rebuttal, TVA lawyer Beverly Burbage asked Bobby. 'When you bought the property, was this back field in corn?'

"'Yes.'

"'Is your land as good as the Davis farm?'

"'No, it is not bottomland.'

"'Well, only good land can grow corn. So you bought some rich land, didn't you?'

"'No, the field was planted in corn. I helped him haul it out to his other farm. He made about twelve bushels an acre. The land had been mined, not farmed. An average yield is sixty-five to seventy-nine bushels an acre on upland soil. That's what a farmer could expect. However, the yield is more today with better seed and fertilizer.'

"Mr. Burbage asked no more questions.

"If it had been a jury trail, I am confident we would have won. Judge Taylor always rules that TVA could not be more than $100 wrong in an objection to their appraisal.[175]

"One of the tricky stunts TVA pulled on us was to sell our rail fence before we accepted their price. I remember Daddy and Granddad stacking the rails higher and putting a woven fence in front of it. One day, a neighbor called Daddy and asked if he had sold any rails. She gave Dad the tag number, and Dad phoned the Loudon law, and they caught the guy coming into Loudon. He was a TVA employee who had bought the rails from TVA. He had a bill of sale, so Dad did not know what to do. We had about fifty cows in that field, and it took us three days to round them up.[176]

"In about three days, TVA men came to the tractor shop and claimed TVA owned the fence. I told them I remembered my grandfather and Dad building the fence. They could not believe that even a dumb hillbilly knew his property lines. I explained that the middle of the county road was the line. One of the men agreed that was traditional and the way it was, but his boss told him to go get in the car.[177]

"TVA claimed the fence belonged to Mrs. Finch across the road. She said that if it did that she wanted her rails. They spent a week with eight or nine men surveying in that twenty-acre field. They drove up stakes and messed. It was a bad deal.[178]

"Mother, Dad, and I went to see Bill Jenkins, who was on the TVA Board and was later director after Mr. Wagner retired. Bill Brock was our congressman, and his assistant was Charlie Thompson. They got us an appointment with Jenkins, who was a real politician. He listened and made no promises, but we did get a little bit for our rail fence.[179]

"I remember the day was hot as whiz when we went to the TVA towers in Knoxville. Outside, it was in the nineties, but the receptionist had on a sweater and a heater under her desk glowing red-hot. It was sixty-five degrees in there. I watched the employees rush out of there to warm up like chickens out of the house every time they got a break. After we were thoroughly chilled, we were sent to the top floor to Mr. Bill Jenkins's office. Going up or down one we were on the elevator with Mr. Red Wagner. I remember a lady employee whisper, 'Is that Wagner?'

"'I've never saw him' was the reply.[180]

"Tubby Hammontree—his name was Claude, and he was on the Monroe County Commission—told me, 'Wagner got upset at a meeting at Greenback School. TVA planned the meeting to prove support for the dam. Wagner told that TVA would build the dam only if the people wanted it. Many of the people present opposed the flooding of the valley. The vocal opposition angered Wagner so much that I predict Wagner will build it to spite the farmers and environmentalists.' Tubby read the meeting right, for that is exactly what happened.[181]

"A lot of crazy things happened over the years of our fight. TVA had a meeting at Vonore school for the displaced landowners. David Freeman of TVA started the organization to find a way to solve the problem of industrial development without flooding the land.[182] The dam was built, and Freeman was chairman of the TVA Board. Somehow, I got put in as president, and there were three or four meetings before John Duncan Sr. pulled his sneaky stunt.[183] The Supreme Court ruled to stop building the dam because of the Environmental Protection Act after David Etnier from the University of Tennessee identified the snail darter as an endangered species if the river was flooded.[184] It looked like people would get their land back. TVA's Displaced Landowner's Association was to figure out how to use the land without flooding the valley. Mr. Freeman and a lot of TVA people believed development could happen without making a lake.[185]

"A better-informed man than David Freeman could not be found. He knew reasons why the dam should not be built. I think he would have returned the land if he had the power. The main thing Freeman and I disagreed on was the price paid. Freeman believed TVA paid a fair price. At a meeting, I asked Mr. Freeman if he knew how much money TVA had taken in rent. He didn't know the land was rented. I explained that Uncle Wilson Davis's farm was rented for $50 an acre for several years. Mr. Freeman always had people there to supply numbers. They paid $250 an acre and had gotten their land payment back by renting the land. Mr. Freeman was surprised that TVA had paid for the property out of rent paid to them after the landowners were displaced.[186]

"I remember the first time I met Zyg Plater. Some folks from the University of Tennessee came to the 'Save the Little T' meeting at Vonore school. I thought he was a college kid because he was dressed in well-worn jeans and was so young. Zyg asked if TVA had cleared the Davises' riverbank. He advised me that we had a good lawsuit if they had. Later, I learned that Zyg was the professor who taught the future lawyers and that he was real smart. Zyg visits every two or three years when he visits Tennessee. TVA got people to write letters saying Zyg shouldn't have tenure at UT, so now he teaches and writes books at Boston University. He still loves Tennessee and helped the poor people put up a fight.[187]

"Zyg Plater, Peter Alliman, and Hank Hill loved the river and the outdoors. One time, Zyg phoned me and wanted to have a tractor parade in Knoxville.

The neighbors called around, and we loaded up forty or fifty tractors. The TV and the radio made a big deal out of the parade. Zyg was a planner and thinker, and it was a sorry deal for UT to let such a smart fellow go.[188]

"The farmers in the Little Tennessee Valley were productive businessmen. They were law-abiding churchmen and worked hard for what they had. No blood was shed in the buying out, but Att Millsaps told me how he showed his .45 revolver to the land buyer. Att was an old man and had a few acres to make a living on. He refused the first offer, and the TVA land buyer came back several times. Finally, Att agreed on a price and told him to bring the papers and cash money. Att said he signed and asked for cash. The TVA fellow said he would get it in a few weeks. Att said he laid his .45 on the stack of papers and threatened, 'You are not taking the papers.' After long minutes, the land buyer opened his briefcase and laid out the cash. Att said that he counted it and advised the man, 'You don't know how close you came to going to hell tonight. I'm glad you brought the cash.' It was a sad time for Att because that land was all he ever had.[189]

"I believe that Tennessee needs people who think and stand up for what's right. My family lost money by going to court, but the Davis family put up the best fight they could. Looking backward, the family affirms that God held their hand and that their fight was possible only because of their faith that God is helping them no matter what happened."[190]

Betty Moser and Earl "Red" Black Tell Their Side

"Let us tell our side of the dam controversy and about our life," the Blacks offer as I look toward Corntassel Road from a wide porch and turn to notice the wavy glass in the side windows beside the heavy front door. From the porch, we see acres of spring grain, wheat, oats, and barley, wearing its proud spring green of mid-March 2006. Oaks, hundreds of years old, shelter the antebellum home. Upon entering the house, Betty points to a bullet hole in the ceiling.

"My great-aunt was coming down the stairs carrying her silverware and her gun when the bushwhackers came up on the porch. I am not sure whether my aunt or the outlaws put the bullet hole in the ceiling, but I still have some old silver. This period is sometimes referred to as the War of Northern Aggression, but those fellows were neither for the north or the south."

In the parlor, we admire the walnut organ that was a birthday gift to Betty's mother in 1900. "I had the internal mechanism redone so I can play it," explains Betty, who plays for the Vonore United Methodist Church and for her sister's church Corntassel Cumberland Presbyterian Church each Sunday.

Betty directs attention to a walnut farmer's secretary.

"My daddy bought it at the Johnson's estate sale in the thirties, and it is surely one of its kind and locally made. The lid extends to make about a forty-eight-inch square work space. Both my kids, Jennie and Brad, say that they don't want this secretary when we die. When they were preschool age, they played on it and broke a hinge. I was so mad that I whipped them both. Then I was mad again and whipped them again. Anyway, they still don't want to touch Grandpa Moser's old desk."

In the broad front hall, a drop leaf pine table holds a round carved cane and a frame with original wood carvings that Red's grandfather, Orville

Bradley Black, carved in resting moments. The cane is of a light-colored wood of unknown species with a symmetrical design carved all the way around the walking stick. Inside the frame, a hatchet and other hand-carved items that may be intended as children's toys show the whittler's skill.

We sit in their large modern kitchen, dining area, and farm office, which is complete with a computer. The boards of the table are wide and solid, but after a picnic, it was rained on and spent years in a dusty shed before Brad Black, their son, refinished it with polyurethane. If their beautiful, but much abused, walnut table could talk, the White and the Black families' stories might burn many ears in the community. Betty says, "My neighbor Gwinn Starnes tried to research the White family but concluded we are dull farmers who work all the time and never do anything else."

Earl says, "That is the original deed to the place in that frame. It shows 160 acres purchased in 1820 for $4 an acre. Uncle Tom White taught me to keep this soil rich and productive. And our son, Brad, earns a living from it now 2006. Uncle Tom and I added to the farm to make 750 acres now. Brad married a fine farmer in his wife, Kim, who cares for a herd of purebred Black Angus. Brad didn't want cattle on the place, but Kim loves her cows. She has about thirty new babies now, and when her cows finish calving, there will be about sixty. Kim works at H & R Block doing taxes for people every tax season, but she and Brad keep this place productive.

"Our daughter, Jennie, is the rural mail carrier and lives in the cottage on Niles Ferry Road. I guess we need Uncle Tom to arrange how to push her into matrimony," Betty laughs.

"Let me tell you," Betty offers, "about this new part of the house."

"Originally, there was a breezeway between the main house and the kitchen. One time, Earl and I had a dance here, and the old floor gave out. Earl tore that part off and built a den, kitchen, and office alcove."

Earl laughs. "Betty had 'one tear' into the carpenter. The ceiling in this kitchen had to be eight feet for the cherry corner cupboard." He pointed to a magnificent cherry piece. "I had to bring it in through the window, but the carpenter kept grumbling, 'You don't make eight-foot ceilings anymore.'"

Betty pointed to a large rounded glass breakfront china cabinet, saying, "Grandmother Margaret White liked to point out that she raised her two children without breaking that glass. I'm glad that I have kept it in perfect shape."

The phone rings, and Earl goes to the farm office and says, "Come on, I'll help you load some corn."

He explains, "That man wants six barrels of corn to feed his fighting roosters. He can sell one for $500 by shipping it to China where rooster fighting is legal. It used to be a big deal near here in Blair's Woods every Saturday night. The attendance got so big that the law made them move. They put four-inch steel spurs on the roosters and let them fight to the death. The money is made on gambling, except for the few shipped to China nowadays."

Earl explains, "The rooster producers only need a used fifty-five-gallon drum to house each rooster, some corn and water, and no training is needed. If you don't mind the cruelty, a family can profit."

Earl feels strongly about gambling and says, "Our Methodist Church was against gambling in Tennessee. I'm the biggest gambler in Vonore. I buy seed and fertilizer and gamble on rain and disease. I thought people ought to be allowed to buy a number if they are that foolish."

Earl expands on gambling, "The new plan is for the Indians to build a casino and chicken-fighting arena where hundreds can bet on the fights. Apparently, it is not illegal for Indians to profit from gambling. You know the Tennessee Valley Authority leased the Indians parts of the Anderson, Carson, and McGhee farms."

Earl and Betty share an interest in community problems. Earl remembers, "There was a time when you did not dare go to Vonore on a Saturday night. A mean drunk might challenge you to a fistfight. A lot of corn whiskey and home brew (beer or ale) was made hereabouts. Our county needs alcohol and drug-treatment facilities. I've never thought the answer for alcohol and drug abuse was to lock people up in jail."

Earl says, "I worked at Alcoa for thirty-one years and farmed. I put in sixteen-hour days. The children could climb all over me and sit on my chest, and I could still sleep.

"Alcoa provided alcohol rehabilitation for employees at Peninsula Mental Health Hospital, but some men abused it. As soon as released from treatment, they would drink again. I hated to fire some of my friends who kept coming to work drunk, but I could not let an accident hurt someone or the company."

Betty recalls, "Earl and I had a strange courtship for around here. We dated for sixteen years. When Earl got out of the military, he used the GI Bill to go to Maryville College. I was a freshman too, but I lived in the dormitory. Earl lived at home with his mother and brother, Reuben, and his wife, my best friend, Beuna Frank Black. Charles Niles had a tuition scholarship but lived at home, so he and Earl drove to Maryville every day."

Earl remembers, "Charles Niles taught me to fish. I learned to enjoy the Little Tennessee and the Tellico River. In the forties, a lot of people set lines from wooden rowboats to fish the spring run (spawning). Then for about thirty years, people would float from below Chilhowee Dam. I don't know anyone who floated with a motor. After the Game and Fish Commission started stocking the river with rainbow trout, people from way off could rent a boat from Hoss Holt for $3 a day. He would pick up his boats at the mouth of Tellico River or at Rose Island. Way back then, I saw a lot of boats on the river. Over at Rarity Bay subdivision, boats are tied up at every home dock, but I rarely see a boat on that lake. I think few fish it."

Earl recalls, "Mowdy Lackey had a Sinclair gas station on 411. That was the company with the green sign and a dinosaur on it. The word was out that TVA was hiring men to build Fontana Dam, which was 1941-1945. Mowdy took a job with Pipman Construction Company and hired me to manage the gas station and Henry Webb Sr. to run his garage across the railroad tracks in Vonore. Mowdy was a construction foreman, so he only got home on weekends.

"Let me tell you about Betty and my getting married.

"Betty's uncle Tom White took me over to his farm on the Tellico River and told me that he wanted me to build him a barn. Then he brought me to this farm and pointed out which trees to cut. I cut the trees, had them sawed, and finished at the sawmill in Vonore, put in the foundation, and built the barn. Uncle Tom never paid me a cent, but he brought me to this farm. He said, 'I want you to farm for my mama.' He pointed to each field and explained how the crop rotation was to go and exactly how he wanted the work done."

Earl smiles. "Then Uncle Tom went to the courthouse and deeded the land where I built the barn to Betty, and he put six cows there."

Betty grins. "We wonder if my Uncle Tom didn't want me to be an old maid, so he made sure Earl could support a family and gently pushed us into matrimony."

Betty explained, "Uncle Tom was a bachelor. In the twenties and thirties, it was a common practice for a big family to send some to their children to live with another family and work. Grandmother White had the McCaulley children—Josephine, Anne, Carol, and Rob. Anne and Carol married, but Josephine had an illness and lived out her life at Eastern State Hospital. Rob stayed and farmed here for forty-five years. People would ask if Tom and Rob were father and son because they grew to look alike. After they died, my sister Margie and I learned there was only nine years difference in their ages.

"After Tom's mother, my grandmother, died, Uncle Tom asked my mama to come back to this house and do for them. She was a widow, but for some reason, this house was built so you have to climb a steep hill from the spring. She told Uncle Rob she couldn't do the work."

Betty and Earl laugh as they think of the men's dilemma. Uncle Tom is reported to have told Rob, "One of us has to get married. It is not going to be me."

Earl says, "I don't know how it went, but Rob found Edna Bell Arden. She was only sixteen years old, but she made Rob a perfect wife. They were married for over forty years and had three children."

Betty says, "I remember the first time they had wheat threshers to feed. Rob got my mama and me to come and help her, but she didn't really need us. Rob had picked and snapped green beans from the garden the night before and planned well. Edna set a good table for Uncle Tom and Rob. That meal, she had ham, roast beef, and chicken for about twenty men."

Earl remembers the area history and tells, "Vonore got electricity in 1932 from the Loudon Power and Light Company."

Betty adds, "Twelve families each had to buy an electric stove for the town to get electricity. My daddy was postmaster and bought one, but it was not hooked up right away. Daddy was postmaster but could not pay the light bill if he let Mama use it, so she kept cooking on the woodstove."

Earl says, "The rural area got electricity about 1940, but this farm had a carbide motor to grind, feed, and pump water. The iron pipes from the springs to the house and barns are out behind the shed. I replaced them with PVC pipe. When I tore the breezeway off and built these rooms, I rewired the entire house and brought everything up to the safety code. In 1820 when this house was first built, every room had a fireplace. For years, Betty and I heated with woodstoves and propane gas, but now we use electricity as a heat and air system."

Betty says, "One thing I hate about the changes the dam made was Vonore losing its high school. I taught at Vonore High School for fifteen years before I stopped to have babies."

Earl claims, "In my freshman class at Vonore, fifty-one started in the fall. But four years later, seventeen graduated. In ninth grade, fifteen girls quit school and married."

Betty remembers, "Forty started in my high school class, but only twelve graduated. Charles Niles was actually a better student, but I was valedictorian. We both graduated from Maryville College in four years and came back to teach at Vonore High School. I always tried to encourage students to stay in school and graduate. I tried to spot the ones who were tempted to quit and pushed some girls to graduate."

Earl says, "In those days, going to high school was a privilege. My daddy was killed when I was young, and Mama moved to her parents on Tellico River. By fall, we lived with my grandpa and grandma Black that is near the apartments on Tennessee Highway 360 now. Reuben and I would cut across the fields and come out where the beer joint Sammie O's is, used to be Giles Grill. The Little Tennessee River Bridge was a toll bridge. But Mr. Niles, the toll keeper, let us walk across free. He could have charged us a nickel each, but he knew Mama had no money. We walked across the fields to Greenback School because that is where we started first grade, and I finished out my eighth-grade year. Walking to Greenback School was about six miles one way but was no big deal for Reuben and me because we could walk behind a mule all day plowing. We walked across the fields, not by the highway.

"One of the jobs I was proud of was building one of the barns on Dr. Foute's farm. His daughter, Frances, married Ben Clark, the farm manager. Dr. Foute used a long rectangular outbuilding for his office. That building was made of the same brick as the mansion, which I understand was built with brick made on the farm by slaves. Dr. Foute waited on my mama when I was born in the Oakland community nearby. Ben Clark's brick silo still stands in that lake. He had a huge dairy and grew their feed and had beef cattle too. Several families worked that farm. Some people look at that silo as a silent scolding to the bureaucrats who forced such change on us."

Earl continues, "The rich men from Kahite community come and buy bales of ryegrass hay for their landscaping. I've been asked why we old-timers resent the newcomers. It is hard to explain, but sometimes, they want to know.

"I try. I picture my farm on the north side of the Little Tennessee River on Baker's Creek in Loudon County. I had 117 acres and was getting it into perfect shape. Mr. Woodward, the land buyer, paid me $167 an acre. He threatened that I would be offered less if I insisted on an appraisal."

Earl continues, "I wanted to fight the Tennessee Valley Authority's stealing, so several landowners and I tried to hire the nationally known Ray Jenkins. Jenkins was raised near the Tellico River and owned a farm near Fort Loudoun Dam. Jenkins was famous for his part in the Senator McCarthy hearings about communists in government. We thought he would represent the farmers against the bureaucrats. Guess what? Ray Jenkins was the first to sell his farm. It is the land where the dam is built. He got more than $167 an acre, and he was already well-to-do as a defense lawyer. I think the poor working farmers really suffered on that land grab. Even thirty years later, I hurt over it."

Betty interjects, "Bob Dorward had maps of the TVA's plan for land buying that showed the land buyouts all the way to Corntassel Road. We think they only took sixty acres of our Tellico River bottoms because of the family cemetery. TVA didn't like to take cemeteries, except they didn't care about the old Indian mounds."

Earl says, "I was trying to reforest some of our steep land before the damming talk renewed. I had planted poplar and pine on about five acres. Dale Brakebill and I planted a bundle of five thousand loblolly pine seedlings from Rose Island. TVA got six acres of that hard work."

Earl reflects, "Land use is curious business. Some of Lackey's farm, most of the Garrens', is in the Kahite development. Forty-six houses are on one-third acre lots. They get $285,000 for one lot. A friend of mine did the Sheetrock on one house and was paid $80,000. A movie theater seats thirty people, and there is a bowling alley. The owner is a German who lives most of the year in Germany and has a similar house in Connecticut as the one here. Betty and I understand the folks in the housing development and in Kahite don't care about community problems. We are sad that our community has become a bedroom community for folks to drive to Knoxville or fly to all parts."

"Earl and I have worked together for fifty years. We wanted to marry, so my grandmother and Uncle Tom's scheme suited us," Betty explains.

Earl picks up her thoughts, saying, "Remember that I was an orphan from a big family. I never lacked for carpentry or farming work, but I couldn't give Betty a home. Uncle Tom fixed Betty and me up by teaching me to farm and by deeding the land to Betty. Betty and I have a good life together. Now we have the satisfaction of watching our son and his wife farming this land. We have deeded it to him. That's our side of the struggle against the TVA."

Earl says, "Stay a bit and let me tell you about our granddaughter, Amy Black. She went to Middle Tennessee State to learn to be a mechanical engineer. After a while, she phoned and said, 'I don't like living in this dormitory. A house is to be auctioned off. Will you help me buy it?' Of course, all four of us went to the auction with Amy. I bid until common sense said enough."

Earl remembers, "We were right up to the college when I saw a For Sale sign in front of a brick house. Brad stopped, and all of us walked around it. Amy liked the location and called the realtor. She got it for $103,000 and, three years later, made $30,000 selling it.

"Now she is in the process of fixing up a house in Knoxville. She is getting a PhD at the University of Tennessee and working in Oak Ridge. Brad said that he would hate to live in such a beehive, but Betty and I don't worry about Amy." Earl smiles.

Earl says, "One more thing I want in the book is about Rob McCaulley. Before Uncle Tom died, he gave Rob a 154-acre farm near here. Like I said, Rob and Uncle Tom farmed together for forty years. Recently, his son was asking $2,000,000 for the farm on Povo Road. Yes, land values have soared hereabouts. But we old-timers do have our side of the societal changes in Vonore, Monroe, Loudon, and Blount counties."

March 2006

Margie Swafford Says Everything Has Its Time

For everything, there is a season, and a time for
every matter under heaven;
A time to be born, and a time to die;
A time to plant, and a time to pluck up what is planted;
A time to kill, and a time to heal;
A time to break down, and a time to build up;
A time to weep, and a time to laugh;
A time to mourn, and a time to dance;
A time to throw away stones, and a time to
gather stones together;
A time to embrace, and a time to refrain from embracing;
A time to gain, and a time to lose;
A time to keep, and a time to throw away;
A time to tear, and a time to sew;
A time to keep silence, and a time to speak;
A time to love, and a time to hate;
A time of war, and a time of peace.

—Ecclesiastes 3:1-8[191]

Margie Swafford believes everything has its time. It is a scripture her mother, Jennie White Moser, quoted to her girls, Betty, Henrietta, and Margie. Henrietta had the favorite passage read at her funeral. Margie, now in her ninth decade, experiences changes in her community of Vonore, Tennessee. The house that she and Wade built in 1956 sits on a gentle hillside looking over her grandmother White's farm. It is the farm that she and Wade bought when her grandmother left her a third of the property. They bought her two sisters' shares and moved to Margie's childhood community.[192]

Margie faced change when the Tennessee Valley Authority bought two hundred acres of their farm. Now her house looks out on a cove, a finger of the lake, made by the damming of the Little Tennessee River and backing up a bit of the Tellico River that flowed through their farm. Now she can say stoically, "With Wade dead, the forty acres the TVA left me is enough. Wade and I fought the dam. I remember when Mr. Woodward, the TVA man, forced us to sign the papers. We sat at this round oak antique table in this room. I begged him, 'Let us keep the land above the water. My sister Betty will give us a road to it.'[193]

"'Impatiently,' he snorted, 'you are lucky I'm letting you keep forty acres. Most people are keeping nothing.'"[194]

Margie recalls, "I blew smoke. I thought violence, but I didn't do anything. We were so helpless. The TVA buyers were so arrogant. They could even make someone who wanted to sell out mad.[195]

"I didn't do much to help fight the dam. My son Mike had a low draft number, 92. I was scared to death that he would go to Vietnam. That was my greatest worry and fear. The threat of the dam hung over the valley since 1937. It flooded pretty exactly to the brass markers the engineers put down in 1937.[196]

"It was not a fair deal. It was cut and dried before any of the landowners knew about it. It was hard to get information because TVA kept their secrets.[197]

"When it was sure the fight was lost, Wade cut the timber. The TVA man, Mr. Woodward, I think, came to the shop. Wade and he didn't do any talking in the house. The TVA buyer threatened Wade, 'You can't cut your timber. TVA is going to buy your land.' Wade heard enough. He picked up a tobacco stick and said, 'You can leave, or I can whop you.'[198]

"Not a blow was struck, for the TVA man left. A tobacco stick is used to hang the tobacco on to cure. The sticks are made of oak and are never thrown away. They are several inches round, and a whop beside the head would do damage. Wade gave ours to Red Black, our brother-in-law, when we lost our land. It is a testament to the farmer's belief in law and order that not a single shot was fired. No one died. The battle was lost in Congress. Our elected officials sold us out. John Duncan Sr. got the final bill passed when few people were there. Jimmy Carter let it become law.[199]

"Another run-in Wade had with TVA was on Dr. Troy Bagwell's farm. Wade had rented some river bottom and planted soybeans. The beans were just coming up. Wade found a man digging with a spade in the middle of the field of tender young soybeans.[200]

"Wade yelled, 'Get out of my beans!' and a few expletives.[201]

"The man warned, 'You don't know who I am?'[202]

"Wade shouted, 'I've got this field rented!'[203]

"The man bragged, 'I'm a TVA lawyer, and I'm digging for arrowheads.'"[204]

Margie recalls, "Wade exploded in a string of words that caught the attention of even a TVA lawyer. He had tromped the beans pretty bad, but he did leave. It was a hard time to be a man in the Little Tennessee River valley. Wade took the meanness but felt stomped like the soybeans.[205]

"As a child growing up in Vonore, my mama kept her girls sheltered from worldly events. In other words, Mama allowed no gossip to be heard by her children. My old grade-school boyfriend phones me, 'Do you remember? They talked about it at the store.' I say no because Mama never let her girls go to the store alone. A lot of local history from the thirties left me out.'[206]

"When I was in the ninth grade, a new teacher came to Vonore High School. The high school was a wooden two-story building, and next to the school was a teacherage. The teachers and the students from too-far-to-walk homes or those riding a horse lived there on weekdays. We had a phone, and the new teacher called one Saturday afternoon. She asked, 'Do you want to go on a hike?' It was a glorious sunny November day. She was a schoolteacher, so Mama said yes. We walked about two miles or so and came to the ford at Rose Island. Several boats were tied up there on the slack side, the south side, of the island. We boldly took a boat and rowed to Rose Island. We poked about, and before we knew it, the water was rising and fast running. Try as we might, we couldn't get the boat to where we borrowed it. We finally gave up and got back on Rose Island. We started hollering and hollering. A farmer who lived near heard us and brought two horses over to the island. The water was up to the horses' bellies, but they carried us safely across. Darkness fell as a cold fog and wind hurried us back to Vonore. It was awful. We almost spent the night with the Indian ghosts on Mialaquo or Great Island.[207]

"That was the first and only boat that I stole. My daddy said I was lucky I didn't end up in jail. As I look back, my teacher-friend who later married Walt Smith was only about five years older than I was. I wish that I could remember her maiden name and who the kind farmer was who rescued us.[208]

"Now that I am old, I wonder how my ancestors survived. You don't think about it when you are young. The Mosers came from an area between France and Germany called Alsace-Lorraine. Some spell it 'Mosier.' My son Tim had work in Paris, France, and took me along. Three pages of Mosers and Mosiers filled the Paris phone book.[209]

"Macular degeneration makes me nearly blind. I read with my ears now. My sister Betty Black and I go to the Maryville library and get tapes for me to listen to. I've listened to *John Adams* by David McCulloch. It has made me think about this country. What these people endured is hard for me to learn about.[210]

"I used to read too slowly. I took Latin at Vonore High School. Everyone did. It makes you analyze the sentences and think about how the plots and characters follow through. One of the books I recently listened to is *Black Boy*. When Wade and I lived in Chattanooga, I remember the black women getting on the bus to ride home after working all day. They had to weave their way back to stand in the back of the bus.[211]

"It was about 1955 when the last black man was bushwhacked in Tellico Plains. They didn't even allow a black to drive a car through the town. This black man was the chauffeur for a rich man, who came to hunt wild boars. The hunters would get all liquored up and have to have a driver and a guide. It is too bad that they murdered him like that.[212]

"Up to the fifties, black families lived in Vonore. The road now called Ridge Road was called Nigger Ridge. I try to say Ridge Road now. When I was a kid, we didn't know the n-word was bad. The Negro church and the Negro school were on that road. The McGhee and Evans families and others lived there before they moved to Knoxville to work.[213]

"Mattie Evans washed for my mama when I was a child. She drew the water and heated it in a washpot in the yard. When it was time for a meal, Mama would always invite her in to eat. She would never come in the house. 'No, me'um, I gots a few more things to do out here.' When ready to start home, her dress would be wet. She asked, 'Mr. Rod, do you have a little toddy you could give me before I start home?'[214]

"When I was a child, I never thought about color and justice. In the summer, Mattie's granddaughter Florence Ruth would come and play with me. We were the same age, but her mama was only thirteen when she was born. Don't hold me to that, but that's how I remember it.[215]

"I'm glad that my boys grew up in Vonore. When they went on a wild hog hunt in the Tellico Mountains, one of the party shot a sow. She had two babies. Wade and boys brought them home, but it was dark by the time they got here. We had no place to put them outside, so we put them in the bathtub for overnight. The next day, Mike and Tim made a pen. Snort was one's name, and I forget the other. They grew up to be big hogs, but their meat was not fit to eat. They grew up in the pen and were fed corn, but if anybody offers you wild hog meat, say, 'Thank you, but I'm a vegetarian.'[216]

"Both of my boys graduated from Hiwassee College after graduating from Vonore High School. Mike finished at Tennessee Wesleyan in Athens, and Tim at the University of Tennessee at Knoxville. Then Tim got his PhD at Mississippi State. For a while, Tim worked as an engineer at Tullahoma laboratories, but now he teaches engineering at the University of Tennessee at Chattanooga.[217]

"Mike says he's retired, but he is only fifty-three years old. He was coming over to talk this afternoon, but he turned the fertilizer spreader over. He has seventy acres that he bought from what was the Garren farm. Mike keeps busy, but he is glad that he sold his store.[218]

"My mama had a scripture or poem for every occasion. One was 'Count that day lost whose low descending sun views from my hand no worthy action done.' That is not in the Bible, and Mama never said who wrote it. If she caught us idle, she would recite that snippet of poetry and put mending, quilting pieces or the Bible into our hands."[219]

"I'm thankful that I grew up in Vonore, raised my boys here, and am living out my aging years here. Wade has been gone for years now, and I miss his cheerful ways and fiery spirit. After the lake filled up, all the wells were contaminated, and the water muddy. Vonore put in a water treatment plant. We got treated water and higher property tax rates. We got city people, monster houses, and idle men who fill their days with golf. TVA built windowless buildings to lease, and folks drive here to work. I am thankful for the prosperity in my community, but my country horse sense tells me that losing soil, fishes, and forests is a mistake.[220]

"Another thing I'm thankful for is my church Corntassel Cumberland Presbyterian Church. My sister Betty Black takes me every Sunday, and she plays the piano or organ for us after she has served as pianist or organist at the Vonore United Methodist Church. The old church membership stays small because so many were moved out, and the newcomers want a big fancy service, so they don't join and come regularly.[221]

"I'm sorry that the Tennessee Valley Authority beat us on saving the river, but that was years ago. I'm making it as a widow and nearly blind. Life goes on. Changes are painful, especially when forced by a government agency. But as the Bible says, everything has its time."[222]

Fred "Fizz" Tallent Speaks Out as Vonore Mayor

A marble plaque of the Ten Commandments sits prominently on Fizz Tallent's desk in Vonore City Hall where he serves as mayor. It is appropriate for a man who can fight for his beliefs and can face defeat. He goes on doing the best that he knows for his changing community.[223]

He announces, "The Seventh-Day Adventist have a radio station here on Dawson Street Highway 360. They gave that plaque to me. I accept the risks of having it on my desk. My faith is important to me. Maybe this little plaque will help me give some of it away. That is a Missionary Baptist tradition, you know."[224]

Fizz "Fred" Tallent serves as mayor and has been for thirty-five years or so. "Off and on," he explains. His bold display of his beliefs reveals his fighting character. His commonsense values reveal his respect and complete belief for his Creator's laws. He said, "To spurn the Ten Commandments is an ultimate rejection of God's love in my nation and my community life, and I don't care who knows it."[225]

Fizz is a working mayor: his desk is evidence of varied projects. His open door invites police officers to seek his affirmation on town business. Fizz Tallent lives in a community experiencing vast changes in economic structure. He recalls, "In the nineteen sixties and seventies, Vonore was a busy village. Two general stores, two barbershops, three beauty shops, a drugstore, post office, a pulpwood yard, a sawmill, a hardware and feed store, mechanic shop, a restaurant, and gas stations. Most of the amenities for comfortable living were at hand. The people visited back and forth between the Baptist, Methodist, Presbyterian, Church of God, and Lutheran churches. In August, my family would visit all the churches' revivals and the decoration days in May. All the churches were small, but they were important for the social life of the young people. I went to twelve grades at the Vonore school, so I knew everyone.[226]

"We didn't have factories. I worked at Oak Ridge National Laboratory and drove back and forth. A work bus took men to the Alcoa plant in Alcoa. Some men went to Ohio or Michigan to work. Some men stayed away a working life, and some men returned when laid off. Their roots were in these hills, and most returned to live out their old age.[227]

"I loved the Little Tennessee River. I had a favorite fishing hole under a shade tree where I would sleep until the water started to go down. Big brown trout in the hole kept me trying. In the spring when the fish were running, I could catch dozen of varieties. That clear, clean, cold water made a delicious fish.[228]

"I was never for the dam. We had no way to fight the Tennessee Valley Authority. My daddy didn't want to lose his farm. My aunt went to her grave bitter that her home was gone. When you put your life into a place like the Tallents did, it becomes you—heart and soul. I tried to talk to TVA about buying some of my daddy's and aunt's places back. They sold the land to strangers, but not the original landowners. The TVA man asked me, 'How many lawyers do you have?' I had none. He said, 'TVA has eighty-four lawyers. You can't win. Take my offer and move.' More than thirty years have passed, no telling how many lawyers TVA has now.[229]

"Some of the old boys who fought in the wars couldn't believe their country would take their land. TVA took 42,999 acres and paid an average of $356 per acre. A lot of it was a land grab and was above water, and they resold or leased it. It was not fair to the people. Industrial development here did not depend on the lake."[230]

Mayor Tallent continued his complaints, "Monroe, Loudon, and Blount counties lost fertile land, good people, and the river. There is still distrust of our government. TVA tells people half of the truth. The half TVA wants the public to know. Aubrey Wagner determined to build Tellico Dam come hell or high water. We got the high water, but the disagreement created deep scars, even in families.[231]

"Now TVA has a special bunch managing the land. TRDA, Tennessee Reservoir Development Agency's purpose is to get around the town of Vonore and the Monroe County Commission and committees. TVA is good at organizing special groups. They have a lot of employees to go around and talk people into going their way. No one can stay elected statewide unless they take TVA orders. John Duncan Sr. got the dam passed by a small number of representatives. He was in TVA's pocket. TVA had sixty-two thousand employees in the seventies. That is a lot of people to get out a vote. They are a clever bunch. They stay on the edge of the law. If they don't like a law or want a special consideration, they tell the Tennessee senator to get the law changed.[232]

"The beautiful river could have been spared. The fertile river bottomland should be farmed for hundreds of years to come. Industrial development can come into an area without a lake. No industries use the lake. TVA built a barge landing. It is past the BFI plant. One barge has come in there. The landing is not in use. Aubrey Wagner promised navigation benefits if TVA flooded the land.[233]

"TVA is planning to spend $46,000,000 on a resort. Here is the plan. They made this beautiful map and named the development Sequoyah Lodge, but the Indians won't own an inch. TVA will lease the development and control who can build or own the business. It is the old Anderson farm. As soon as the gambling bill passes, TVA will put a casino there. Docking facilities will be available for yachts, kayaks and canoes. It will be possible to come or go all the way to New Orleans by way of the Big Tennessee River and Fort Loudoun Lake. It ought to bring in a lot of tax money.[234]

"It was 1979 or 1980. I had a picture around here, but I can't find it now. I invited the TVA Board to visit Vonore. I cooked ham, red-eye gravy, and biscuits and had a real county meal. The TVA Board came in two helicopters. I had persuaded TVA to grade us off a ball field for the children. This was my thank-you to them. I paid for everything myself. The town of Vonore had no money.[235]

"The helicopters had turned off their motors. The two Freemans, John Duncan Sr., and other officials got off. A TVA man passed the loudest, stinkiest burst of gas I've ever heard. Joe Bagwell, editor of the *Madisonville* paper, was at my elbow.[236]

"He asked the TVA man, 'Is that your opinion of Tellico Dam?' It was well known that there was disagreement within TVA on the cost-effectiveness of building the dam from the start," Tallent remembered.[237]

"A nice crown of protesters gathered outside. I knew they would be there. I passed ham and sausage biscuits out the back door to them. I fed the TVA Board in the dining room.[238]

"Quite a few people helped TVA by telling what the preservationists were up to. TVA paid them off handsomely when their land was bought up.[239] Few people had debt on their land. TVA pulled a slick one by using the 1950 tax assessment to determine land value. That hurt the poor people. It did look like TVA could pay current land prices or at least 1970 land values. A lot of small poor landowners got hurt in the buyout. You got less if you let them condemn you. The TVA men kept telling people to take their offer or they would be sorry. Now places like Rarity Bay resell three-fourths of an acre for $200,000, and rich people build half-a-million-dollar mansions.[240]

"The people at Rarity Bay don't even know what river was destroyed to make the lake. Their fancy seven-color map calls the dam the Tellico River Dam. It was the Little Tennessee River that was dammed. The Tellico River flowed into the Little Tennessee River and was not backed up much.[241]

"My country lost a lot by the flooding of the Little Tennessee River valley and the big land grab. I've served as mayor since the seventies off and on, over thirty-five years. TVA wants locals to agree with their plans. The industries have brought in sales tax, but property tax goes up every year or so. It is mixed bag of curses and blessings. TVA gives the foreign people tax breaks, so the county doesn't get land tax from the monster buildings built for industry.[242]

"I try to be helpful to the rich people who move in. They are interesting to listen to. I know there is change. I welcome some changes. I hold to the eternal truths and watch the economic changes."[243]

Herbert and Edith Millsaps Talk

"When I think of the Little Tennessee River, my baptism comes to mind. The Baptists used a spot near where the Tellico River came into the Little Tennessee. That's where the old Niles Ferry Bridge was. I never forget my baptism. It is as clear as yesterday. It was a few days before Christmas, and I was twelve years old in 1932. Fouch Sloan, the Mills brothers, the Pinkerton boys, and I were baptized at the same time.

"I'm the oldest living male member of the Vonore Missionary Baptist Church. I've held on to my faith through all the turmoil and problems in my community. I have health problems now, and it is a comfort to know God is with me. I read my Bible every morning and at bedtime, but I don't memorize the Bible. I never could.

"Except for the three years I was in the U.S. Army, I'm at church. I've served as deacon, treasurer, and trustee. Nowadays, I'm a seat warmer and an inactive deacon. In good weather, Edith and I are in church for Sunday school, worship, and Sunday night service, and Wednesday night services. When it rains or if I can't drive home before dark, we stay home. I don't see well enough to drive at night or in the rain nowadays.

"Charles Niles has been my Sunday school teacher for nearly sixty years. He was seventeen years old when he started, and I was about twentysome. Melvin Sheets and one or so others of the original bunch are there most Sundays. As I said, I'm the oldest male in the church, so everyone is younger than I am. I was never a public speaker, but I do believe in the Bible. When I needed to give a current-event report in high school, I would stay home to work on the farm. There was never enough brass in me, so I would stumble along when I gave church reports. That is the hardest part of being church treasurer, but I did it for years.

"I was never on the Little T River in a boat, and I never went swimming there either. The river was near our farm, maybe three miles more or less. I have fished from the bank and caught nice fish. People talked about floating the river from Hoss Holt's, but I never did, and I never went fishing for trout. I knew about the Association for the Preservation of the Little Tennessee, but I never went to a meeting. It seemed foolish to fight it if TVA wanted to dam it.

"My first six years, I grew up near Fort Loudoun and played on the ruins. It didn't seem worthwhile to try to keep the history place from flooding. No, I was not bitterly for preserving the river. I didn't value it. I figured I would gain nothing by opposing TVA. In fact, I thought fighting it would get the community further into a hole, and there was no use fighting something that couldn't be stopped.

"I knew my farm was too far upland to be flooded by the dam. Edith's daddy, Mr. Pressley, knew his land would be flooded. They lived near Loudon. Some of Edith's childhood farm is Tellico Village now. They left her some rough land that joins it. Mr. Pressley feared driving to Maryville to the land office, but he was worried and anxious to know when he would be bought out. I drove him to the land office, and he asked me to go in and listen with him.

"The land buyer told Mr. Pressley there were no plans to buy his property right then. But he looked at me and said, 'Mr. Millsaps, your farm will be bought in the spring.' I turned white, and you could have pushed me over with a finger. I didn't expect to be bothered.

"Edith and I began the struggle to find a place to move. Since I worked at Alcoa in addition to farming, we looked in Blount County. It was impossible to find a farm. My farm was in perfect condition. I worked it as a boy and bought out my brother's share. I had thirty-two acres, house, barn, and sheds. I cannot say TVA bought me out. They took my farm, and I got $32,000.

"We decided to get as near our home communities as possible, so we bought this three and a half acres on Oak Grove Road. The payment was not quite enough to pay for this house and land. I have room for a big garden and a woodworking shop in the basement.

"Now it is time for Edith and me to downsize. We have looked at condos and independent-living places in the Atlanta area where our son lives. I don't want to drive in Atlanta, and I hate to leave our community and church. We have heard that an independent-assisted living and nursing home may be built near Tellico Village. Our house is full of antiques that our son's family doesn't want. We dread moving again. We have lived here thirty-five years now.

"The changes in this area of Monroe County came swiftly, and the people were unprepared for what happened. My father was farm manager for the

Carson farm. When he saved enough money, he bought his own farm, the same thirty-two acres TVA took. The small farmer had a hard time, especially during the depression years when I was growing up. Edith scolds me for being busy every minute, but that's how I was raised.

"When I was about four months short of my fifteenth birthday, I left school at noon on May 1. My daddy had lumbago. He was in such pain that he had to sleep in a chair because getting in the bed made him hurt more. In time, he improved and worked again. That May Day, I hitched up the horses and started plowing so I could plant corn. I worked the tobacco too that year. Wheat was already planted, and I got that in. I did a man's work that summer. It hurt Daddy to see what I was doing and be unable to help. When I plowed near the house, he would lean on the fence and cry. It was a hard, hard time for our family. My brother, Clarence, was ten. And he couldn't stay with a job long. He tried, then got tired and mad and threw clods at me. I would work until dark, so about five o'clock, Mama would come to the field with water and biscuit or corn bread. She made a snack to hold me until supper, which was after dark. I grew an acre of cotton so Mama would have batting for her quilt making. Even my younger brother, Clarence, could pick the seeds out of the cotton. Not many fifteen-year-old boys can say they did what I did that hard summer.

"Sometimes, a neighbor would pay me a dollar a day for plowing his corn with horses. That is a daylight-to-dark day, but they fed me a good noon meal. Sometimes, on Saturday, Daddy would give me a quarter. I would walk to Vonore, about five miles, and buy a pack of Ready Rolls cigarettes or an ice cream and Coca-Cola.

"Between my junior and senior year of high school, I rented on halves on a half acre of a neighbor's tobacco allotment. The land was where the pharmaceutical factory is today. I made a good crop and paid the landowner $50 and put $50 in the Vonore Bank. With that money, I bought a suit of clothes for graduation, my class ring, and went on the class trip. I could write a check for a dollar and have spending money when I needed it.

"When I was in high school, the school system had no money for substitute teachers. If a grammar school teacher was sick, the principal would come and get me. I never did just sit there. I made them do their lessons and put in a good day's work. My brother, Clarence, and his friends would show out. But I kept order. I guess that is why I got sent so often. The principal had his grade to teach, but he depended on me in a pinch.

"I usually carried my dinner to school in a four-pound metal lard bucket. Mama made big country biscuits, and my dinner was usually ham or side meat.

The town kids would have peanut butter on store-bought bread. Sometimes, I would swap my ham biscuit for their sandwich. At times, Mama would give me fifteen cents to go to Charlie Frank's store. I could get cheese, bologna, and a Coca-Cola. Mr. Franks gave us crackers. That made a filling, special dinner.

"During my school years, I got to know John Mowdy Lackey. I called him Lackey. I bought many agallon of gas from him. He loved the Vonore community and helped out the schoolchildren. He was always up on the goings-on in the courthouse in Madisonville and in Washington. The Democrats kept an eye on the Republicans and vice versa, but my energy went into my farm, I didn't think politics would touch me.

"When I was twenty, I got on at Alcoa, the Aluminum Company of America. Daddy had a 1929 Chevrolet and gave it to me to sell so I could buy a car fit to drive the seventy-mile round-trip every day. I was able to buy a good used Chevrolet.

"Alcoa was essential war work, so I was deferred from the draft. All my friends were going to the service, but Alcoa would not let workers go. In fact, they were shorthanded. Then the national Selective Service Board ruled that no one under twenty-four years of age could be deferred because of essential work.

"I went into the infantry and trained at Fort Benning, Georgia, and was shipped to Germany. I was in the army for three years and in seven countries in Europe: Scotland, France, Germany, Czechoslovakia, Austria, and Switzerland. I saw beautiful Switzerland on a furlough, but all the other countries were torn up by the war.

"My squad was for replacement soldiers. Every Monday morning, we would line up. Six names would be called to replace men who had died. This went on for weeks until there were few of us left. The sergeant announced that six of us were going to the signal corps. I was never shot at, and I learned a lot about telephones. We could hear the fighting at the front. It is no fun not knowing if you will ever see home again. Now I can be glad that I had the experience.

"Alcoa gave me seniority for the three army years and put me back to work. I worked there a total of thirty-seven years. When work was dull, I was transferred from the machine shop to the rolling mill. I am thankful I was never laid off due to dull work times.

"When I got home of an evening, I set to farming. I bought Daddy his first tractor, a used John Deere. When our son, Ken, got started driving it, Edith wanted me to sell it. That model could rear up and kill a man. I got shut of it and got a Ford that was safe for a boy like Ken to drive. As I could, I bought good farm machinery for Daddy.

"My parents made every penny count. But my brother, Clarence, and I never felt poor. We had all we needed and as much as our neighbors. Mama had a sewing machine and made me beautiful shirts. You could buy a pair of overalls for a dollar.

"My mama traded eggs or a chicken at the rolling store. It was a truck loaded with groceries. He would take butter, eggs, and chickens in trade for flour, sugar, cornmeal, and other basic needs. He had coops in which to put the chickens. The rolling store helped the women who had no cars and needed basic groceries. Mama could get a large bag of hard candy for a nickel that lasted us a long time.

"Mama and the neighbor women always had quilts going. When we were eating or not quilting, the quilt hung on the ceiling. That kept the room warmer in the winter. She did beautiful work, and the neighbors would come of an afternoon in the winter, or she would walk to their houses to quilt. It was a social thing as well as good covers.

"One thing my parents always did was support the church. When I was a child, the preacher came twice a month. His son brought him and returned for him after the evening service. Somehow, Vonore was always peculiar about inviting the preacher to eat. Daddy would wait, and if no one asked the preacher to dinner, he would say, 'Preacher, get in the car.' Mama would cut a ham or go out and kill a chicken. She would have a great dinner on the table in no time. She always baked a cake or pie on Saturday for Sunday dinner. We always made the preacher feel welcome and at home. We would take him back for the evening service.

"I'm grateful for good parents. My mama died at fifty-two years of age, but Daddy cooked and took care of us. He got better from that painful lumbago, but he suffered a bad heatstroke. He was never strong after that and left more to me and to Clarence.

"It is a miracle God has brought me through eight surgeries. One year, Edith got after me to stop making a garden. I went to my heart doctor for my six-month checkup. I told him that Edith was after me to stop gardening, and I had promised to ask him about it. He said, 'I'll write you a prescription.' It said, 'This man is able to make a garden.'

"From beans to watermelons, I like to grow everything, and we give away to everybody we know who doesn't have a garden. I could say asparagus to zucchini squash. At church, they say, 'Lock your car, or Herbert Millsaps or Charles Niles may put zucchini or cantaloupes in it.' Nowadays, I put a nitroglycerin tablet under my tongue before I go to my little garden. Clarence, my brother, dropped dead in his garden.

"I'm grateful to God that Edith and I are living out our last days here. The changes in my community are vast and were unwanted, but now no one needs to drive seventy miles a day to work. Maybe the only way to change the Little Tennessee Valley was to destroy it and move the upland farmers like me away. It was one way to force change on a satisfied, contented people."[244]

Mary Fay Maynard and son Ricky Maynard Reap Change

Let us not grow weary, while doing good,
For in due season we shall reap
If we do not lose heart.
—Galatians 6:9 NKJV

Mary Fay Maynard and her son Ricky greeted me with warmth and friendship. We sat on the shaded porch of the old house that John Mowdy Lackey had moved there. The yard abounded with trees and shrubs. Mary Fay identified several as gifts from Ms. Johnnie Bell Lackey. She remarked that she received a Christmas card from John Jr. and a picture of his newest grandchild. Ricky served me an iced glass of Mountain Dew.

I asked Ricky to tell me of his first memories of John Mowdy Lackey. "He came to Soak—that's in Monroe County, off Ball Play Road. Daddy agreed to move to his farm. I was about ten years old, and we had to catch all our chickens. My older and younger brothers and I thought it was a great sport.

"Lackey taught me to drive his tractor. I was ten years old, and he sat with me until I could feel in the seat of my pants how to drive. We always called him Lackey, never Mr. John or Mowdy or Mr. Lackey. He had an exact way to do the work, and we learned his way. He treated us like men, but he did make us go to school.

"The farm grew wheat, oats, barley, and soybeans. We had a tobacco crop and always grew an acre of green bell peppers in the fall. One of my jobs was moving the irrigation on the peppers and in the spring on the tobacco. Lackey was proud of his cattle. He named them and knew them. That's not easy with white-faced cattle. He knew how he bred them and whose calf belonged to

88

what mama cow. We also had pigs and a milk cow. We made hay all summer. Lackey depended on Daddy to take care of the farm and cattle.

"After Lackey lost his farm, I worked construction. When I was twenty-four years old, I went to Michigan and got a job at a General Motors factory. We turned out thirty Cadillacs each day. City life was hard after being raised to be responsible for the life of animals and crops since childhood. I lived on a street with houses an arm's reach away. To be alone, I had to drive away somewhere.

"General Motors closed the factory in 1985 and moved it. I came home and took care of this place. Lackey deeded about three acres to Dad and Mother. I raised a big garden and kept an eye on Mama. Daddy went with cancer some years ago. After Lackey lost the farm, my daddy worked for the city of Vonore."

Mary Fay Maynard's fair blond complexion indicates an Irish ancestry. At seventy-two years, she remains a clear blue-eyed, strawberry blond with few wrinkles. Her well-toned, strong body serves her well although she admits she needs blood pressure medicine these days.

"My mama delivered nine children at home, and all were born healthy and lived to adulthood. I was Mama's last child. The neighbor woman didn't get there, so my daddy bragged that he helped me get born.

"When I was growing up, I attended school at Green Bell, Ball Play, and Antioch—all in Monroe County. Daddy moved us a lot. Jack and I lived at Soak in the Ball Play area of Monroe County. Lackey brought a big truck and two pickups. He moved us to this house, but it set where the lake is now. When he lost his farm, he moved the house here. Lackey put in a good word, and Jack started working for the town of Vonore.

"Jack and I had ten children. The last two were born in a hospital. I had a granny woman, a midwife, when my time came for the first eight births. All my deliveries were natural and normal. All my babies were born healthy, and all my children grew up healthy. God blessed Jack and me. I never had a miscarriage or a stillbirth. We were young and strong and worked from daylight to dark. I never saw a doctor with the first eight, and the children were strong"

"Lackey and Jack and our three boys worked the farm. When they had a big job, I would feed Lackey too. I remember one time, I had skinned poke stalk and fried them. He said he was going to get Miss Johnnie to fix him some at home. You gather poke in the early spring. If he and Jack got especially dirty, he would leave his coveralls here, and I washed them with Jack's. At some time, I got an automatic washer and dryer, but for years, it was heat the water for a wringer washer, and dry the clothes in the sun. We always had a freezer full of pork and beef. I froze vegetables from the garden and canned my beans.

"All my girls married and have families. They came about two Sundays ago. April 18 was my seventy-second birthday. I have twelve grandchildren and four great-grandchildren. It was good to see them all at once. None of them live too far away. I'm thankful for that.

"I lost William Randal in a car wreck several years ago. My other nine children are alive and healthy. God truly blesses my life and family. In some ways, I miss the simpler time. Jack and I never had money or fine possessions, but we loved all our children and life on the farm.

"Lackey's heart failed him. His little house in Vonore is in ruins. It is a sad sight. He fought with all he had to save the river and the rich farmland in the Little Tennessee River valley. Our way of life is lost forever, but now people don't work so long or so hard." Mary Fay smiled, and we sipped our icy drinks and enjoyed sitting on their front porch.[245]

Earl Melson Muses

I say to God, my rock,
"Why have you forgotten me?"
—Psalm 42:9a NKJV

Hope in God; for I shall again praise him,
"My help, my God."
—Psalm 42:11b NRSV

When asked to talk about the Little Tennessee River, Earl Melson muses, "We might as well forget it. We have to. We got beat on it, but we gave a good fight."

Earl thinks back and says, "My grandparents' farm bordered near the Mountain Settlement and the Citico area. The Little Tennessee River flowed nearby and was controlled by the Chilhowee Dam. Our farm was about twenty miles from Vonore. The Mountain Settlement is in Monroe County across from the Chilhowee Dam. Below Chilhowee Dam, the Little Tennessee flowed free until the Tellico Dam was closed more than thirty miles down the river. The Cherokee National Forest borders the Citico community, so for travel purposes, the county road ends there. The forest is open for camping, hiking, and, in season, hunting and fishing.

"Polly and I tend the graves of our ancestors in the Citico Baptist Church graveyard. We contribute money and our labor to prepare the cemetery for Decoration Day. Decoration Day is an important church service in rural East Tennessee. Brush is removed, the graves mowed, and flowers are placed on the graves. A memorial service is held at the church. Dinner is on the grounds, which means a shared picnic, and family ties are cemented and renewed. Cousins get reacquainted, and new babies are admired, and nobody wants to miss it. Polly and I will rest there when our time comes."

Earl points out, "The old two-room schoolhouse is used as a community center now. Before Monroe County had school buses, the Citico school provided an elementary education. A big cast iron stove stood in the center warming the room. In warm weather, mountain breezes blew through the large windows on either side of the rooms. I remember I was in first grade when the area got electricity in 1946. Ms. Evalena Cannon was the teacher, and she had a long hickory switch in the corner. I never got a switching that I didn't deserve, but I'll not elaborate on my misdeeds.

"Ms. Cannon started school with Bible reading, prayer, and the Pledge of Allegiance to the Flag. I still have the Bible she gave me for memorizing John 3:16. Her goal in teaching reading was for each child to be able to read the Bible, and I believe each parent approved.

"First thing one morning near Christmas, she asked who could go get a Christmas tree. Carson Williams and Carson Cooke got their hands up first. It was near time for school to be out when they drug in a cedar tree. We glued cotton to it and thought it was so beautiful.

"In Citico, Jerry Millsaps's store and Johnnie Bell Kirkland's restaurant were meeting places. Jerry and Dealie had most things you needed: gas, coal oil, cow and horse feed, and groceries. The families kept a tab and paid up each month or when they sold tobacco in the fall.

"William Reilly Williams was Carson's daddy. WR was a farmer, the preacher, and the mailman for the Mountain Settlement. He rode a horse and carried the mail in leather saddlebags. In winter, the road up that way was impassable for a car or a truck. WR was preacher at Citico Baptist. At some time, he was the preacher at Mount Pleasant Baptist Church in the Mountain Settlement. In his last days, he had a farm on the Blount County side of the Little Tennessee River, below the Chilhowee Dam. WR influenced my life, and I want people to remember him.

"A ferry out from Jerry Millsaps's store was a shorter way to Maryville than going through Vonore. That was Niles Ferry at Vonore, and then a bridge over the river for U.S. Highway 411 came later. The ferry near John Gray and his brother was Bacon's Ferry, and it was heavy used but still a day to travel to Maryville.

"That was the best land in Citico. John Gray and his brother farmed the bottom near the ferry. They grew the best corn and soybeans. It killed John Gray to see the water cover that fertile valley. The water from the lake is over the road where Jerry Millsaps's store stood. The land is rich up the Mountain Settlement way and not flooded, but it is idle now. TVA will lease it for farming if anyone thought they could finance a crop. It is hard to make a living on rented land, and no hope of ever owning it.

"When I graduated from eighth grade, my family moved to Blount County to work on a dairy farm. I graduated from Porter High School. I got up every morning at 4 AM and milked. I dressed for school, was a kid all day, but was home by 4 PM to milk again. I knew my math, but algebra and geometry were a challenge. I even took Spanish. I remember how the teacher would walk around algebra class and tell me, 'You can do it. You can learn anything you want to.' I believed her, but there was so little time to study or read at home. Dad and I worked until after dark." Earl remembered his struggle to get as much education as he could.

"I was planting potatoes for my grandpappy and grandmaw when Bob Dorward and Jerry Millsaps came. Bob needed men to start the Rose Island Nursery. I grew pine seedlings for years. When TVA won the battle over the Little Tennessee River, I went to Etowah to work for Hiwassee Land Company and Bowater. We did all we could to stop the TVA from building that dam, and I think many people did not realize how much it would flood. I read a map real good because I take crews to the woods to fight fires, but until a man sees the flooding and destruction of the land, he doesn't believe it.

"Polly and I have three children and a few acres near Madisonville. She works for banks, retires from one, and gets called to work at another. It's her talent, so I keep quiet. I worked for Hiwassee Land Company for thirty-eight and a half years. Bowater planted millions of trees, and I am proud of what I did. The bean counters at the mill (accountants and bosses) decided to sell the company's land and stop planting the cutovers. They gave me the golden handshake, but I enjoy retirement. Bob Dorward and I fished the Hiwassee River. I would get tangled in the bushes. He called that squirrel hunting. Mostly, I like to grow a garden.

"Monroe County is still about half-Democrat and half-Republican. The two parties united to fight for their land and way of living, but now it is back to half-and-half. Our struggle was long ago, and some people believed TVA would make the country rich. Every year, Monroe County raises property tax. Outlanders come in and build $500,000 houses and pay $200,000 for a lot. It doesn't seem to help the county government. TVA, who only pays in lieu of taxes, owns much land. The county used to get money from the sale of timber on the Cherokee National Forest. Outsiders put an end to timber sales. The trees just fall and rot. It is like the farmland that the government owns in the Mountain Settlement that grows nothing. I like to grow and tend the soil, but in the winter, I read history books. Two of my daughters are schoolteachers. And Jerome, my son, is a lawyer in Knoxville. My family likes to differ about the long-term effects of the changes that Polly and I tell them about." Earl grins.

"TVA promised to bring industries to Monroe County by getting rid of the farmers and old-time families, and it has brought in some industries near Vonore. TVA got Japanese and German companies to lease land and build buildings. I don't know any Monroe Country men who work here. There must be some. People come from Knoxville, Maryville, and Loudon County to work in the factories. If I had my way I would like to get a big dozier and push those buildings and asphalt into the lake, but I don't think that Jerome is the kind of lawyer that gets folks out of jail." Earl laughs at his joke.

"I doubt TVA will show a profit in their land grab. They destroyed so much. The fertile land cannot be restored. The pretty clear rushing water is gone forever. People get over the mad, and make the best of whatever happens. I count my blessings every day and thank the good Lord for the bitter and the sweet."[246]

Billie Curtis and son Tom Curtis Provide School Buses

Hear my child, and accept what I say.
—Proverbs 4:10 NIV

Billie Curtis remembers the night she met with other women in Ms. Johnnie Bell Lackey's parlor to plan a chicken barbecue for opponents of the dam that threatened their lifestyle. "I agreed to make a sheet cake, and about two hundred neighbors came to the meeting at Rose Island. That was over thirty years ago."

Billie and Raymond had bus contracts for Vonore school. Billie explains their business, "Monroe County did not have money to buy buses, so people like us invested in buses." Billie recalls that Raymond's first route was on the north side of the Little Tennessee River to a school named Little Tennessee School. "The county wanted more children to go to high school, so children were bussed from the Citico and Lakeside areas to Vonore High School. Gradually, the county closed the community schools like Toqua and Little Toqua (pronounced toe co) and we provided more buses.

"Raymond farmed Mrs. Grace McCammon's farm, his uncle Wayne Curtis's, and his uncle Clayton Curtis's farms. Some years, he rented acreage from Dr. Troy Bagwell, so he worked hard. All that rich bottomland is underwater or grown up in briars and trash trees now.

"That property across the road from my house was the beautiful Grace and Francis McCammon's farm. Today, it is wasted land and used for nothing. TVA gave it to the Fort Loudoun State Park. Part of Uncle Clayton Curtis's farm is not underwater and is sold to a housing developer, but that development is not complete yet. I think only one or two houses are finished, but the roads and waterlines are in place."

Tommy Curtis is fifty-seven years old now and is a stout forceful businessman. "I contract with the Monroe County schools to provide seven bus routes and three shuttle buses to Sequoyah High School in Madisonville. I keep three additional buses ready for emergencies and for athletic events and field trips," Tommy explains his work.

Billie says, "I'm proud of Tommy's management of the business."

Tommy says, "We never knew why TVA did not buy our farm and business. Daddy thought it might be because of the gas tank down by the road. It showed on the TVA maps. We thought that might qualify us as a business and make our place worth more than the farmland, Anyway, we got to keep our land. TVA took everything from the road in front of the house to the river.

"I started driving a tractor when I was ten years old. I've plowed and mowed the McCammon farm, Uncle Clayton's and Uncle Preston's farms. And for a few years, Daddy rented some of Dr. Bagwell's place. I'm about the only man left here who knew this soil and land. It was a rich valley and really produced, but Daddy and I worked hard.

"I've been swimming in the Little Tennessee River, but we didn't have a boat. I never floated it as a teenager. The plowing, planting, and harvesting kept us so busy that I never thought of going fishing or floating."

Billie says, "For some years after they moved everybody out, our school enrollment went way down. Some of my route is now underwater, and the roads are closed. I drove the school bus from 1960 until 1976. I drove from the time my daughter started first grade until she graduated from the University of Tennessee, Knoxville."

Billie Curtis is a hero and a role model for the hundreds of children who rode her bus. The hour's bus ride is a learning part of school for the children who lived so apart. On the bus, they socialize and learn to behave under her watchful eye. Recently, Gail Galyon, Debbie Lane, and Elaine Dorward recall the fun of bouncing over the Vonore railroad tracks. Don Keeble remembers his first-grade sweetheart, Elaine Dorward, and the teasing at home because he roared like a lion for her as they bounced on the long back seat.

Billie Curtis continues her story. "Raymond and I divorced in 1976, and I worked in sewing factories for fourteen years in Tellico Plains and for ten years or so in Madisonville. The factories moved overseas, and I found myself unemployed. If I got a GED (general education degree), I stood a chance of a job in Vonore Industrial Park and could receive unemployment benefits as long as I was in school. I took the training and studied hard, but I did not score high enough to get a diploma. I was seventy-nine years old, so I haven't worked since the sewing factories closed. I'm eighty-two now, so I don't mind staying home. I help Tommy by sweeping out the buses on Saturday."

Tommy remembers the buyout period. "Tennessee Valley Authority was buying Uncle Wayne's farm, and the TVA man found the hammer mill in which feed is ground for the cattle. The TVA man didn't know what to appraise it for. So he had Bob McCammon, the equipment dealer from Maryville, to come and look at it. He allowed Uncle Wayne $2,000 for it. All told Uncle Wayne got $200,000 for the land, sheds, barns, and house. Dr. Bagwell, Griffin Martin, and the Curtis family had the best soil, so TVA did better by them than a lot of folks."

Billie says, "One of the Toqua (pronounced 'toe co') community changes was the closing of the Toqua Presbyterian Church. The Bob and Johnny Carson families, Griffin and Nancy Martin, and others were moved out. So the presbytery sold the building. Lately, I've realized that one day I will need a preacher for my funeral, so I moved my membership from the Fork Creek Presbyterian Church to the Mount Zion Baptist. My childhood church, Fork Creek Presbyterian Church, has only a retired preacher. And he takes frequent vacations and trips. Mount Zion is up our road a few miles, and I've known the preacher since he was a child. He works in the box factory in Sweetwater and is rarely absent from his pulpit. That move has put my mind at ease concerning my funeral.

"I believe any woman can drive a school bus if she sets her head to it. My neighbor Betty Sparks drives an eighteen-wheeler from Pennsylvania to Florida. I'm eighty-two, and Betty's about sixty by now. I hope that Tommy never has to call on me to drive again, but I know I can."[247]

Muriel Shadow Mayfield Testifies to Congress

Muriel Shadow Mayfield has fond memories of their Citico farm. The Mayfields lived on a dairy farm in the Eastanaille Creek Valley in McMinn Count and Scott's brother, Tom, managed the creamery, milk, and ice cream plant in Athens. This McMinn County farm has been in the Mayfield family for five generations, but the level fields were small. Scott was the farmer and in charge of milk procurement for the Mayfield Dairy factory.[248]

Charles Armstrong from down the valley told Scott about a fine farm on the Little Tennessee River in Monroe County. The soil was fifteen to twenty inches deep, and the fields were broad and flat. After seeing it, Scott was so excited he could not sleep because he wanted the farm so intensely. His brother, Tom, was indifferent at first but then became a part owner. The tract was seven hundred to eight hundred acres from the original McGhee land holdings. Mr. Perry sold it to Scott. The farm manager was a Mr. Shirk and lived in the large old house on the property.[249]

Every weekend, the family would don overalls and work shoes and go to their farm. They rented a cabin on Citico Creek from Johnnie Bell and Ruele Kirkland. It was a two-room cabin with a wide porch, swing, and outhouse. The Kirklands had a grocery and restaurant. Johnnie Bell was known far and wide for her delicious home-style cooking. She took the Mayfields and their three children into her community family. She and Ruele were known for their generous nature and kindness to all the neighbors. In time, the Mayfields remolded a house on their farm for their weekend farming adventures.[250]

Their fertile fields produced corn and soybeans. There was a broad flat area next to the river. About fifteen to twenty feet higher, another broad, flat area was also under cultivation. After rains, many artifacts would wash to the surface revealing the site of ancient civilizations. The fishing would sour when it rained, so fishermen often walked the fields in search of artifacts.[251]

News that the Tennessee Valley Authority planned to flood the valley shocked the farming community of Citico. Appeals to the Mayfields to stop the proposed damming of the Little T stirred Scott and Muriel to go to the *Knoxville News Sentinel*. In vain, they tried to describe the valuable natural resources of soil, pure water, and priceless archaeological evidence of ancient peoples. To their dismay, they learned TVA had presented all the newspapers and public officials with graphs, facts, and figures that indicated great wealth would come to the valley by creating a shallow lake and buying land for TVA to sell. Pleas to save the Little Tennessee River were never printed in the *Knoxville News Sentinel*, for the editor had given his word to support TVA.[252]

Mrs. Alice Milton was aware of the history of the Mayfield farm because of the McGhee ties in her genealogy. She worked to influence historical groups to write letters to Congress. Muriel Mayfield spread information about the treasures of land, history, pure water, and the fishery. The Mayfield family all worked to get the letters of opinion and information written to Washington and to the *Knoxville Journal* and other newspapers.[253]

Muriel Mayfield vividly remembers, "The TVA meeting at the Greenback School was a hot one with the lunchroom packed to the walls. Aubrey Wagner, director of TVA, told the farmers and business people why the dam should be built but said, 'TVA would proceed only if the people wanted it.' Many spoke against the project, and no citizen spoke for it. The next day, Willard Yarborough's story in the *Knoxville News Sentinel* failed to reflect the emotions and oppositions to the damming of the Little T.[254] The failure of the media to give fair coverage hurt the people trying to preserve their farmland and history. No one, certainly not the Mayfield family, opposed industrial development. But I did not want the land destroyed by another dam. Twenty-two dams were within a fifty-mile radius of this area. Seventy-two thousand acres of industrial sites were already available in Tennessee as I remember it.[255]

"TVA's method was to request funding from Congress each year for a part of the project. Tennessee Congressman Joe Evins of Smithfield headed the House appropriations committee when the opposition started. A group headed by John Lackey, Judge Sue K. Hicks, Mrs. Grace McCammon, and I testified before the committee."[256]

Mrs. Mayfield says, "I remember the graciousness of Justice William O. Douglas. He entertained us with tea in his office in the Supreme Court building. The building and his office were elegant and in refined good taste. He and Harvey Broome of Knoxville knew the river, the mountains, and valued the natural environment. Justice Douglas got an assignment to write an article about the river and valley for the National Geographic Society. The rumor was government agencies would make it hard on the National Geographic Society if they criticized the TVA. I never knew why National Geographic refused to oppose the destruction of the priceless valley. Anyway, Justice Douglas published his article in a smaller magazine, *True*. Unfortunately, the priceless natural resource and different ways to develop the area for fishing, farming, and tourism got little attention.[257]

"Our appeal to the ways and means committee resulted in Congressman Joe Evins putting the funds requested for the damming of the Little T in a bill to study a dam on the Duck River in his district. Our meager and weak appeals to reason and conservation were heard by the farmers and environmentalists in West Tennessee, and those people prevented the building of that dam on the Duck River. The Tims Ford was that project.[258]

"Some far-thinking and smart people at the University of Tennessee realized the beauty and value of the river and land. Fish biologist David Etnier found a small fish. In Meigs County, I think we called it a hornyhead, but this was different in a biological way. He called it the snail darter because it ate snails from the bottom of the riverbed.[259]

Zyg Plater, a law professor, argued the case and won the case to stop the closing of the dam. By this time, the dam was built and a lot of land bought up.[260]

"TVA knew their power, however, and kept buying small tracks of land and kept on with the dam. TVA went around the new Endangered Species Act by changing the law so that it did not apply to this project. One advantage TVA has is a lot of employees. Only about three hundred families expected to be flooded. I made the one trip to Congress, but two years later, TVA brought up their funding request again. People, even in my family, were discouraged. Mr. Lackey went back to protest as president of the Association for the Preservation of the Little Tennessee River, and I guess the Fort Loudoun Association helped with some money. I think that Scott did. One thing about John Lackey was that he could go to Washington and spend about $300 in a week. I don't know that our representative John Duncan Sr. served him refreshments, but other congressmen and senators who were interested in agriculture and the environment did.[261]

"Scott and I went with others to visit with Senator Albert Gore Sr. By that time, he had forgotten the people in Tennessee and was deep in the pocket of TVA, just like John Duncan Sr. Gore was old, and his head was in Mexico and international politics. At his next election, we managed to defeat him. And he went to work for a strip-mining company, Peabody Coal Company in Kentucky.[262]

"I like to think that the long hard work that Scott and I did to save the Little T served as a spark. We didn't stop the destruction of the free-flowing river and fertile soil, but I hope that our efforts made the citizens aware that such make work or pork barrel projects can be bad. God is making no more land. Land with such deep and rich soil is scarce and cannot be replaced.[263]

"When I speak about farming, I come from a personal farming heritage, and the Mayfields' value and encouragement of purebred cattle and good practices are known in East Tennessee. There is no food or milk without good cows and fertile soil for growing soybeans, hay, and corn.[264]

"My father came to Meigs County as county agricultural agent in the twenties. I grew up on a farm with my five sisters. My mother was one of the few registered nurses in the county. She did anything she was called on to do. Once she delivered triplets. She took cardboard boxes and a light bulb and made an incubator to keep the premature babies alive. I remember how small they were, but all lived. Mama delivered many babies, sewed up wounds, set broken bones or whatever she could.[265]

"As farm agent, my daddy worked to make conditions better in Meigs County. A Delco system in Decatur, the county seat and only town, supplied some electricity. Worth Lillard and Daddy organized the Volunteer Electric Cooperative. They went to Washington to get help on buying electricity. Norris Dam, the first TVA dam, made electricity from water. Daddy and Mother were friends with the Norris Dam engineer Johnny Hershey from Pennsylvania. When he and his wife Betty visited us, they brought Hershey kisses. We five sisters loved their visits. After they returned to Pennsylvania, my parents took me to visit them. I was the middle child. My two older sisters were near in age. My twin sisters were much younger than I, so I didn't have a sibling buddy. I was spoiled by being picked for trips with my parents according to my sisters.[266]

"My mother worked to get school lunchrooms in Meigs County. She helped to start the library in Meigs County. My family worked hard on the farm, but we never felt deprived or put upon by our hard child labor.[267]

"When Scott and I raised our three children here on the Mayfield homeplace, we taught our children to work. My son, Scottie, who you can see selling Mayfield Dairy products on TV, says the worst job that he got was to sling blade the ditches by the road. The farm workers would be busy with important seasonal work, and when he was a child, the farmers mowed their own roadsides. Today, he uses the dairy barn as a woodworking hobby shop. I refinished old furniture and like wood, especially pine. I wish families today could teach their children the satisfaction of growing plants and making things. It is my family joke to call Scottie our Sanford and Son from the old TV show about a junk man. Scottie can see value in old things and make them beautiful and useful again.[268]

"When TVA came to buy our farm, Tom and Scot tried to keep the land not flooded to farm. They offered to give the bottomland if they could keep the above-the-waterline land. The buyer came back and said, 'No TVA would buy all the eight hundred acres.' The ancient village of Chota was on the higher level. TVA brought in backhoes and dug down to reveal where ancient peoples had lived. Posts for dwelling and stone tools were revealed. UT took the artifacts to McClung Museum to be cataloged some day.[269]

"Years later, a relative of Johnnie Bell and Ruele Kirkland came to Scott and offered to sell about sixty acres left of their holdings. Johnnie Bell and Ruele had gone to be with the Lord by then. Scott talked to our lawyer, Bill Biddle. They agree to form a company, Scobile, and buy it. Scott has been dead for about six years, but Bill Biddle and my three children still own it.[270]

Mrs. Mayfield says, "I am glad to have known the wonderful people in the Citico and Chota mountains and to have lived among them. They lost their land, farming, and timber-harvesting lifestyle. But I hope our stand against the damming of the Little T sends a signal. The message I want to speak is that people must oppose government projects that are questionable. We must stand against get-rich-quick projects, especially when land and timber are taken from the powerless. Lies as to benefits must be exposed, and citizens must keep asking questions. Our fight was lost. But I hope people will someday value pure, clean, free-flowing water and rich, deep, fertile soil."[271]

Ben Snyder Questions

Democracy should accommodate a great diversity of tastes.
Rivers and forests need humankind's protection.
    —William O. Douglas, *My Wilderness*

My first visit to Farnsworth Firearms was during deer season. The parking lot was jammed and business was brisk that cold, damp day in December. Ben Snyder invited me to come and talk when things slowed down.[272]

In midsummer, a Border collie and spaniel mix greet me with a wagging tail. The black dog with a white bib and collar follow me to Ben's counter. High on the wall, heads of deer, wild boars, and even a ram look over the rows and rows of hunting rifles along the wall and center of the building. Both large and small pistols are in showcases, but unlocked, Ben says. Accessories for hunting, even a bear trap, and all hunting needs pack the business.[273]

The store looks like a burglar's paradise and a shoplifter's dream. No dog or person guards the priceless inventory at night, but an expensive alarm system can summon the police who are a few blocks away.[274]

I first met Ben when he was a teenager. Snyder's General Store supplied basic needs for a spread-out rural community. My son, Bruce, had a fast-growing wide foot. Ben, whom I called Bennie then, would fit and order the best size. The Snyder family did this for all the community. With three children in four years, the caring service helped me and everyone who depended upon them.[275]

Ben's mama was the businesswoman of the family. His dad worked at Alcoa and farmed the family land. Ben reckons he is the fifth generation of Snyders to rear a family in Vonore. The first Snyder was a Moravian preacher, who also farmed. Ben had a brother and several sisters. His three girls are on their own and doing well. Ben still gardens but plans to cut back on his planting next year. One suspects his labor at the gun shop is pleasure and a means of keeping his mind sharp.[276]

As we talk, he stops to discuss hunting rifles with customers. All assure him that they are just loafering on this rainy day. "Loafering" is a Monroe County expression for time-out from hard labor to enjoy oneself. In the Not for Sale cabinet is the gun that Ben borrowed as a young teenager to go hunting in the Tellico Mountains.[277]

"Tubby 'Claude' Hammontree always loaned me his gun. Years later, I asked the aged Mr. Hammontree if I could buy the gun for old time's sake. One day, I looked out and saw Mr. Hammontree put something in my truck. Mrs. Hammontree frequently sent vegetables or jelly or something, so I thought nothing about it. Mr. Hammontree came into the store and said, 'Bennie, give me $30.'

"I thought he had left home without money and handed him $30. One of my little girls was standing behind the counter, and Mr. Hammontree handed her the $30.

"Puzzled, I asked, 'Why did you do that?'

"'You never give away a gun. It is bad luck. The old rifle is in your truck.'"[278]

Ben says, "I treasure my memories of those many hunting trips to the Tellico Mountains with my brother, Darrell, and my dad. Mr. Hammontree made them possible. He served for years on the county court, now called the commission. As a young man, he ran the Niles Ferry across the Little Tennessee River."[279]

Ben tells me, "I hate to remember the limbo that the three county areas experienced for years because of the threat of the valley flooding. Then the moving out took six to eight years, but the families had a twelve—to eighteen-month period to reinvest their money in more land. The Tennessee Valley Authority promised our community a great future. The Snyder family got $300 an acre, but many people got only $170 an acre.[280]

"It is possible my great-grandfather Preacher may have paid as little as $5 an acre, so the family avoided a capital gains tax by finding land to buy. Land now sells for $250,000 to $300,000 an acre. Now our land taxes are so high that old families are hard-pressed to keep the family farms. For generations close-knit families were common. We are still the same water, but different branches.[281]

"My mama was a Sloan. Before it was Snyder's General Store, it was Sloan's General Merchandise. The Sloans are business families from gas stations to used cars to farming and cattle and real estate. My roots are working people, who worked to have a good name in the community and in business."[282]

Ben remembers, "I floated and fished the river many times. The age of the river impressed me and stirred my imagination. I could picture Indians making the fish traps, standing on the rock traps, and spearing or netting the fish for drying or eating. I will draw you a picture of the fish traps as I can see the long piles of rock laid in a parallel slant to the bank."[283]

Snyder frowns before he smiles, "Local folks did get it, as to how, Washington is where the power is to destroy a community. Congressman John Duncan always stopped at Snyder's store on his reelection tour. I remember how he would buy a slice of bologna. My mama or daddy would make him and Ed Bailey, his front man, a sandwich. Congressman Duncan Sr. had a countryside and convinced everyone that he really cared about his people. I think Duncan was a good man but got caught in politics in approving the final money for the dam. He would try to solve any problems that he could. His front man, Ed Bailey, was a former pro baseball player and visited a lot for Duncan."[284]

A hint of regret and sadness is noticeable in Ben Snyder's tone as he ponders today and the past. "The great future is what TVA promised, but it is not here yet. The wages in the industries TVA brought in are low considering the rest of the United States. Lowe's Hardware and a drug company use Vonore for a shipping place. Loading and unloading trucks isn't the job the old farm boys expected. Taxes are higher, and some of the second-home folks buy little locally. Farnsworth's Firearms does well from the local folks. And the old farms are a haven for deer, squirrel, and rabbits. But productive farming land is lost. Things are looking up, so maybe the next generation will see the great future TVA promised when change was forced on my community."[285]

Juanita Wolfe McCollum Says Repay No Evil

Repay no one evil for evil.
Have regard for good things in the sight of all men.
If it is at all possible, as much as depends on you,
live peaceably with all men.
                                        —Romans 12:17-18 NKJV

"My husband Beryl and I owned twenty-eight acres on the Little Tennessee River and up Island Creek. We were paid $28,000 for the land, house, barn, and sheds. It was hard to get information. TVA promised to help the displaced find new land but failed to help us. Every time we asked one of them a question, they said someone else had to answer that. It was as if the right hand did not know what the left hand was doing.

"I've been here thirty-two years. Sinking Creek Road and Greenback are a good place to live. Beryl has been gone twenty-two years, and I miss him. I'm glad that Shirley has an apartment in the basement. I work three days a week for the U.S. Forest Service in Tellico Plains. I'm in the information office. I've been there for years and glad I have the job.

"I know there is going to be change. I go to Vonore and walk with my friend, Mary Kidd. I still support the Vonore United Methodist Church. I'll bet that you remember this and held up a bumper sticker that said Save the Little T. It looks like new, but I saved it from the time many cars and trucks had them.

"I could not save the Little Tennessee River, but my life has flowed on, and I enjoy a serene maturity."[286]

Shirley McCollum Brown Sees the River Die

Our culture must fight intrusions
that destroy our natural rivers, soil, fish, and forests.
With easy justification we blithely drown another river,
disembowel another mountain
with gouge-and-get out strip-mining, and we further pollute
our air and streams, as we pack tighter the cities
and slice smaller the wild land and the cultivated land and forests.
                                              —Harvey Broome, *Earth Man*

"Day after day I saw the Little T die. I worked in Sweetwater and drove across the dam from Loudon County. It was 1980, and the gates were closed. Each day, I watched the slow death of the once free-flowing river. I was so sad that tears welled up, and my throat hurt.[287]

"My extended family fought a long fight to preserve their land, but TVA decided the rednecked farmers did not need their land. The threat of the dam was discussed from 1937 but actively pushed from the mid-sixties. Industrial development was possible without destroying the farmland. The dam forced people to move away because the government required the money to be reinvested in land.[288]

"My grandfather was Dr. McCollum, and he gave my daddy forty-seven acres on the creek that flowed into the river. I guess that is Island Creek. Grandfather McCollum gave my aunt Johnnie Bell Lackey the farm on the Tellico River. For a time, my mother's parents, the Wolfes, farmed that land. It was one of the best farms anywhere.[289]

"By the time the fight with TVA was hot, I attended Hiwassee College. Uncle Mowdy was president of the Association for the Preservation of the Little Tennessee River.[290] The congressmen and senators demanded letters from the people as to whether to destroy the land and water to develop industry or to keep the farmland and free-flowing river. Few people in the three county areas wrote business letters or had typewriters. Uncle Mowdy would bring the handwritten letter to me, and I typed them. My teacher at Hiwassee knew what I was doing and allowed a friend and me to type after class. Bob Dorward at Rose Island Nursery typed a lot of the letters for people. And Alice Milton, the historian at the Fort Loudoun site, also typed for people. That was my part in trying to stop TVA from destroying the water and land in my area.[291]

"As more than thirty years have passed, TVA has developed Vonore as a shipping hub. Products are shipped in an eight-hundred-mile radius from a drug company and Lowe's Hardware and others. You don't need a college degree to know this could be done without a six-thousand-acre lake and the forced sale of acres above the flooded land. TVA can do this with the law of eminent domain. Thus far, the unions are kept out of the industries, so wages are lower than in the Northeast. Many jobs pay $8 or $9 an hour for loading and shipping at the distributing centers. Some of the industries are reported to keep hiring new people and getting rid of the older workers to keep wages down. People get let go so the companies don't have to pay benefits. The businesses rely on a lot of temporary labor. I must give the Tennessee Valley Authority and the Tellico Reservoir Development Agency credit. Jobs are available.[292]

"I am grateful that I grew up in Vonore. My sadness at seeing so much wasted is because I love my country. Not just this small three-county area, but all of it. In all directions, my family was and still are Democrats, but both parties share blame for the foolish mistakes. After all, Republican John Duncan Sr. slipped the final money through Congress with the exemption of TVA from the Endangered Species Act. Democrat Albert Gore Sr. was afraid of TVA, and he did their bidding without hearing a word of the people's commonsense pleas. Senator Howard Baker got the bill through the Senate. President Jimmy Carter, a Democrat, signed the final appropriations bill. And Democrat Jim Sasser pushed for the dam.[293]

"Growing up in the Little T Valley was a unique experience. I treasure it. Butch Atkins was a town character. He went barefoot and wore cutoff, ragged overalls, but he loved children. He would come by our house and ask Mama if he could take me to town. Mama had four younger children, so I took his hand, and we walked several miles to the Vonore Drug Store. Butch bought me an ice cream cone, and I would settle into the magazine rack. Dr. Troy Bagwell, Uncle Mowdy Lackey, Claude Hammontree, and, of course, Bill Kikpatrick, the druggist, would talk about world events. I was only five years old, but apparently, the men thought early reading no novelty. After Butch got the news, we would walk home.[294]

"A place of interest in Vonore was the yellow Italian brick building. An Italian was dating one of the Hughes girls, an aunt of mine, and he made the yellow bricks in an Italian style that they used in Italy. Downstairs, Sam Tipton had his leatherworks, and upstairs was a dance hall. The building was built with an elevator. The story goes that the Baptist Church was praying for the sinners at the dance hall, and the elevator stopped. I think stairs were built later, but that ended dancing in Vonore. Later, the building burned.[295]

"My uncle Bobby Wolfe would come by and ride me on a mule to my grandparent Wolfe's farm near the joining of the Tellico River to the Little Tennessee River. My grandparents moved away from that farm in the fifties. The Jack Maynard family farmed it for Uncle Mowdy and Aunt Johnnie Bell until TVA bought it. Most of it is underwater now, except for three acres or so that Uncle Mowdy deeded to Jack.[296]

"I was in the first grade when the elementary school was built on the Highway 411. Vonore always had a huge PTA and enthusiastic fund-raisers, especially talent shows. The parents knew the teachers, and the teachers knew the families from way back. The teachers lived in the communities and really cared for the children. Vonore High School had the best percentage of students graduating from high school in Monroe County, but it needed improvement. Many of the graduates went to college and became professional people.[297]

"After I graduated from Hiwassee College, I worked in Madisonville at the Citizen and Farmers Bank, and then in Greenback at the Merchant and Farmers Bank. After my son was born, I stayed home until he was school-age. I was bookkeeper at a manufacturing company in Sweetwater for thirteen years. After Mark grew up, I divorced and wanted to travel and do some other kind of work. I went to Florida and was hired to look after the housekeeping and maintenance of a large hotel. Each spring and fall, Aunt Johnnie Bell paid me to deep-clean her house. This experience came in handy. I knew how a room should be taken apart and truly cleaned. Then I spent a year at a dude ranch in Colorado. There were 160 units, and I hired thirty college students to clean.[298]

"The hills of Tennessee beckoned me home, and like a true hillbilly I returned and found a similar job at the Comfort Inn in Oak Ridge. I enjoyed that for seven years before I wanted to come home to Vonore and Greenback. I earned my real estate license, surrendered my politics, and tucked up my knowledge of the past wrongs.[299]

"Before I left my insurance coverage at the Comfort Inn, I decided to get a checkup. The doctor found cancer, and I had surgery and radiation. Now I'm as strong as that old mule Uncle Bobby and I used to ride to visit Grandma Wolfe.[300]

"If I had not indulged my emotional state and anger about TVA winning the battle, I might have gone into real estate earlier. It was years before I would visit Vonore. Now I love being back. Old high school friends remind me of my basketball-playing successes. I already knew the lay of the land, and my years of looking up deeds of trust and taking loan applications at the banks stands me in good stead. I find real joy in finding the best home for people and helping with the financing.[301]

"I predict this area will continue to grow. When the Indians put a casino on their leased land, and more hotels and docks are built, land prices will increase. I advise my friends and clients to hold onto their land for more people will be moving here and needing homes. It is exciting to work in Vonore and keep friendships from childhood and to meet new people who recognize a good place to live."[302]

James Riley "Junior" Pugh Loves His Land

Yea, they [the heathens] despised the pleasant land,
they believed not his [God's] word.
—Psalm 106:24, KJV

Junior Pugh is emphatic as he says, "TVA's offer for my 235-acre Rose Island farm was insulting. I'm still glad that I went before their kangaroo court of three judges that the Tennessee Valley Authority picked. It didn't help me financially, but I'm glad that I put up a fight.

"I went to all the local meetings and helped John Mowdy Lackey and Beryl Moser go to Washington, but I never went myself. As our struggle dragged on for years and people were forced out, attendance at our meetings dwindled out. Folks whose land wasn't bought didn't care and couldn't see industrial development didn't depend on a lake.

"As I see it today, young people still go out of the area to work. Sea Ray boat company tests a few new models in the lake, but the other companies don't use the lake. I still get mad and hurt when I remember how the Tennessee Valley Authority treated people like me"

"My daddy had two hundred acres of hilly-pasture-type land on the north side of the Little Tennessee River. He had a large dairy herd and bought the north end of Rose Island to grow feed for the cows. Daddy used Nine Mile Creek to cool the milk. He covered a spring to hold ten to twelve ten-gallon aluminum cans. Each day, he collected Ben Clark and other neighbors' milk and drove to Knoxville to sell it. He was one of the few men around here with a truck, so when neighbors needed to go to Maryville, they rode along. He picked them up on the way back.

"When the TVA land buyers got to north side of the river, I got a big shock. I was offered no money but could keep fifty acres of my two hundred acres. I knew the messenger was acting on his orders from higher up, so I told him, 'No deal.'

"The next offer was better than my rich island farm, and this farm is hilly pasture. I was let keep fifty acres and the homeplace across Highway 72."

Junior points to the land across an inlet and explains, "That housing development over there was my farm. TVA forced me to sell it to them, and they turned around and sold it for a big profit.

"I built that dock off my front yard so my grandchaps could fish or tie up a boat. I had to pay TVA $5,000 for one hundred feet of shoreline in order to put the dock there and walk to the water. That water was Nine Mile Creek before the impoundment in 1980.

"I loved the Little Tennessee River all of my life. I rented a boat from Hoss Holt and floated with my buddies. One boat would float on each side and scare up the ducks. We mostly got green heads, which are good eating.

"Canadian geese try to come up in my yard, but I try to keep them wild by not feeding them and shooing them off. I see a flock of wild turkeys, plenty of deer, and the coyote packs come and go through this farm. I watch the red foxes and the yellow foxes in summer and notice how the yellow foxes turn into gray foxes in winter.

"I love living near Vonore. For thirty-three years, I drove two hundred miles a day to Oak Ridge where I worked in management in the weapons laboratory doing top secret work. Since I retired, I built this house, my son a house. And today, I worked on Shelia Wolfe's house.

"Shelia Wolfe's grandfather, Max Wolfe, taught me to farm. Ben Clark was overseer for the Rose Island farm because I was only seven years old when my daddy died. My mama managed the two-hundred-acre farm and the dairy herd on the north side of the Little T. Mr. Max Wolfe rented the Rose Island farm for years and knew the land and how to cross the river. We had a checker planter that I got rid of only recently. A check planter plants two rows at a time so the corn or soybeans can be plowed in two directions. A metal marker was set, and the machine dropped the corn or beans evenly in two rows. Both Mr. Max and his son, Estel, could do this perfectly. Many farmers planted in the checkered pattern in order to make keeping the weeds clear."

Junior remembers, "I never went back to look at my soybeans without seeing where an artifact hunter had walked the rows. Rose Island was lived on for longer than I can imagine, but it had to be a large strange artifact for me to get off the tractor and pick it up.

"I recently sold ten acres and the homeplace house to my sister, who is the family historian. I do know that the first Pugh came into the Nine Mile Creek and Baker's Creek area about 1770, but I leave the kinfolk details to her."

Junior and his wife live on a knoll overlooking the Tellico Lake or, as Junior calls it, the flooded Nine Mile Creek. Besides building houses, he restores vintage cars and, like an authentic Appalachian American, has a passel of cars near his home. He says,

"I want you to write my story so that my grandchildren will remember that rich sandy soil that was as fine as the Nile Valley of Egypt before it was flooded. My country's loss is bitter to me because I know industrial development was possible without losing the land and river." [303]

By His Hand, We Are Fed by Anonymous

In order to protect kinfolks from embarrassment concerning the family history, all names used in this narrative are fictitious.

The ornament in the middle of the dining room table reveals Colonel and Hetty's way of looking at life. It states, "By His hand, we are fed." They are grateful to God for the comforts, peace, and love they enjoy in their mature years.

I ask them to tell me about growing up in the Little Tennessee River valley. Hetty begins, "I grew up at Little Toqua and Colonel at Nottchey Creek. Life was hard, very hard." She dropped her head and fought back tears.

"I was born in 1937, and ways to earn wages were sporadic. There was no electricity or car. My daddy would work a job for a while, and then he was back to Grandpa's farm and his family. I was the oldest child, and Daddy's two brothers lived with us. My sisters, Carrie and Florence, and my cousin Jean made a house full. Grandma Watts had six children with Grandpa Watts and six by her first husband."

"We loved our daddy, who was kind and good to us and did all he could for his family. He had only one bad fault. He cussed until he got saved, and then he stopped his foul language. It was a miracle, for it was his way of talking all the time. I remember when I was three years old. Daddy was at the apple tree, and I yelled, 'Bring me an apple with a string of oaths that would set a fire!'

"Daddy picked up a switch and started after me. My grandmother stopped him. 'She is talking like you do. It is all that she hears.' Shamed, Daddy turned away.

"My grandmother was a godly woman. She would sit in the front room and pray and read the Bible while the men poured up the whiskey in the kitchen. None of her boys ever served time in prison. I think a Mama's prayer protected them.

"One time, Carrie and I put two kittens into the cast iron teakettle that was on the floor beside the big old woodstove. Grandpa caught us and switched us. I have the old kettle that reminds me of Grandpa and to be kind to animals. I think I was about four years old and Carrie, three.

"On cold winter mornings, I think of that Jersey cow that I had to milk starting when I was nine years old. Grandpa would wake me up at five o'clock to go to the barn. He believed that a Jersey cow gave more milk for a woman and that a cow could know whose hands milked her. Maybe so, she gave me a heavy bucket every morning. Every frosty winter morning, I thank the good Lord that I don't have a cow to milk before dawn.

"One year, we grew so much corn that Mama pickled a fifty-gallon wooden barrel of corn on the cob. It sat outside by the back porch. The men who worked the upper still would go by and reach in and get a cob to eat as they climbed up the hill to work. Mama would get so mad because their hands were dirty. Grandma and Mama had that crew to feed for dinner, so it was hard work for them. Mama cooked on a woodstove, and water was carried from the spring. It was sulfur water and took some getting used to. She and Grandpa worked a garden. And Grandma canned, dried, or pickled all summer. Mama was pregnant or caring for a baby during those years.

"When I was six, I had a five-mile walk over a knob and through the woods to school. It was an old Indian and deer path and no real road. Mama got up a petition to the Monroe County School Board to build a school at Little Toquo. It was named Touquino and was torn down years later. Mama became the teacher at Touquino. Her parents could not afford to send her to her last year of high school, but she got on a government program for poor youth. She worked in the records at the courthouse in Madisonville and saved every penny possible. The next year, she and her sister graduated from high school as valedictorian and salutatorian. Mama loved teaching and had positions at Mount Pleasant, Citico, and Antioch and other one—or two-room schools in later years. Her last year, she taught at East Sweetwater, an eight-teacher school. But her politics were wrong, so she lost that job. Back then there was no tenure, and the county was about half-Democrat and half-Republican. Both parties used the school-teaching jobs for patronage.

"I went to school to her, Ms. Edna McMahan, and Ms. Garnet McSpadden at Touquino through eighth grade. By then, Monroe County had a school bus to take the high school-age children to Vonore. My mama and daddy rented our house at Little Toquo and rented a house near the school bus route. The house was near Jones Bend and might have been owned by Doc Gray. My ninth grade at Vonore High School was the worse humiliation and pain a kid could suffer. Every day, I begged to quit. Every morning, Mama marched me to the school bus with a big hickory stick in her hand. Every kid on the bus saw this. It is no wonder I failed a semester of English. I was a stubborn brat, but Mama was determined her girls would go to high school. Many of my grade school friends did not, especially the girls.

"I had only a pair of old ladies' comfort high heel shoes, two pairs of jeans, and a short fur jacket. My aunt bought me the shoes, and they were exactly the style she wore. I thought the high block heels and laced-up shoes were terrible. The children from Citico had few clothes. On days I had to stand up before the class and give a book report, I played sick and stayed home. The teacher would hear them laugh and giggle at me and say nothing.

"My cousin Jean helped me get through high school by sending a box of clothes and a pair of loafers. She was my uncle Howard's daughter, and they lived in California. Mama and I were the same size. Every night, we brushed and aired what we wore that day. Once a month, we went to Madisonville and had our clothes dry-cleaned. I remember a corduroy skirt that made me look better. Mama and I wore it for years. Mama taught school. But there were Carrie, Florence, and my cousin Jean for Mama and Daddy to dress and feed. They tried to treat us all the same.

"A new teacher came to Vonore High School when I was in my senior year. It was Mrs. Betty Moser Black, and she was determined that I graduate. I took ninth-grade English for one semester for the third time and eleventh-grade English for the second time and senior English. She convinced me that I wanted to learn it and could. Another thing that helped me was that Mama and Daddy decided I ought to drive the car to school so the four of us could get home earlier to work. Having the car raised my status at school, and I made a friend. Like I said, many of the girls I went to grade school with did not go to high school or dropped out after the first year. Now I am glad for Mama's big hickory stick and for Mrs. Black's encouragement and belief in me so that I did get to graduate.

"My uncle Howard, he's the one who moved to California, had the best whiskey business. He bought a farm at Kingston, Tennessee. By that time, I was fifteen years old and had my driver's license. On Sunday afternoons, Uncle Howard would drive over in his big DeSota car. He asked, 'Would you girls like to drive over to Kingston to the farm?' It was a pleasant drive of about fifty miles one way. When my two sisters and cousin Jean got there, he always asked, 'Will you go to the store and get some eggs, bacon, milk, and bread?' Off I would go, proud to drive the big, old DeSota.

"In the months to come, driving the DeSota was risky. I was stopped and searched every time I took the dry-cleaning to Madisonville. The police recognized the DeSota. Uncle Howard used his nieces to haul his whiskey to Kingston. He buried it on the farm until he could sell it. The meanness of him using me to haul his whiskey makes me furious to this day. It has been fifty years or so. He knew the law was onto him, so he moved his family to California.

"In the fall, after I graduated from Vonore High School, I enrolled in Knoxville Business College and studied bookkeeping. I rode the bus to Knoxville each day and walked several blocks in the dark of winter to the school. It was a dangerous route, but I was almost fearless at seventeen. The college let you pay for the training after you got a job. I got a job at Fletcher Meatpacking Company after one semester. My bookkeeping has proved helpful in many ways.

"Mama moved us to Michigan the next summer. Daddy had a job in a car factory. I got a job in a restaurant and saved my money. When the time for school to start came, Carrie and Florence wanted to go home, so we moved back to Mama's house in Toqua. My hardworking daddy stayed in Michigan, and Mama worked in a rug factory in Sweetwater.

"I used my savings from the Michigan work to buy the restaurant equipment in a restaurant in Vonore. The Greenback Merchant and Farmers Bank loaned me the balance of the money I needed. Now I wonder about her loaning money to a nineteen-year-old with little experience. I ran it for three meals a day seven days a week. After ball games at the high school, the place would be crowded. I made chili by the five-gallon pot. Colonel would stop in and buy a cup of coffee. He and my daddy would help me after ball games. Colonel worked building the Chilhowee Dam. I made a good day's work when I married him. I paid off my note at the bank and sold the restaurant.

"We could buy a salvage house from Oak Ridge and put it on some land Colonel had at Howard's chapel. With the money from the restaurant sale, we went back to the bank. And Ms. Kennedy set up the payments for $1,600, so we could pay as we could. The way she explained it was that if we got laid off, the bank would not take the house. As it happened, that was a smart plan. The building was a twenty-four feet by twenty-four feet flattop, and later, we put a roof on it. We moved in, and I carried water from a spring.

"Colonel was building Chilhowee Dam and staying up there weekdays. His friends liked for him to make a little home brew, a kind of beer. He had some going in a crock in the bathroom with a siphon to a bucket of water. The hose is called a thumper because of the thumping noise it makes. You could hear the gas coming off, and our house smelled like beer. The time came for it to come off. Colonel said for me to take it off and bottle it. I was raised to obey my husband, and we were newly wed and still on our honeymoon. I locked the doors and pulled down the shades. I strained the workings out and bottled it in quart jars. It was really mellow and beautiful home brew. Right up to 1975 when the people were moved out, most of the families up Citico and Toqua made corn whiskey, or they made home brew. It was a way to get cash and to give a gift to a special person.

"Now whiskey making is a lost art, but one of my uncles could shake a quart and tell if it was made on copper coils or aluminum. An experienced ear can hear a certain beat and know if it is good corn whiskey. There was bad stuff made by using shortcuts, like Draino. Colonel can tell about finding a jar in the woods and taking a sip that made his nose bleed. You can bet that he threw it up fast.

"One of the great places at Citico was the swimming hole at Citico Creek. It was cold, but not as cold as the Little Tennessee River. I remember the J hole where the men stopped after work and took a bath. They washed and swam, naked as a jaybird.

"Colonel and I loved to eat at Johnnie Bell Kirkland's restaurant. It was the best place to eat. Folks would drive from Knoxville and Chattanooga to eat at Citico. She put platters and bowls on the table, and all her food was delicious. She fed Mrs. William O. Douglas and the *National Geographic* photographer when Justice Douglas was writing a story about the river. TVA got to *National Geographic* magazine, and the editors did not print the article. It was in *True* magazine and a good article. Unfortunately, the Little Tennessee was not saved or preserved."

Colonel nods and explains, "I worked construction, but it was off and on. In winter, I pulled pine seedling at Rose Island for Bob Dorward and Bill Keithley. One day, I was laid off from construction and a-sittin' by the road watching the cars and trucks go down Highway 411. We country boys called it loafering. Bob saw me and told me to go to the nursery. I worked full-time. TVA took the nursery, and we moved it to Georgia. You can't move something like that in a day, so we were back and forth for months."

Hetty picks up, sharing her feeling about this time. "We would come home to Mama's every weekend. All the way back to Georgia, I bawled and bawled. I did this for five years. I thought I would die because we were so homesick. We hurt so for people we knew. One Sunday, on driving up to our little trailer, the Lord revealed to me that it is not where you live, but how you live. After eight years, we were able to sell our house in Vonore.

"That Sunday, God spoke to me. I looked at our little trailer and the trailer park. I decided to make it home. We fixed up the yard, planted a garden, and made friends. By the time we built a house at Fairmont, Georgia, every person in the trailer park was our friend.

"One day, a man came and asked me to work in his rug factory. I worked for him for twenty-one years. Now we go back and visit our Georgia friends. They come to Vonore to see us. New people come to Vonore now, and Colonel and I try to make them welcome."

Colonel explains, "I make sourdough bread. Hetty and I take it to new folks, the sick, or folks having troubles that we hear about."

Hetty shows a bottle of detergent that she had dressed in a shamrock apron. "My Sunday school class at the Vonore Missionary Baptist Church fixes stuff for our shut-ins. It cheers them up.

"While we were still in Georgia, we bought this land in Vonore. It was part of the farm of the mean old English teacher who did not know what to do with the rebellious little thirteen-year-old in the faded jeans and old-lady high heel shoes. Now only three-fourth of an acre of the land near here sells for $200,000, they say."

Colonel and Hetty laugh. "Who would have ever thought we would ever sit on our front porch and watch grown men play golf? Our little five acres is across the road from a golf course." Colonel explains, "It is made like the Link in Scotland, and they call it the Link. I watched some Mexicans dig a hole and put sand back into it. I walked over and asked them what they were doing, and they said it was a sand trap. The rich men get their ball in the trap and knock the sand out. Sometimes, I see one throw it out and give up. It is a show to sit up here and watch. They named the development over there Heehee. Nobody knows how they made up the name, but it is supposed to be Indian. The homes in Heehee are huge, and some of the people only live here part of the year.

"Vonore has industry now after about thirty-five years since everyone was moved out. They brought businesses from Japan and Germany. The buildings are concrete over cinder blocks, big rectangles with no windows. A few are aluminum siding, but they are smaller. The TVA arrangement is strange. The business gets the place rent-free for ten years. They get some sort of tax break from the county. After ten years, some of the industries move. Several are large and cover acres, and many people work there. It is good that they are there because when Hetty and I grew up, there were few jobs. The available work paid little. The risk of prison was real for whiskey makers because a still cannot be hidden for long.

"The plus side was that we knew everyone, and everyone knew us. At Toqua, Little Toqua, and Citico, we didn't need a gated community. We knew our neighbors. Our dogs knew to bark if a strange car passed by.

"God is good to us. The Vonore Missionary Baptist Church has grown. Hetty and I welcome the new people who retire here or come and go for a few months each year. Our church and our hearts are big enough to share our faith with them. Maybe God sent us away so that we would have sympathy for the people who have no roots and no family here. They chose a good part of God's beautiful world. TVA did not drown our spirits, but the changes made us depend upon the good Lord. We thank the Lord every day for bringing us through the hard knocks of our childhood and young-adult years without bitterness or hatred."

Betty Jo Steele Shows Faith and Courage

Joey Steele urged me to meet his mother, Betty Jo, and all the brothers and grandchildren, who gather every Sunday for dinner with his mother. October 1, 2006, was a gloriously beautiful East Tennessee day, and the house was packed with folks from her eight-month-old great-granddaughter (Joey's granddaughter) to her oldest son, Frankie.

Perhaps, the sorrow and hardship of their father's early death and their mother's honesty about their money cemented the family. Frankie and Don were teenagers; Sherrie was thirteen, and Joey, eight, when their daddy died on June 2, 1972. Before the family recovered from that blow, the Tennessee Valley Authority forced Mrs. Steele to sell their home and boat-rental business in September 1972.[304]

Betty Jo sadly remembers, "I argued that the payment wasn't enough for the land, the store, the dock, and another five-bedroom house."

"The buyer told me, 'You don't need such a large house.'"

Betty Jo said, "But I knew my teenage daughter needed her own room."

Her brother-in-law Junior found a house on Highway 129, and she borrowed money to buy it. Frankie already had work experience with Hoss Holt's grocery and boat rental, so as soon as he was old enough, he found a job rebuilding and relocating Highway 72. A memorable part of that job was setting the explosives in the rock. He also learned to operate a Bob-cat, and in between temporary TVA work, he rented a Bob-cat and landscaped the yards for the new folks, who were moving into Tellico Village at Loudon. Frankie has his dad's adventuresome streak, so TVA maintenance and repair service valued his work, such as hanging by a belt over deep water to work on a dam.

In 2006, Frankie is a self-employed carpenter and plumber. He is married to Pam and has adopted her three sons. Their son Steven prayed before the meal for his large extended family. He is a high school senior and expects to get a football scholarship. His career goal is mechanical or electrical engineering.

Steven showed surprising maturity by agreeing with his grandmother that he would not play a pickup football game with his cousins because he could not risk an injury. He also said, "I told coach that I would not play basketball this year. I want to protect my ankle that I twisted last year."

Pam and Frankie introduced their son Brandon who is a freshman at the University of Tennessee at Knoxville where he is a premed student. Brandon packed a care package of his grandmother's turkey and roast pork as he explained, "I can study better on the weekend at home. I work part-time with a medical laboratory on brain tissue research."

Frankie's firstborn son is Tillman, who works as a jailer at the Monroe County Jail. Tillman had a sister, Hailee, who died at age five, after an extended illness. Both Tillman and Hailee are special to Grandmother Betty Jo because they were with her during their early years. Pam and Frankie have a twelve-year-old daughter who favors Betty Jo with her beautiful blond hair and skin.

All three Steele sons have suffered disappointments in youthful marriage. Recently, Don Jr. rescued his divorced wife and put her and his stepdaughter in his nearby house, and he and his son Cody moved in with Betty Jo.

One of Don's first jobs was as a Monroe County deputy sheriff. Don did not recall an adventure of his own, but remembered his great grandfather Joe Steele. As a deputy sheriff, Joe Steele once had to raid and bust up his brother Hal's still on Four Mile Creek, which is up Highway 72 East. Family troubles did not result since brother Hal was not at the still, therefore not arrested for bootlegging.

Billie Jo's love story with Don brings smiles. She and her sister left their flat south-Georgia home to work for the telephone company in Atlanta where her sister introduced her to Don. They hit it off, but Don was soon off to the Korean War. He returned with only one leg and damaged by several bullet wounds but was able to woo Betty Jo. She agreed to marry but would only live in Tennessee if he built her a house on level ground. She was sure that she could never live on a hill. The difficult requirement forced some looking, but Don found six acres in the river bottom on the Little T and near his brother and father's property.

When pregnant with their first child, she decided she wanted to be with her mother for the delivery. The men planned to build her house as she had sketched it. She returned with her six-week-old Frankie. Betty Jo described her father-in-law as a builder of sorts. First, she noticed no room had a closet.

They could fix that. To her surprise, he had reversed the kitchen so, as he put it, "you can see the river while at the sink."

"With the old man's revision the dining room had no view of the river," Betty Jo smiled.

Betty Jo saw Don's wild and happy streak when he surprised her by arriving at the Blount Hospital to pick up Don Jr. in a red Corvette convertible. The nurse refused to let the baby ride home until Don put the top-down. The year was 1955, and even nurses believed the wind caused babies to get earache.

Don liked his brown mule, Jake, but bought his boys a donkey to ride. The boys named her Christine in honor of their aunt, and Don proposed to teach the boys to ride. Betty Jo says, "We think it was because of Don's one leg, but the donkey bucked him right off." Christine always let the children ride her, but the boys still laugh about their daddy's spill.

Betty Jo frowns. "Losing our house and business was hardest on my youngest son, Joey. He had started third grade at Vonore, so I took him to school and met the bus at the Little Tennessee train station near the Allegany Mountain in the afternoon."

"Lib and Homer Kirkland had sold their restaurant, the Teddy Bear, to Alta Eggers, and she needed help. I have cooked thousands of hamburgers between dropping Joey off at school and picking him up after school"

In time, her sons bought some land off Highway 360 (Citico Road), and she sold the house on Highway 129. As their means permit, the boys improve the property. Their future project is hardwood floors for the dining room and living room. We talked on her spacious front porch, which all three sons built. Joey has applied stucco to the original house but chose logs for his own house.

When Betty Jo's mother suffered a stroke, she moved to Georgia to nurse her. Her sons turned to and added a bedroom and bath with a walk-in shower and bought a hospital bed. The young grandchildren called her Georgia Granny, and she knew each of her great-grandchildren that Betty Jo was raising. She never regained her speech and died in about six months but was happy to have her family with her.

Betty Jo is a member of the Mount Zion Missionary Baptist Church near her present home. Even with the twenty or more families coming for Sunday dinner, she had attended her worship service. Her plan was to clean up the kitchen and be at her church for the evening worship. Her son Don Jr. recently had a heart test that showed a healthy heart. Betty Jo knows her prayers and those of her church family are answered, and this is one example.

We sat on the broad front porch in sweet, pure mountain air as Betty Jo and I rocked in stout homemade wooden rockers. "I rocked all the babies," she allows as Don Jr. put a fretful great grandbaby into her arms. I thought, "Betty Jo shows so much love and care that she makes all the family sorrows and the hard times of poverty seem small. She had mentioned that she had legal custody of several grandchildren and that through the years others were left in her care permanently."[305]

Joey Steele Misses the Lost River

Joey Steele wants the world to remember the Little Tennessee River. It was his childhood playground, and his parents' means of supplementing his father's pension. His daddy, Don Steele lost a leg in Korea and suffered four different injuries in six months. He returned the most decorated veteran in Monroe County with four purple hearts for wounds and two bronze stars for heroism under fire.[306]

Don Steele remained a handsome and strong man, so he won Betty Jo Slatton's heart. They built a house, a store for serving boaters, two barns, and two wells on Highway 72 on the north side of the Little Tennessee River. In time, they had three sons, Frank, Joe, and Don, and a daughter Sherrie. The family lived on land near Don's brother, who was always called Junior.[307]

The land was farmed by Joey's grandfather, who was moved out by the building of the Fontana Dam in the forties. Ancestors of the Steele family came into East Tennessee in the seventeen hundreds. The family story is that the family ran a toll bridge in Cades Cove before they felt the power of the law of eminent domain when their land was purchased for the Great Smokey Mountain Park in the thirties. The great-grandparents walked to their new home near where Fontana Dam is now. They took turns carrying their young son, Green Lee Hill, who grew up to be a storyteller of Appalachian folktales.[308]

A family story recounts that Grandmother was walking from the spring when grabbed by a bear. She untied her apron and ran away. Joey attributes some of the Steele men's spunk to their full-blooded-Cherokee great-great grandmother, who was hidden by her white husband when the army came to remove the Cherokee from Cades Cove. Joey does not know the names or exactly how the Steele's are kin to Elijah Hill, Harriet Hill, and Green Payne; but somehow, their descendants came to the north bank of the Little Tennessee River after the purchase of their land for Fontana Dam. Other Steeles, Hills, and Paynes settled along Nine Mile Creek and Baker's Creek well before the forties. Joey cites as evidence the Baptist Church cemetery where many are buried.[309]

Joey Steele has much to live up to as he remembers his father, Don. His daddy loved to fish. So he rode Jack, their mule, onto a shoal and caught fish from his mule's back. Don Steele's truck was a straight shift, so he used his cane to work the clutch.[310]

The Chota mound and bottoms were on the south side of the Little Tennessee River and across from the Steele's dock. The Steele's named their boat dock, Chota and put, "Have boat, will float" on their sign. A trip from their dock to the mouth of the Tellico River was four hours, or to their friend, John Patrick's pasture was two hours. Joey remembers that John Patrick had played in Dolly Parton's band in Nashville.[311]

Joey's brother Frank worked for Hoss Holt's boat dock, which was nearer Chilhowee Dam. That float trip was at least six hours. Don Steele would guide guests on fishing trips. His brother Junior had some cabins, which he named the River Breeze. One guest that Joey remembers was Archie Campbell of the *Hee Haw* television show.[312]

Joey Steele loves to recall family stories that would make his grannies say, "Hush your mouth." "Uncle Junior had a beer joint or club. He and my daddy liked a drunken brawl; even with daddy's balance on one leg he could fistfight. I remember that if a keg of beer got stale, we fed it to the hogs. We had fat and tender pork."[313]

"Uncle Junior owned vending machines for gambling in beer joints all the way to Georgia. He had three clubs in Knoxville where poker was played in his private parlors. He entertained politicians and Knoxville businessmen in his private games. Men came to the River Breeze for poker and to relax, and many to fish."[314]

"My parents sold bait, gas, and drinks from the store, and we rented the boats. My parents kept no secrets from us kids. When I was eight years old, I knew how much the light bill was. At ten years of age, I could clean a boat and mop a floor. So our store was clean, and our boats were ready for renting. By the time my brothers were fourteen years old they could drive the truck to fetch the boats after our guests floated to a take-out place."[315]

"Money was tight, but in the summer Daddy would run a still on an island in the river. The island was so small that when the leaves were off, you couldn't make a run."[316]

"I was born in 1965, the year Mama and Daddy got a letter from the Tennessee Valley Authority that they would buy our land. When I was nearly nine, Daddy suffered a massive heart attack because he was messed up inside from his war wounds. The Tennessee Valley Authority paid Mama $23,000 in 1973 for the business, two wells, boat house, the store, two barns, and our five-bedroom house. Mama moved us to a run-down place on Highway 129, but she had to go into debt to pay for it."[317]

"Then my family got the second blow. Daddy's pension for his army service stopped. For five years, my family got nothing. Mama did not go to Washington with Beryl Moser or with Mr. John Lackey, but she fought to get Dad's pension back by appearing before committees in Washington with other widows. After five years, it was re-instated."[318]

"After the buyouts the area was really dead. TVA sold the Davis farm near Loudon for a housing development, Tellico Village, but Vonore was lifeless for years. Finally, TVA got some foreign companies to invest here and new people to move here."[319]

"My brother bought this ridgetop back of my store building on Highway 360 where we are talking. We moved back here about 1979, and I got to go the Vonore High School. When the gate closed on the dam, my friends and I went every day to measure the flooding waters. The snakes and fish were crazy. They couldn't feed or know what to do. Many died, but fishing as I knew it was destroyed."[320]

"I had a wonderful high school experience at Vonore High School, and I grieve that we lost not only the river, but our high school. I was captain of the football team but played basketball and baseball too. They say it is our Cherokee blood that makes the Steele men so scrappy. All my brothers were captain of their football team."[321]

"Today, some children have to get on the bus at 6 AM and ride for hours. Our schools need improvement, especially I want Vonore to have a high school. TVA promised us prosperity, so why can't we get money for our local school?[322]

"I think that TVA sold the people out to the land development companies. They get the land TVA forced people to sell and resell it for profit. The original landowners and even their grandchildren aren't helped."[323]

As we talk, we sat under a life-sized oil painting of Jesus, a valley, a stream, and sheep. The artist, Marvin Church, wrote, "The Lord is my Shepherd; I shall not want," across the top of his painting. Joey says, "I rented this building to an antique dealer, and he left the picture."[324]

The Bible verse suits the Lost River Restaurant and reminds all who eat there to depend on the Lord. On another wall, the 1763 map by Timberlake is framed, and each menu has the map on the cover. Billy hopes to put pictures of the 360 families who were displaced by the dam on a far wall.[325]

"I built the restaurant on Highway 360, formerly Citico Road, with rough sawmill pine." One wall has diagonal paneling and windows. The large dining room has game machines for children, two full-sized pool tables, a game table, a huge TV set, a rocking horse, and for a quarter a massive gum ball will roll and roll into the child's hand. It is a family place with the Steele stamp of hospitality. Alcohol is not served, and on a Saturday morning almost every booth or table is used several times for breakfast.[326]

Old-timers feel welcome, but Joey says, "The newcomers ask me about the lost river. I tell them the stories as best I can, but I want a book that tells how the families made it when forced out."[327]

Part Two

The Second Wave of Attack to Save the Little T

Introduction

Outsiders Take Up the Fight

The local residents were successful in raising some support for their cause outside of the immediate area and from those not directly affected by loss of property and home.

The Tennessee Game and Fish Agency entered the protest against the destruction of the finest cold-water fishery east of the Mississippi River.[328] Still later, the University of Tennessee law school students and a professor and an ichthyologist saw the need to stop the loss of a unique fishery. A new species of fish (snail darter) was identified,[329] and in 1973 using the new law concerning endangered species,[330] lawyers started a suit, which went all the way to the Supreme Court.[331] The Supreme Court ruled to halt the dam,[332] but despite this order, the Tennessee Valley Authority never stopped buying land and preparing to flood the valley.[333] In time, TVA had the law changed so it did not apply to this project.[334]

Although in some ways more sophisticated and having at their disposal a different set of tools to work with, these opponents to the dam found their way blocked in much the same way as had the local opponents. The stories that follow reflect their courageous actions often taken with risk to themselves, their reputations and livelihoods.

Zyg Plater Faces the Giant with a Fresh Appraisal

Zyg came to the University of Tennessee to teach law, but lived out his passion for the law for the entire world to see. He came to the Association for the Preservation of the Little Tennessee River dressed in worn blue jeans and a turtleneck cotton shirt. Casual dress had not reached the Little T valley, and the farmers and fishermen wore a crease in khaki pants and an ironed shirt, hat or cap. To the fighters he looked young to be taking on the sacred cow, the feared monster, the Tennessee Valley Authority.[335]

Like David in the Bible, Zyg faced the giant knowing full well its might. Zyg became a tireless advocate for land, water, all animals, but especially a little fish, called the snail darter. TVA had broken the will of the landowners and citizens affected by the destruction of the valley. Plater was a fresh voice who had no fears of TVA. He arrived in Tennessee in 1973, thirty-six years after the farmers first heard of the dam in 1937. His defeat by the giant resulted in a determination to do what a lawyer is supposed to do, uphold the law. He learned how the press can silence or slant truth, and sadly how a politician can avoid the law as upheld by the Supreme Court.[336]

Like the farmers, fishermen, and historians, he was moved out also. Zyg's "moving out" was different, since he owned no land, had a different ancestry, Polish and English, and an education at Princeton and Yale. Education and a worldview were the help the country folk needed to carry their problem to the nation. Plater was a law professor at the UT Law College when his students invited him to the River.[337]

His students, Hank Hill and David Scate, kept saying, "Come fishing. You must see the Little T." They marveled at the placement of the English Fort Loudoun on the Little Tennessee River near the mouth of the Tellico River. Hank anchored near Howard's Bluff near where huge cedar timbers formed a V-shaped fish trap. Long ago, it was here women and children netted fish during the spring runs. Zyg's imagination spun as he realized the long history of the river valley. Seeing the bottomland farms, the native flowers and trees, and believing the new Endangered Species Act was important for the world, the three lawyers resolved to try to stop the flooding of the valley and the destruction of the habitat of many fishes and wildflowers.[338]

From the first, he understood the resentment of the "old boy" bureaucrats opposed to the new ideas of preserving endangered species. Zyg was called before the dean of the College of Law and told a petition against him charged that he violated the ethics of the law profession. Zyg's response was that he was doing what a lawyer was supposed to do, that is, seeing that the law to protect an endangered species is enforced. The funds to file suit to protect the snail darter came from his pocket, the sale of tee shirts, and a collection from some landowners.[339]

It was agreed that the only way to stop the flooding of the valley and the destruction of the snail darter habitat was to get national attention. The Tennessee city newspapers did not use news items criticizing Tennessee Valley Authority. The county or small-town newspapers feared to oppose TVA, but locally the court of public opinion opposed the Tellico Project in spite of surveys by rural editors. TVA had many employees to go to the newspaper writers and present TVA stories.[340]

TVA let the College of Law know there would be no TVA money for scholarships to the Law School if Zyg Plater stayed on. Zyg was devastated when Joe Cook, another law professor told him that he did not have the moderation expected of a University of Tennessee law professor. He found a job at the University of Michigan.[341]

His new job freed Zyg to take the battle to Washington. He knew the battle would be won outside the Tennessee Valley. For the next two years, Zyg lived *the dam*. His classes were taught on Monday and Tuesday, and off he flew to Washington to educate the committees and legislative aids about the environmental protection needed for the snail darter, the water, soil, and people of the Little Tennessee Valley.[342]

Ann Wickham gave him a bed. Ms. Wickham worked for Friends of the Earth organization and had a two-story apartment next to their office. After weeks of sleeping on friends' couches, he was happy to accept her upstairs bedroom. Ms. Wickham was in a wheelchair and could not use the room. For the next two years, Zyg laundered his shirt in the bathtub, washed and dried his hair, and put on his best face to visit the hill.[343]

A citizen's petition was required to list the snail darter as an endangered species. Zyg remembered, "I had the flu and a 104-degree fever, but I sat in bed with two cats on my belly and my sleeping wife beside me and drafted the petition. Point one: The snail darter exists, appendix 1, a picture. Point two: A description of the fish and where it is found, appendix 2 with map of the river and shoals, and so on. The petition was filed in 1975 as administrative procedure 563."[344]

The first legal step was federal court before Judge Robert Taylor. Judge Taylor accepted the facts presented but ruled against the suit on legal questions. This meant the federal court agreed that the species was jeopardized, and the habitat would be ruined. Judge Taylor ruled against the petition on legal grounds, so this meant an appeal could be made to District Court.[345]

Great and justified was the fear that Senator Howard Baker would get a rider attached to a bill that preempted TVA and the Tellico Project from the Endangered Species Act. Zyg, Hiram "Hank" Hill, and Peter Alliman kept the administrative assistants, representatives, and senators aware that the suit was in the courts.[346]

A committee of government officials, including the Department of Interior, Corp of Engineers, the Department of the Army, Agriculture Secretary, Environmental Protection Agency, and others were appointed by Congress to study the snail darter. The committee was informally called the God Committee because of their power of life and death. To the dismay of TVA, the God Committee ruled to stop the closing of the dam.[347]

The case to stop the destruction of the Little Tennessee River valley was argued by Zyg Plater before the Supreme Court on June 15, 1978. The TVA side was argued by the Attorney General of the United States. The ruling was that the law to protect the endangered species included the snail darter.[348]

John Duncan Sr. found himself up against a rock (TVA) and a hard place (the people and the river). Zyg remembers meeting Beryl Moser visiting congressmen and asked him where he spent the night. The answer at Congressman John Duncan's house seems strange thirty years later, but many people were on both sides of the issue.[349]

Congressman Duncan lost his integrity with a dishonest act. He took a rider written by TVA and added it to a bill during a late-afternoon and poorly attended session. The rider was not read in its entirety and was added without a point of order being raised.

Many people including Congressman Duncan's typist thought Zyg, Hiram Hill, and Peter Alliman and others who lived the fight knew about the rider. It was a slick, crooked political trick that closed the dam and flooded the valley.

President Carter wanted his Panama Canal Treaty passed and needed all the votes he could get for that. President Carter let the bill and its rider become law. TVA hastened to close the gates, and the flooding began.[350]

In 2006 Professor Plater is at Boston University, Newton, Massachusetts. He was a participant in the lawsuits against the Valdez oil damage and Exxon Oil Company. He has worked on suits in Africa. At present he is writing a detailed story of his personal battle in environmental protection, especially the Cherokee heritage and the soil, water, and people of the Little Tennessee River valley.[351]

Peter Alliman Makes a Difference

"I was working on a double master's degree in law and in planning when the Endangered Species Act[352] was passed. My love of the river and my passion for the new law put me in a position to visualize economic development for the valley without covering the vast area with a shallow, broad lake."[353]

"I learned that Dr. David Etnier identified a unique species.[354] We formed an alliance to stop the closing of the floodgates. Our slogan was 'Snail darter—it's more than a fish.' New hope arose for saving the River, and I agreed to serve as secretary of the new organization, the Little Tennessee River Alliance."[355]

In alliance were the following organizations: Tennessee Conservation League of the National Wildlife Federation State Affiliate, the Sierra Club of Tennessee, the Tennessee Citizens of Wilderness Planning, the Tennessee Endangered Species Committee, the Smoky Mountains Hiking Club, the Tennessee Audubon Council Inc., the Great Smoky Mountains Chapter of Trout Unlimited, Ann Arbor Group of the Little Tennessee River Alliance, the Tennessee Outdoor Writers Association, and the Tennessee Environmental Council. "The people in these groups did not live in the area to be flooded or bought for economic development. They were idealists who found the unique free-flowing river priceless. Floating the river and fishing in the quiet and peaceful pastoral scenes healed the wounds of academic or business stress. These outdoor lovers wanted to save the valley for future generations," Alliman said.[356]

The landowners and civic leaders were weakened by years of struggle and the reality of the loss of land and community. The business people and farmers were shocked and unbelieving that a little fish could influence, much less, hinder the plans of the mighty Tennessee Valley Authority.[357]

"I agreed to serve as secretary of the new organization, Little Tennessee River Alliance, and William Chandler of Oak Ridge was president. Our plan was to take the fight to Washington. As secretary I wrote many letters to senators and representatives and made many trips to call on the senators and representatives."[358]

"The law students and I fought the second battle to alter the Tellico Project. The farmers, business people, and historians were impoverished and worn-out by years of struggle and little encouragement from outside the valley. Folks in the valley were divided as to whether to accept what could not be stopped and confused as to whether TVA's buyout was the way to a better life.[359] The outdoorsmen, fishermen, hikers, students, and professors saw a way to alter the Tellico Project and keep the free-flowing river. A passion to prevent the closing of the gates of the dam developed."

"Professor Etnier found the unique species, and law professor, Zyg Plater, students Hank Hill, several dozen other students, and I believed the new law that protected endangered species could stop the closing of the Tellico Dam. Judge Robert Taylor ruled against saving the Little Tennessee River and the snail darter, as the new species was named."[360]

"However, the University of Tennessee lawyers saw a way to argue the case in the U.S. Supreme Court. Hiram Hill and Zygmunt Plater argued for the law that protected fish and other wildlife from extinction by building dams and roads. The Supreme Court ruled against TVA, and construction of the dam was stopped."[361]

"We young lawyers underestimated the power of the Tennessee Valley Authority if we thought the river was preserved as free-flowing. At a late-night session Representative John Duncan Sr. introduced a rider to exempt TVA from obeying the Endangered Species Act. This procedure was irregular as amendments usually go through a committee process. However, this late afternoon, political maneuver allowed TVA to close the gates and flood the valley."[362]

"As a conservationist and outdoor man, I recall the powerful arguments for developing the river as a cold-water fishery. Such a free-flowing river would be the only one in the Eastern United States. The second regret I have is the destruction of the deep, fertile soil. Industrial development was possible without the flooding and destruction of the river. I practice law, but I have a master's degree in planning, and I believe this, thirty years after the flooding of the valley," Alliman stated.[363]

"I have respect for the ancient civilizations that lived in the Little Tennessee Valley. A grateful client prepared this beautiful shadowbox of artifacts. Beside the usual arrow points, a stone fish hook and a perfect stone tobacco pipe make an impressive statement on a red background. The artifacts came from the Ball Play neighborhood."[364]

"My law office in Madisonville is about fifteen miles or less from the former wild river that I tried to save for future generations. Like many of the losers in the long battle, I still believed Monroe County is the place to live."[365]

Hiram "Hank" Hill Practices Law
in East Tennessee

Hiram "Hank" Hill started fishing the Little T when he was thirteen years old. He loved the water, knew the shoals and ripples, the fort, the rock bluffs, and fertile fields in seasons. At the University of Tennessee he had many friends who were game and wildlife management majors, but chose law as his profession.[366]

His wildlife and game friends feared the destruction of the Little T, which was developing as a trout fishery. Hank knew about the Environmental Protection Act of 1973 and was searching for a topic for a term paper for his Environmental Law Class. One afternoon he and Robert Smith returned from a quail hunt in McMinn County and discussed writing about nuclear emissions and the First Amendment. His honest friend advised it was the dullest topic anyone could research. Why not study the snail darter? The next day, Hank visited Dr. David Etnier, who identified and named the snail darter. Dr. Etnier thought the topic suitable for the Environmental Law class.[367]

Geeky little environmentalists were derided in the law school, but Hank read the Endangered Species Act. He learned only two lawsuits had been filed. The first was for a cave fish at Devil's Hole, New Mexico where it was feared agricultural use of water would reduce the aqua table so much the cave fish species would be completely killed. The other case involved the nesting habitat of the Mississippi Sandhill Crane. Both cases were solved by compromise. Moving an interchange of Interstate 10 away from the bird's traditional breeding area solved the Sandhill crane problem.[368] After his initial research and selecting his term paper topic, Hank invited his professor Zyg Plater to fish the Little Tennessee River. Zyg was impressed with the beauty, power, and history of the valley. Professor Zyg, Hank, Peter Alliman, and Don Cohen became tenacious, tough, and shrewd opponents to the destruction of the last thirty-three miles of the mighty river. As expected, the mighty Tennessee Valley Authority reacted violently.[369]

The lawyers stepped into the long line of fighters who struggled before their start. They took their vision to keep the free-flowing rivers to the courts and to Washington. It was long and difficult work, especially for financially handicapped students and the professors. The courts judged TVA's first environmental statement inadequate.[370]

Dr. Etnier and Wayne Starnes had a grant from TVA to survey the fish in the Little Tennessee River. The purpose of the grant was to establish what species would be influenced by the closing of the dam. Dr. Etnier found the unidentified little darter and knew it was unique. It is ironic that this was before Congress passed the Endangered Species Act. Later, TVA used Dr. Etnier's report for their part three of an environmental study.[371]

Hank explained, "The snail darter had some first cousins west of the Mississippi in the stargazing darter, but is a unique species. Speciation means that it will not breed with other fishes that are not snail darters. The last seventeen miles of the Little T was the primary breeding and living place of the snail darter. It took a long time to get the snail darter listed as a unique and endangered species."[372]

"In the mean time the Tennessee Valley Authority ignored court orders to stop the dam and went to work twenty-four hours a day to cut all the trees and vegetation from the river valley. This helped to demoralize the people who had not sold out. They also spent as much money as possible so that they could report the largest possible amount as the cost of the project. They did exactly what a public agency should not do."[373]

The lawyers went to Federal Court and argued that the snail darter was a unique species whose breeding habitat would be destroyed by flooding the valley. Judge Robert Taylor allowed a former TVA employee, and at that time, the University of Tennessee general counsel to call out from the audience and answer how much money had been spent. Judge Taylor ruled that too much money had been spent to stop the project.[374]

An appeal made to the Sixth Circuit Court enjoined the Tennessee Valley Authority to immediately stop work on the project. The court order pushed TVA to work harder to buy up remaining farms and to clear the river of vegetation. Hank remembers one of the sad actions was the destruction of the huge river beeches at Coyatee Springs where the Cherokee Indians signed a treaty. [375] This was an area above the flood line. Another disgraceful incident was the bulldozing of Mrs. Asa McCall's homeplace without removing her possessions as promised when the federal marshals removed the old lady from her home. The house was not in the area to be flooded either. TVA wanted the land above the flood line for second homes for wealthy people.[376] Hank observed, "It is simply wrong to steal one man's land to give it to another man."[377]

Hank reported, "TVA bought thirty six thousand acres for the twenty-thousand-acre reservoir at an average price of $300 an acre.[378] Some people tight with TVA did quite well, such as lawyer Ray Jenkins of Knoxville. What you were paid depended on your politics and the debt on the land.[379]

"TVA planned Timberland as a model town. These Midwesterner agri-Democrats planned to teach the rednecks how to be civilized. Walter Cronkite of TV fame was to be the spokesman. Boeing Corporation was to build the houses and stores. When they understood the project and its socialist implications both Cronkite and Boeing Corporation pulled out. I suspect the plan to force the poor to sell so that the government could resell it smelled to them."[380]

"The next spin that TVA made was that so much money was spent the work must go on. By that time, TVA had spent about $50,000,000. The concrete plug for the dam was $2,000,000-$3,000,000. The remainder of the cost was for the roads and land acquisition. More was spent for the roads than for the land. The roads could have been through the finest farmland in the eastern United States. Views and access to the beautiful, clear, free-flowing river were better without the shallow, still lake. The deep river bottom soil was a match for the Central Valley of California."[381]

"Development of the Little T as a trout fishery had continued for years. The native brown trout reproduced in the river and the brookie in the creeks that flowed into the valley. Rainbow trout stocked by the Game and Fish Agency thrived. The stocked fish grew faster in the river than in a hatchery. After a few years in the pure, clear, fast water, the stocked rainbow trout was as delicious as a river-born fish. I know from fishing the river."[382]

"The closing of the dam and the destruction of the river fishery impelled me to take a semester off from the University of Tennessee. I fished 310 days before the destruction. Each day, I could, I took people to float and fish the Little T," Hill said.[383]

"One day, after passing my bar exam, five others and I traveled in a Toyota pickup with a camper cover to Cincinnati, Ohio. The TVA lawyers flew in an eight-passenger jet. Young, full of salt and vinegar, the six lawyers were ready for the court case. Judge Anthony Celebreeze ruled the snail darter was an endangered species and enjoined TVA to halt the closing of the dam. TVA continued to buy land and clear the riverbanks of vegetation. Alternative ways to develop the valley were not seriously worked out by TVA.[384]

"I recall another long trip from Knoxville to Memphis to a Wildlife and Fisheries meeting. We traveled in an UT Rambler station wagon while TVA arrived in a jet with pretty girls and public relations officials. Our numbers were small against the mighty bureaucracy, who was reported to have eighty-two lawyers on staff, but our strength and intelligence coupled with our idealist's beliefs to save the environment gave us courage to keep on fighting.[385]

"Our next step was to argue the case before the Supreme Court in Washington DC by Zygmunt J. B. Plater. We young lawyers were outnumbered by the experienced TVA lawyers, who had Attorney General Griffin Bell to argue their case. I thought Attorney General Bell looked foolish in his morning coat and striped pants. The Supreme Court ruled by a six-to-three vote to uphold the lower-court ruling and to continue to block completion of the Tellico Project.[386]

"I remember, Thurgood Marshall and Rehnquist had blank, puzzled looks as they heard the testimony. Marshall voted for the snail darter, but Rehnquist along with Powell and Blackman voted for TVA to close the dam. Justice John Paul Stevens understood the Endangered Species Act and the issues.[387]

"The Tennessee Valley Authority and Senator Howard Baker were outraged. Their plan was to get Congress to change the law and to overturn the Supreme Court ruling. Senator Howard Baker and Representative John Duncan were deep in the pocket of TVA and disgusted by the Supreme Court order to stop the Tellico Dam project. They decided to try to amend the Endangered Species Act by forming an Endangered Species Committee of nine officials, such as the secretaries of Agriculture, Interior, and Army. The committee had the power to grant exemptions to some federal projects. Because of the power of life and death over certain species, the new committee was nicknamed, the God Committee.[388]

"The committee met and took testimony in Washington and in Knoxville. Finally, a vote decided unanimously to defeat the petition to exempt the Tellico Dam Project from the Environmental Protection Act. Baker and Duncan decided to get a congressional act to exempt the Tellico Dam from the Endangered Species Act. The protection fighters for the valley began a period of visiting the Congress and presenting their information for saving the valley and fishes.[389]

"As often as I could I visited congressmen and their assistants. I found support for the National Endangered Species Act in Senator Jim Buckley of New York and in John McMurphy, chairman of the Merchant Marine and Fisheries Committee. Repeatedly, the senators and congressmen told me to get a member of the Tennessee delegation to support the Endangered Species Act to preserve the Little Tennessee River, valley farmlands, and the fishery.[390]

"I was excited when Al Gore Jr. was elected congressman. In campaigning, he appeared to want to protect the environment. I rode the elevator up four stories and climbed the stairs to Gore Jr.'s office. It was about half the size of this one office in my Chattanooga Law firm. Gore graciously thanked me for coming to see him and said he supported the river and snail darter 100 percent. After a bit of talk about the National Endangered Species Act and fishing, I thought Gore was the Tennessee delegate in opposition to the Tennessee Valley Authority.[391]

"As I walked back to Representative Murphy's office, I thought of Albert Gore Sr. After losing the election for failing to represent Tennessee, Gore Sr. took a job as chairman of Peabody Coal Company, a strip-mining company. I didn't get off the train yesterday, but I hurried to Congressman Murphy's office hoping the son was not like his old daddy.[392]

"A secretary ushered me into Congressman Murphy's office, and I heard his speaker phone. Gore was upset that these wackos, communists, ecology freaks, and crazy nuts would try to stop a much-needed project. Al Gore Jr. had lied to me face-to-face, and I heard his tirade to Congressman Murphy.[393]

"The lawyers and the ordinary folks of the river valley were hit with more disappointment. John Duncan Sr. of Knoxville and Marilyn Lloyd of Chattanooga presented House Resolution 455 to exempt the Tellico Project from the Environmental Protection Act in March 1977.[394]

"Jimmy Carter of Georgia defeated Nixon, so we persistent and diligent fighters hoped the new administration would care about the farmers and fishermen's point of view. At every chance I visited Washington to talk to the senators and congresspersons. One day, I missed my direct flight to Washington, so I was rerouted to Atlanta. When I reached Atlanta there were no seats in the coach class. An airline official assigned me to first class. Immediately, I puzzled, 'Who is the man across the aisle?' Someone famous, I was sure. The six-foot-two man was drinking diet Cokes as fast as the attendant could replenish them. The lightbulb flashed as I realized it was Hamilton Jordan, Carter's chief of staff. I wrote a one-page list of reasons to oppose the dam project. I apologized for interrupting his work and asked him to read the one-page list.[395]

"Hamilton Jordan was on his way to Washington to set up the Carter White House, but he was interested in the Endangered Species Act, the snail darter, and the impact of the destruction of the Little Tennessee and Tellico

Rivers and the valley land. We talked for thirty minutes, and I hoped for Carter's support.[396]

"I remember John Duncan Sr. as the dirtiest and sneakiest politician Tennessee ever produced. President Carter had a meeting with Anwar Sadat of Egypt and addressed a joint session of Congress. The Senate adjourned; the House remained in session although I remember that only a few representatives were in their seats. Others say a near-empty House of Representatives. The 1980 public works appropriations bill was up for a vote and John Duncan Sr. rose to offer an amendment. Then Duncan moved the reading be waived. Tom Bevill of Alabama seconded the motion. A voice vote exempted the Tellico Project from the Endangered Species Act."[397]

Hank explained, "The next step was for Senator Howard Baker to push the bill through the Senate. That accomplishment put the land, river, and fishery into the lap of President Carter. We, Zyg Plater, Peter Alliman and many others, worked to get President Carter to veto the bill. Senator Jim Sasser informed Carter that if he vetoed the bill he would support Ted Kennedy as the Democratic candidate for president in the Tennessee Democrat primary."[398]

"An apologetic President Carter phoned Zyg Plater and me from air force One that he felt forced by Sasser to sign the 1980 Public Works Appropriation Bill," Hank said.[399]

"I remember the opponents fired one more shot. A suit was filed to protect the river valley for Cherokee religious services. The suit was laughed out of court."[400]

"I feel this period of my life convinced me that the general population should take more interest in what goes on in Washington. This is a bumper sticker that the environmental lawyers and landowners sold to finance our long fight. My collection of articles includes this *Atlanta Journal* article on the struggle with a full-page cover picture of the snail darter," Hank said.[401]

Hank bid me good-bye to interview Kenneth M. Murchison of Louisiana State University. He is writing a book about the actions of the tenacious young lawyers and their defeat. A vast source of information is available in this tough, strong man who regrets his country's loss.[402]

Dr. David Etnier Pronounces a Happy Ending for the Snail Darter

When I interviewed Dr. Etnier, I found him in a lab set aside for the retired scientist (zoologist) by the University of Tennessee in Knoxville. The one-story brick building is set near the street a bit away from the gyms and stadium familiar to Vol fans, who jam the streets for games. Fish are sent to him for identification from all over the world. He advises several master degree candidates but explained, "A doctorial candidate needs a professor who will be available for the entire length of his research. I'm in my seventies now and want to be able to follow a student to completion of their research."[403]

Dr. Etnier identified himself, "I finished my PhD at the University of Minnesota in an area where I liked to catch walleye. From childhood, I read about the *Field & Stream* magazine fishing contests. I caught eight—or nine-pound walleye often, but the requirement to enter in Tennessee was a fifteen-pound walleye. This was exciting, so when a job opening at the University of Tennessee appeared, I applied and was hired."[404]

Dr. Etnier explained, "The impoundment of Norris Lake no longer produced big walleye, so I never won that prize. I did find an exciting fish on August 12, 1973. Although insignificant in size and appearance from other darters and sculpins, the snail darter stopped a mighty government agency from damming the Little Tennessee River until politics won."[405]

Etnier remembers, "A National Environmental Protection Act was passed by Congress, and one court hearing on the accuracy of TVA's environmental impact statement was held. The court ordered a temporary injunction to stop the impoundment of the Little Tennessee River. TVA responded by buying land and clearing the riverbanks at a faster pace. It was widely reported TVA felt above a court order, so near the dam's closing.[406]

"I testified at the first hearing, 'Species of fishes and insects that lived in the clear, flowing water would be affected by the impoundment of the Little Tennessee River. A second hearing before the federal Judge Robert Taylor was set. As a scientist, I wanted concrete and exact species to back up my testimony. My graduate student Bob Stiles and I went to the Coyatee Spring areas and found the clear water difficult to use a seine. We put on face masks and snorkels and floated. I reached down with my hand and scooped up a fish. Without the water magnifying and reflecting, I instantly knew that I had a unique fish. I waded over to a sandbar and called Bob Stiles. We agreed it was a unique specimen. Study in the UT lab proved the initial impression was correct. We found about twenty-nine species that day that would be adversely affected by the dam, but the snail darter was a fish that had never before been identified scientifically.'"[407]

"I learned, 'The lower Little T contained some five thousand darters, and they were one of the most abundant species in the lower twenty miles of that river before Tellico Dam was closed. They have not been seen there since the closing of the dam in November 1979. The life span is about three to four years. Many are sexually mature at age one, and all are by age two. Maturing adults move upstream to gravel shoal areas to spawn, with migratory movements up to twenty to thirty miles. Peak spawning occurs in early to mid-April. About six hundred eggs are laid per female. The young hatch in fifteen to twenty days and after absorbing yolk sac and "swimming up," drift passively downstream with the current to develop in deep pool areas. Adults and subadults feed primarily on small pleuroceridae snails, with diet supplemented by blackflies and caddis flies, especially during the winter months. The maximum size is seventy-five millimeter total length. Their closest relative is *Percina uranidea* of the Missouri and Arkansas Ozark region where it is rare and localized.'"[408]

"I wrote up my findings and prepared for the next court appearance. However, a large number of persons wished to testify, so I was not called. My scientific description of the snail darter was submitted to the Biological Society of Washington. Three scientists reviewed the work, and the Department of the Interior agreed that an original and previously unidentified species was described and published the paper."[409]

Dr. Etnier says, "TVA was required to meet the court requirement for a better environmental impact statement. They used my testimony from the first hearing in an appendix when they made a full disclosure concerning the ecology of the river and to predict change. It did save the taxpayers some money by not sending their own biologists out to repeat my findings."[410]

"The National Environmental Protection Acts of 1966 and 1969 were weak, so Congress passed the Endangered Species Act in December 1973. Hank "Hiram" Hill, a graduate student of Zyg Plater, came to talk to me about a paper that he was writing. He wanted information on the snail darter. The 1973 act made it possible for citizens to sue federal agencies, which threatened any species listed by the secretary of the Interior as endangered. I told him that I thought he had a case."[411]

"I felt puzzled. Judge Robert Taylor of the Third District Court set up the ground rules for the second hearing. He required that nothing to do with economics could be used. That ruling prevented questioning about the cost/benefit ratio that the Tennessee Valley Authority claimed. In the end Judge Taylor ruled the project should proceed because he did not think a major project like this dam should be stopped because so much money had been spent. However, the court agreed the fish was an endangered species and would become extinct. General Manager Lynn Seeber refused to stop the timber cutting even though many people complained that all the bull dozing was causing silting in the river and hurting the fish."[412]

"I remember saying to the other zoologists, 'It is hopeless, and we were so downcast.' However, Zyg Plater, Hank Hill, and Peter Alliman and the other lawyers were elated. The law said to save the endangered species and nothing about the cost of a project. The lawyers recognized grounds for an appeal to a higher court. The lawyers went to the circuit court of appeals, and that court of three judges ruled in favor of saving the snail darter, the river, and the soil of the valley. The Tennessee Valley Authority appealed to the Supreme Court."[413]

"On June 15, 1978, the Supreme Court announced its decision in TVA v. Hill. By a six-to-three vote (Powell, Blackman, and Rehnquist dissented), the Court upheld the lower-court ruling and continued to block completion of the Tellico Project. The ruling was in favor of endangered species and barely touched on the project's merits," Etnier remembers.[414]

Etnier thinks, "Politics disregarded saving species, free-flowing water, and fertile soil, especially our Tennessee senator and representative. Senator Howard Baker of Tennessee wanted the dam, and John Culver of California worried about the Endangered Species Act. They created a cabinet-level committee, known as the God Committee. The formal name was the Endangered Species Committee, and the group had life or death over a species when there were irreconcilable differences concerning a project.

The committee was not weighted toward the environmentalists, the Department of the Army and every cabinet office composed the committee.

They ruled in favor of the endangered species. I bet that Senator Howard Baker was furious and couldn't imagine anyone would disagree with him. I remember reading in the newspaper that Director of TVA Aubrey Wagner said that TVA was unwilling to discuss alternatives to Tellico Dam."[415]

Dr. Etnier explained, "Senator Baker and Representative John Duncan Sr. prepared a rider to a big public works bill that exempted Tellico Dam from all federal legislation. It passed in a poorly attended session. I feel naive about the working of politics, but President Carter was in the midst of a battle with Congress. Carter wanted a new Panama Canal Treaty passed, and he needed every vote. Carter feared a veto of the huge public projects would cause Senator Baker and Representative Duncan to work against approval of his treaty. Carter felt the Panama Canal Treaty was the landmark of his presidency. Carter reluctantly signed the bill. Within half an hour, plans to close the gates of Tellico Dam proceeded." [416]

Dr. Etnier said, "I sympathize with the landowners who lost their property in order to justify the flooding. I remember how the land was bought as cheaply as possible so it could be resold or leased for huge waterfront homes and the upland for businesses. The reselling of the land allowed TVA to develop a cost/benefit favorable to the project.[417]

"The court battles plodded along for years. Academics agreed with the common opinion that TVA could not be hindered. Wayne Starnes, a doctoral student, and I went to the Tennessee Valley Authority and said, 'You are going to win, but how about financial help in studying the biology of the snail darter and in finding suitable habitat for transplanting the snail darter.' Many fishermen searched for similar environments as the lower Little T, and we began to introduce snail darters. I knew the caddis fly was found in only the Little Tennessee River, the Hiwassee River, and the Etowah River in north Georgia. Darters are hard to recognize and do not thrive except in free-flowing water with adequate oxygen."[418]

Dr. Etnier said, "I am glad that TVA saw a way to prove that the snail darter was not endangered if we could transplant it elsewhere. Wayne Starnes was allotted $750,000 to locate places the snail darter could be relocated. TVA was looking for snail darters in creeks and in other places, but one place they failed to look was the lower reaches of the Hiwassee River. I knew the caddis fly thrived there, so as a zoologist and fisherman, I figured the snail darter would also. Time has proven me correct. I foresee a project for a doctoral student to study the genetic code of the snail darters we planted, and some I discovered a bit further up the Hiwassee River. I suspect the two groups of darter have some genetic differences, such as the number of anal fin rays.

From June 1975 to February 1976, 710 snail darters transplanted to the lower Hiwassee River. At the last count, a population of three thousand or more is doing fine. It is a happy ending for the snail darter."[419]

"One victorious planting is in the Holston River near Strawberry Plains. The Cherokee Lake water when released from the lake has almost no oxygen, but by the time it reaches Strawberry Plains it has picked up some oxygen. Some snail darters from the Little T were left over from the plantings, so rather than flush them down the toilet, Starnes and I decided to introduce them into the Holston River. It was a poor habitat, but the fish lived in the oxygen-poor waters for ten years. At that time, the biologists at TVA decided to improve the oxygen-poor water of Douglas and Cherokee Lakes. A perforated hose was placed in the tailwaters and a tankard of liquid oxygen was pumped into the still and low water of the reservoirs. This dramatically improved the fish populations. Snail darters reproduced and increased with some drifting-down to the mouth of the Little River at the 411 Bridge and some drifting to the right to the French Broad River. They are doing well almost to Douglas Dam and Interstate 40 at the Holston River," Dr. Etnier reported.[420]

Etnier believes, "More fish are doing well in 2004 than before the vast network of dams on the Tennessee River. I believe the snail darter thrived in the oxygen-poor but flowing waters. They were threatened with extinction because of oxygen-poor water below the dams and in the reservoirs. The snail darters in the Little T had found an oxygen-rich environment and plenty of caddis flies. I figured this out from an unplanned find. I had a contract with the Forest Service to do a study in North Georgia on weekends. Each time my students and I crossed South Chickamauga Creek someone wondered what life lived in that creek. One Sunday, work was stopped in the early afternoon, so the group left the interstate and parked behind a supermarket. A seine haul brought up some interesting fishes: mountain marlin, sucker mouth minnows, a few darters, and a little catfish.[421]

"I said, 'Let's go seine that ripple up there.' A downstream haul brought up six snail darters. The South Chickamauga Creek is muddy, littered, and slow-flowing. The habitat is completely different from the Little Tennessee River. As soon as I reached Knoxville I phoned the snail darter recovery team. The team consisted of two TVA biologists, Tennessee Wildlife Resource Agency's Dick Burch, Etnier's office staff, and Wayne Starnes. I explained my new findings. Likely areas were the lower ends of creeks that flowed into the Big Tennessee River."[422]

"The lower Sequatchie Creek looked likely, but access is possible only by boat. The team put in and went upstream to free-flowing water. It was

February and very cold, but the team waded and seined. One of the men, Jerry Dinkins, stepped into a hole, and water went into his hip waders. I built a fire and left him to wring out his clothes, and the team kept working and found a few snail darters."[423]

"The team found a few in Big Sewee Creek, Meigs County, Tennessee, near where the water flows into Chickamauga Reservoir. A few were found in Paint Rock River in Alabama, about two in thirty years. It appears that is as far south as possible. Some were introduced into the Elk River in middle Tennessee, but that is too far downstream, and they died," Dr. Etnier remembered.[424]

"It is a happy ending for the snail darter, but the taxpayers, landowners, and trout fishermen paid a high price. The snail darter is important in the food chain. The snail darter eats snails, digests the inside and defecates the shells. All kinds of good happenings are resulting from the oxygenation of the tailwaters of Norris Dam. Endangered snails, clams, and Lake Sturgeon stocked by TVA, UT, and the Tennessee Aquarium are reproducing. The reason the species are endangered is the low oxygen. I am confident the project will have a successful outcome and hope to live to see the results. Lake Sturgeon females have to be fifteen years to reproduce, and the males are ten years old. This fish gets up to 1,200 to 1,500 pounds, so this is exciting to watch. I started out to find a way to defend the beautiful Little Tennessee River but found endangered species. One little fish is now helping the entire lake and river systems of Tennessee," Dr. Etnier exclaimed.[425]

Dr. Jefferson Chapman Explains Tellico Archaeology

The Little Tennessee Valley was an archaeology laboratory for young Jefferson Chapman. He studied at the University of Tennessee in the winter, but in summer he led crews of students to dig near the Little Tennessee River. The valley had not been property studied although the farmers, fishermen, and hunters would pick up worked stone artifacts. Many farmers had a few buckets of Indian rocks in their barns, for the arrow points and pottery were special and invited collection.[426]

As a high school student, Jeff Chapman's first formal dig was before Barkley Lake was closed in 1959. After graduating with a degree in archaeology, he taught at UT for six years before returning to graduate school for his PhD. In 1967, he started a field-study group for high school students. In the summers of 1970-1971, the group stayed at a church camp on Highway 72 and explored Icehouse Bottom. Evidence of Early Archaic Period inhabitants was found and is extensively described in his book *Tellico Archaeology* published by TVA and UT.[427]

Chapman completed his PhD and was hired to work on the archaeological excavations in the valley in 1975. The Tennessee Valley Authority planned to inundate the valley as soon as congressional appropriations were available. Chapman worked in the valley from 1975 until 1982 when the shallow lake covered the remains of ancient civilizations. Chapman was the principal investigator, and the research focus was the Woodland period from 1000 BC until 8900 BC. He looked for a clear relation between the Hopeland peoples and the evidence found in Icehouse Bottoms.[428]

Chapman found evidence of rich archaeology areas for research focus. His first interest was the relationship of the Cherokees to the Mississippi culture and of evidence of the Hopewell culture in the Ohio River valley to the Cherokee trading habits. Chapman was the chief investigator from 1975-1982 when the water seeped slowly over the soybean fields hiding the ancient civilizations forever.[429]

Chapman spent five to six years investigating Rose Island where he found extensive evidence of Early Archaic civilizations, 6000-7000 BC.[430] Such evidence was also found at Icehouse Bottoms.[431] Half of Rose Island was farmed by Ralph Lane and owned by James Riley "Junior" Pugh, and half was a pine tree nursery. Millions of dollars were spent by Hiwassee Land Company, the forestry management company of Bowater Southern Paper Company, to develop a pine seedling nursery for reforestation of the southeast United States. The Hiwassee Land Company in cooperation with North Carolina State University engaged in a research project to improve southern pines. Superior trees were located in the southeast and grafted to established rootstock. The seed orchards produced seed for the millions of seedling shipped out of Rose Island each year.[432]

Occasionally, a seed tree would die, and the roots were removed by a machine, which balled up the roots. This left a deep hole, which revealed levels of civilizations.

In 1978, National Geographic Society sponsored investigations of the valley from Chilhowee Dam to Bussell Island at the mouth of the Little Tennessee. Both sides of the river were studied using a toothless backhoe. Chapman claimed, "I was one of the first archaeologists to use this method. I quickly figured out that my forty students were not going to dip deep enough to learn much in the summer weeks of work".[433]

Chapman and his students found one of the few air-conditioned places in Vonore, the Teddy Bear Restaurant. He made friends with Elizabeth Kirkland, the owner and cook. Lib and Homer knew everyone in the area, so Chapman and John Hammontree made a deal for leasing his backhoe. Cecil Fowler, who lived on the Blount County side of the Little T proved to have a real feel for archaeology. Mr. Fowler devised a toothless backhoe and had an innate feel for finding sites and bringing up material for study.[434]

Following the prolonged studies at Rose Island, the work returned to Icehouse Bottoms, which is located between Toqua and Fort Loudoun. Barclay McGhee damned Little Toqua Creek with logs so that it froze solid in winter. A trench thirty-feet across was scooped out, and the ice cut from the creek, stored in a hole, covered with sand. The ice would last all winter according to a McGhee descendent, Barney Ray. Barney Ray owned the site until purchased by TVA. The original McGhee land purchase by Big John McGhee in 1819 grew until he owned acreage estimated variously at from fifteen thousand to seventy-eight thousand acres. The higher number included land bought only with mineral rights.[435]

Toqua, located on the Griffin Martin farm, yielded an enormous amount of information. Dr. Chapman, curator of McClung Museum at UT, Knoxville, has a wall picture of the Toqua village and a replica of the village in wood to tell the story of the excavation. On the six—to nine-acre village, Dr. Chapman found a mound from the Early Archaic Period. The purpose and uses of the mound were lost by the time of the Cherokee, for dating indicated it was very old.[436]

Another place of archaeological interest was the port of Morganton in Loudon County. When Dr. Chapman and his toothless backhoe operator, Cecil Fowler, reached the site, the TVA crews had leveled the old buildings. "It would have been easier to reconstruct what went on there if I could have studied it before TVA destroyed the old buildings." Morganton was an important ferry and shipping point for farm produce. It is now underwater.[437]

Jefferson Chapman recalls, "I grew to love the beautiful river and valley. The archaeological sites I identified could have provided study for many years to come. In an effort to prevent the destruction of the river and the valley, I testified before both House and Senate committees. I still remember how strange it felt to be testifying against the agency that paid my salary."[438]

Chapman says, "I admire the diligent work of Mrs. Alice Warner Milton to preserve the history of the valley. Her broad understanding of the historic significance of Fort Loudoun and of the genealogies of the local people helped in the struggle to prevent the destruction of the valley. Although she made a real pest of herself for years, the English fort to protect the East from the French and Indians is now underwater. Her many alternatives to the flooding of the valley were disregarded by TVA. As a result of the loud complaints of the historical associations in East Tennessee, a replica of the original fort was built, and a dike made to protect the area. It is now a Tennessee State Park."[439]

Jefferson Chapman is now (2005) in charge of McClung Museum on the University of Tennessee campus. He laughs. "For many years I paid for an obituary in the *Knoxville News Sentinel* on the date of the closing of the gates of the misnamed dam."[440]

Part Three

The Observers

Introduction

Can't Fight the Government

Some people resisted the vortex of societal change by taking no part in the struggle to prevent the destruction of the valley. Appalachian Americans face problems in a straightforward way. Since the thirties, the Tennessee Valley Authority had moved farmers out of the river valleys. So historically, they were right to bite the bullet and let happen what might happen.

The stoic nature of some Appalachian Americans, formerly called hillbillies, may be illustrated by a single memory. A young adult approached the Rose Island house one Saturday afternoon with a wicked steel fishhook embedded in his right muscular forearm. He refused a trip to the hospital, so I seated him at the kitchen table with a bottle of rubbing alcohol, gauze, and adhesive tape. I worked the barb out causing pain and bleeding, but he was back at the nursery to work on Monday.

The issues concerning the flooding of the rivers were conflicting and confusing. Thousands of good, smart people fell into being politically and environmentally inactive and/or neutral. Their previous experiences had taught them that you "can't fight the government," so these folks stayed on the sidelines in the fight despite caring deeply about their land and homes.

Melvin Sheets Was a Sawmill Man

Melvin Sheets states, "I am one of the last of the Vonore boys with whom I grew up. Gone are Bob Carson, Henry Webb, Leon Harvey, and other childhood companions. I am not as active as I look, and my tough and strong appearance hides a hip replacement and several episodes with blood clots. Every day, I am at work at my woodyard and sawmill on New Hope Road. I buy hardwood. The white oak is sold to Havco Wood Products in the industrial complex where it is used as flooring for box trucks. Other hardwood is sold to companies in North Carolina and Virginia, particularly furniture manufacturers.

"My father owned the hardware store in Vonore in the twenties and until after World War II sold boxcar loads of wagons, buggies, farm equipment, feed, seed, and anything a farmer might need. Vonore provided all the amenities for genteel living. It was a thriving prosperous little town. Railroad cars unloaded freight and carried away lumber, corn, tobacco, and soybeans. A large flour mill made flour from the local wheat. A general store sold food and dry goods. A blacksmith made horses' shoes and farm implements. Barber and beauty shops, a bank, post office, garage, and gas station were busy. Back then Vonore had every thing we needed," Mr. Sheets recalls.

"After I was about thirteen, my folks sent me to work on the Carson farm every summer. Their son Bob was in my grade. We plowed corn with mules and put up hay. I learned to drive a tractor and adjust and repair equipment. I was paid room and board and $5 a week. That was 1934 to about 1939 when I graduated from Vonore High School."

"As a boy growing up in the village of Vonore I kept busy. We climbed trees and played ball. In the summer about five of us would walk to Citico Beach. That's about twelve miles up there. I played horseshoe because that icy water was not for me, a non-swimmer. The road was narrow and curvy, but we seldom saw a car or truck. We walked part of the way and ran part of the way."

"When I was in high school, John Lackey hauled the baseball teams many miles in an old truck. He never got a penny for gas or time either. He would get an old bus for the trip to Copperhill. That's about a hundred miles. Lackey was very civic-minded and always the leader and worker on community projects. He was the natural leader for the Association for the Preservation of the Little Tennessee River. It was too big a project for him and farmers of limited education and finances. Lackey would take the bull by the horns and try to do what he thought was best."

"I was never the leader myself, but I was glad for him to be. My talent is nothing but hard work. I got it from my mother. She was always digging in the yard and always had flowers for the school events or for church. She was a Cardin and was born at Ball Play in Monroe County. Mama and daddy came to Vonore to have the hardware store.

"After high school I worked at Alcoa, the Aluminum Company of America, for two years, 1941 and 1942. Margaret Evelyn Johnson and I went together some before I left for the navy. I was never off a DE destroyer escort for a year. I mean, no shore time. Then I was fourteen months on another destroyer. It was rough-riding, but I never got seasick. I saw a lot of action in the Pacific Ocean."

"After the war I couldn't settle down. I didn't belong anywhere. Looking back, I wonder if I saw too much war. A buddy and I took off for California. We would work awhile and get gas money and go on. I had four uncles in Idaho, so we worked for them awhile."

"When we finally got to California, I got a job in an English walnut grove. I was an experienced tractor driver from my high school years on the Carson Farm. I put a chain around a tree and shook the tree. The walnuts fell and were picked up. Each evening I took them to town to sell. After a few years I came home and found Margaret Evelyn. We married in 1947."

"Margaret Evelyn was a beautiful woman and as good inside as outside. We loved each other dearly. I try to see her nearly every day. She's been in a nursing home for five years now. She has Parkinson's disease and is getting weaker and losing muscle tone."

"I was not happy trying to farm with my brother-in-law, so I started logging. Margaret Evelyn taught history and was guidance counselor at Vonore High School. I bought walnut trees and exported them to Germany. We trucked them to Sweetwater, since the depot in Vonore was closed. I could only ship the butt end. That is the part nearest the ground. Later, I found a man who could use the tops to make furniture. Now I cut or buy other hardwood. These days I buy a lot of oak and resell it.

"Margaret Evelyn hated to lose the family farm. She was attached to the land. Some people fought TVA tooth and toenail. We didn't want it, and it was a big deal for her to lose her homeplace. I knew there was no stopping TVA. I searched and searched and talked to everyone. The man I sold walnut tops to asked me, 'Why don't you buy my farm?' I had no idea that he would sell. I wish I remembered his name. We torn down the old log house he lived in and built a house. I sold the old Johnson house for $1,500 after TVA bought the land. Some people were allowed to keep their houses and move them, and some were not."

"As near as I can tell, our old house set about where the golf-club house at Rarity Bay development sets now. All but about fifty acres of the Johnson farm is underwater. That land is in the Rarity Bay subdivision."

"I don't look back. My work is my life. People bring hardwood to my modern sawmill. I have the best crews anyone could want. They can fix anything and keep the work moving. Today, the chipper is broken down. While we are talking, they are fixing it. The Havco Wood Products is a good customer and pays me well. That account lets me pay my men on time and well."

"This area did not need a lake for any of the companies here now, but there is no going back. I thank the good Lord for the work I have and for the jobs my business provides."[441]

Beuna Black is a Superior Teacher

Beuna Frank Black is a teacher who was unafraid to put into practice the techniques that worked for her. "I married and was armed with a high school diploma when I answered an urgent plea to come and teach at Toqua School. I had the first four grades, and despite my youth and lack of a college degree, it was a good year for me and the children," Beuna Frank Black said.

"The following summer I enrolled at Hiwassee College, a two-year college, and after many summers I graduated from Tennessee Wesleyan College, Athens, Tennessee, by studying each summer."

"One of my interesting experiences was teaching at the Little Tennessee School, a three-teacher school with an auditorium and a kitchen. Each week the three teachers planned the menu for the coming week. The school got government commodities, and the cheese was especially delicious. The pretty white clapboard building did not have a dining room, so everyone carried trays back to the classroom. It was a time for the children to socialize and to learn table manners. I always ate with the children and drank milk to serve as an example to the children. The school was located on Highway 72," Beuna said.

"A speech teacher visited the school, and I observed how she taught the sounds. Because of my questions, the visiting teacher offered to teach my class phonics. Thereafter, for more than twenty-five years I used the first thirty minutes of each day for phonics. I applied the basic lessons to reading and spelling," Beuna said.

Some of her former students Don Keeble, Gail Galyon, Debbie Lane, and Elaine Dorward attribute their spelling and ability to pronounce any word to their second-grade teacher, Ms. Black. They believe that all children could read and spell better if they had a Ms. Black to lay the basic foundation for their education.

Beuna says, "My favorite subject to teach was mathematics. My own college education was gained along with my practical experience. When I learned the new math, it made sense to me, and I began teaching it without a textbook."

She says, "I always said that you carry books, but you regroup numbers. I never let my students say they carried when adding. I had red plastic disks that they worked with until the concepts, like expanded notation, were learned. Then I let them add on paper. My students loved math because I taught for understanding."

"When Monroe County got the new math books, I taught in-service lessons to the other teachers. I was the only teacher who taught phonetic reading and spelling, but some teachers used the new math methods."

"I grew up in Vonore where my father built the first, and for a long time the only, gas station and garage. Betty Moser lived next door and was a special friend. When the four-lane highway was finished, but not open to traffic, we skated from Vonore to the Little T Bridge several times in one day. The six-mile round-trip jaunt was our first time to enjoy skating on pavement and on such a wide road."

"I wonder if Betty remembers the time we were struck by lightning. We were walking to school under my umbrella in a rain and thunderstorm. Why we were not injured or killed, no one could understand. About seventy years later I still marvel to tell how we stood in the road giggling about our narrow escape."

"I had five siblings, so our mother planned carefully. When we got home from school, the warming closet over the blue enamel wood range had baked sweet potatoes lined up for our after-school snack. Another childhood memory is that the Frank family put in the first bathroom in Vonore. The house had a porch all the way around it, so my father made a bathroom on part of it.

"When I grew up, I married Reuben Black, and my friend, Betty Moser, married his brother, Earl "Red". We enjoyed becoming sisters by marriage. Reuben has been with the Lord for many years, but Earl and his son still farm. Reuben farmed his mother's farm, and the brick home where I live is near the old family homeplace. The house looks out on the Tellico Lake, and next-door the old tobacco patch has an apartment building. The former gravel road, now Highway 360, provides a busy racetrack for hundreds of cars each day," Beuna said.

"One of the joys of my life is my nephew, Charles Scott Frank. His brother was injured in a motorcycle wreck and required years of nursing care in the home. Each Friday after school, I picked up Scott to visit the farm. One fine day he came with his fishing pole and his bait. I volunteered to fry his catch but did not expect him to catch any. Scott returned from the Tellico River with a bucketful of fish. I fried up two pans at a time. That cold, swift water grew delicious fish," Beuna said.

"After I was widowed Scott lived with me for a time after his college graduation. He had a girlfriend that I liked. To encourage the courting couple I would have a picnic basket prepared for them to take to the Fort Loudoun State Park. I always insisted that I was too busy to go with them. Scott is now a father himself. His daughter, Brittney, spent Valentine night with her great-aunt so her parents could go out to dinner. When Brittney has a school problem to share with me, we climb up to the attic to find related school material that I filed."

"Scott is employed by the TRW Company in the Vonore Industrial Park. He is an engineering graduate from Tennessee Technical College in Cookeville and lives in the Hopewell community near Vonore," Beuna said.

Beuna says, "I did not participate in the struggle to save the Little Tennessee River. I attended no meetings, wrote no letters, but decided the best thing to do was to be neutral. Today, I regret there are no fish to catch in the new lake, and I wish the large white oak tree that was hundreds of years old had not been cut down by TVA crews. The changes in the environment and community are still not of interest to me. However, the property that Reuben and I once farmed is now valuable."

"When the Indians build a casino and other amenities, my property will border it. Not a week goes by without a phone call from a real estate developer, but I hope to remain in my home as long as I am physically able to live alone," Beuna states.

"Each day, I go to my brother, who is blind, and help him. I play rook with the senior citizen group and enjoy their covered-dish dinners. Every Sunday I worship at the Vonore United Methodist Church where I have been a member since childhood. As a volunteer I take books to a group home in Vonore," Beuna says.

Her personal library is extensive as would be expected for the woman who taught over a thousand children to read and to understand math. The Vonore community has a hidden pearl in this modest woman who says simply, "I loved to teach."[442]

Lib and Homer Kirkland Lived in Health and in Sickness

Thou wilt keep him in perfect peace,
whose mind is stayed on thee:
because he trusteth in thee.

—Isaiah 26:3, KJV

Elizabeth Hunt Kirkland grew up in the Toqua community where her father was the blacksmith and had a gristmill. Homer grew up in the Citico community where his family had lived for several generations. His roots go to Nathan Kirkland, who hid many of his blood during the removal. Now their home faces the lake and is beside the lively, growing Toqua Community Church, formerly the Toqua Presbyterian Church.

The building sat idle for several years after the moving out because of the flooding of the valley. Harold Gudger organized the nondenominational church that welcomes Lib and Homer. Lib recalls her pastor and several people canceling a vacation in order to be at UT Hospital when Homer underwent open heart surgery. Lib explained, "A nurse came out and said that Homer was oozing blood, and they could not close him up. Right there in the hall we joined hands and prayed. The doctor said it was the power of prayer that brought Homer through that danger point."

Lib married Homer when she was sixteen years old and he was twenty-four years old. Lib has stood with Homer when he had throat cancer and thirty-four cobalt treatments and the four bypasses on his heart. Today, he is active mentally and physically but relies on a feeding tube for nourishment. Lib scolds herself for being too protective, for she times the six daily feedings as any protective wife would.

Lib remembers, "It was 1956 when Homer and I bought the Teddy Bear Restaurant. I had the Grandview Restaurant about three buildings south of where Mr. Gray built the Teddy Bear and asked me to run it. Homer had the gas station next to it. We hadn't had it too long before we put in a drive-in awning, and a few years later we added a dining room onto the side of the building. I had such wonderful help in those days and enjoyed a rich, fulfilling life. High school seniors would work for me. The twist was the popular dance. I was only a little older than the high school children were, so I would twist and jitterbug when we cleaned up. I didn't go to high school, but I enjoyed the excitement and their ball games and gossip. Most of the business was the high school children and the travelers on Highway 411."

"I named the restaurant the Teddy Bear because I have to hold back from buying a stuffed animal when I'm shopping. I have hundreds now but try not to give in to my compulsion to buy more. As one of eight children in a family where extras were scarce, I didn't have a teddy bear or doll as a child. Now I like to hug one. When I get old, I'm going to donate them to the police to give to children when they have to arrest their parents and take the children to foster care."

"Becky is my only child. Since Homer is Rh-positive and I am Rh-negative, we lost a baby. We did have Becky, but the doctors advised us to have no more children. I'm sorry that we didn't adopt, but I worked seven days a week and long hours at the restaurant. My mama and daddy lived with us, so Becky had loving care, but I wish I had been there for her when she was a baby.

"I miss my busy working years. After the people were moved out by TVA our business slacked off, and I closed up. Homer bought the De Ville restaurant and motel south of Madisonville. That was too much work for me, so we got rid of that business."

Homer said, "I was for the dam. TVA promised to make us all rich and prosperous by bringing in industries. It was slow happening, but eventually businesses were established on the above-the-flood-line farms that they took. TVA got foreign companies to come here."

Lib said, "It doesn't seem right that they took people's farms and then sold the land for huge mansions. They forced the people to sell and paid what they wanted. Before Homer got so weak, I liked to work at the BP station. The new dam people would treat me like dirt. Never a smile or a thank-you, and they didn't want to talk to me. I wasn't used to people looking right through me like I wasn't even there. I wanted to say, "I wear shoes and read. I didn't marry my cousin either."

"Everyone expected Vonore would thrive, but Ollie Williams, Charlie Frank, Burch Harrison, and Snyder-Sloan General Store burned down. The big pulpwood yard is closed too. John Hall's Hardware has a flea market in that building now. Instead of the Teddy Bear we have a Hardee's chain restaurant, in place of the Vonore Drugstore we have the Wil-Save Drugs, which is a branch drugstore, and no place to sit and visit. Sloan's BP station has a big fresh-meat market, groceries, horse and cattle feed, and various essentials, such as carryout fried chicken. Despite what I said about snooty newcomers, this is still a good place to live."

"Times have changed and I'm glad Homer and I shared in the changes. Many people live in this area and work in Knoxville and Maryville. The businesses that TVA brought in here make a lot of jobs. Our son-in-law Buddy Silvers works in the manufacturing plant, Sea Ray."

"Another good change is that we got city water this year. Our well water is iron water. Sometimes, the clothes would be all pink. Now the many septic tanks in the area won't make anybody's water bad. Of course, a water-treatment plant could have been built without destroying so much land and making the water still."

"Homer likes to say that he took me out of the cradle and raised me right. Truth is we have worked together these fifty-seven years that we've been married. I would like to have a party and invite all the people that worked in my restaurants, the Grandview, the Teddy Bear, Ox-Bow, De Ville and our ice cream-hamburger stand in the yard over there." Lib pointed to their last business in their front yard.

"God has been good to us. That's why I always answer the phone, 'Hello, God bless you.' Homer is a walking miracle, and who knows what work God has for him and for me to do yet."

One Saturday night, the writer was answering the Contact Helpline when a woman was crying that she needed gas money to drive to Sweetwater Hospital for surgery on Monday. She attended the Toqua Community Church, and I asked if she knew anyone there. Within the hour, she called back that Lib promised her the needed $3 for gas and would have it for her at Sunday worship.[443]

The Homer and Gladys Woods Duncan Family of Citico and Beatrice Duncan Bivens

Children are a heritage from the Lord,
The fruit of the womb is His reward.
—Psalm 127:3 NKJV

Bea Bivens recalls her parents fondly and without criticism or rancor. Homer is pictured with dark brown hair and eyes; broad, muscular shoulders; thin frame; and short stature. Daddy was stern and severe enough to keep his eleven children at work in providing vegetables, fruit, meat, eggs, and milk for the family. He was never idle, for the family farm demanded unending toil.

The farm was in a hollow place between two mountains and aptly named Duncan Hollow. His fertile flat fields were watered by three or more springs that flowed into Duncan Branch and then to Citico Creek in Monroe County. The family planted corn, tobacco, sugarcane, and vegetables. The corn went to Granny Welch's to be ground into meal for bread and cereal. The tobacco brought cash for shoes, flour, coffee, cow and pig feed, and fabric.

Homer demanded modest behavior and dress from his daughters. Bea remembers the three times each year that she and her sisters were allowed to wear pants: berry picking, sorghum making, and beehive robbing. Berry picking was fun and meant a picnic up the mountain to the blueberry bald with Mommy. Sorghum making was distasteful, for Bea's job was to push the dusty cane into the grinder as a mule turned it round and round all day. To this day, she believes the world could do without sorghum or honey. For honey taking she wore a beekeeper mask, long sleeves, and her pant's legs tied tightly at her ankles. The work was done near noon on a hot day while many of the bees were away from the hives. Chewing the honeycomb wax was her meager reward while the family strained and bottled the honey.

Daddy Homer was strict with his seven daughters. They must sit with their knees covered, and their homemade skirts could not be too short. They were permitted no makeup or jewelry. Bea and her mother insisted she was ready to marry at sixteen and a half, but the dour Scotsman pleaded for his little lassie to wait. She had found her true love and pledged her troth to Wilburn O'Dell Bivens. Her dad reluctantly blessed the union and loved another son.

Gladys Woods Duncan and Homer married as teenagers at the Citico Creek Baptist Church. Gladys was a skinny woman with dark brown eyes and black hair, but Bea never heard any talk of Cherokee blood. The couple enjoyed their secluded hollow and a fruitful, serene life together. She was rarely without a baby on her lap or in her womb in her childbearing years. All of her eleven children were born in the Duncan farmhouse, and their births were attended by her neighbor, Laurie Williams. Bea suspects she was a self-taught midwife. Fortunately, all of Gladys and Homer's babies were straightforward births and full-term, lusty babies. All grew to adulthood without inherited diseases, which was a special blessing for the families were far from modern medicine.

Homer and his family farmed without electricity, gasoline motors, a tractor, or a chain saw. He used an ax, a handsaw, and a bow saw. Two men used a five-foot saw to fell a large tree, and the mules dragged it to the barnyard to be cut into fireplace logs or split for the kitchen range. The land was rented from Ms. Pattie Houston of Vonore, who was paid a percentage of the tobacco crop.

One of Gladys and the children's spring jobs was to clean the springs. In case of dry weather, three springs were maintained. The leaves were swept out, and a box of salt was poured on the rocks lining the springs. The rocks were swept until they shined clean and white. Each day, the children carried the pure, clean water to the house.

Bea says, "The life was a rough go, but we kids had a lot of fun in Duncan Hollow. Hugh grapevine swings were special fun. We climbed young, limber hickory trees and rode them to the ground. We gave the game no special name, but the daring, bucking tree challenged our courage. Another special miracle from the Lord was that no one broke their bones. The piles of sawdust from the wood gathering for winter heat and year-around cooking and laundry were an exceptional thrill. Now I wonder why we didn't stick a splinter into our tough hides, but it was a great place to hide, jump, and slide. In summer we dammed up a hole in Duncan branch and swam, splashed, and enjoyed the water after working in the fields all day."

Much of Homer and Gladys's life was a tough struggle to provide food and necessities for their brood. Bea accepts that their school days were brief in the autumn after crops were laid by. The children walked along the branch to the Citico Road and up the hill to the Citico School. Eight grades were taught, but Bea says that her brief school days left her only able to write her name. She never learned to read and neither could her parents. In winter the narrow path was slick and icy, and in the spring all the children were needed for planting.

Gladys worked in the fields alongside the children and her husband, but she was also busy with canning and drying fruits and vegetables. She cooked all their meals on a wood range and washed and scrubbed their clothes and bedding with water the children carried from a spring. Gladys's method for making leather breaches beans was for the children to thread a thread through each bean and hang them on the porch to dry. When dry she stored them in a cloth sack with sassafras twigs to keep the bugs out.

Bea's method differs a little. She snaps her beans, dries them, and stores them in an electric freezer to keep the bugs out.

By 1957 a neighbor told Homer and his brothers Jessie or Jet, and Ernest that workers were needed near Vonore at Rose Island. It was winter work taking up pine seedlings and for the Duncan brothers about fifty miles round-trip. Bea says that her father walked to the Citico Road because he never owned a car or tractor. The brothers were accepted and saw Dr. Kimbrough in Madisonville as the first doctor visit in their lives. Dr. Kimbrough pronounced them fit for the labor. Bob Dorward, their young boss, taught Homer to write his name on his time card. It was a strict company policy that no one could do this for an employee and that an *x* was unacceptable. Bill Keithley, who kept the time card and reports each week said an exception was made for one brother.

When Homer started working for the Hiwassee Land Company, Gladys and her son, Millard, farmed. By the time TVA planned to move all the river-bottom farmers and businesses near the Little Tennessee River out, Homer was sick. It was throat cancer, and Gladys wanted to get nearer a better road. The land was sold for a campground, and the buyer put up a sign that read Duncan Hollow. Bea thinks it still marks the road her daddy made.

Daddy Homer died at fifty-seven years of age, but Mummy lived to be eighty-four. One year, all of her children packed picnic baskets and enjoyed the new picnic tables and good road into Duncan Hollow.

Bea says, "When I tell about my childhood and how my mommy and daddy lived, it sounds like a rough life. A bright spot was church on Sunday. We worked all week, but on Sunday our family walked over the mountain to the Citico Missionary Baptist church. A mule and sled could make that road, but our family walked it in about thirty minutes. After crops were laid-by, the family went to revival. It was a time to see the neighbors, kinfolks, and new babies, and to experience spiritual renewal."[444]

Charles R. Hall Cooks for Vonore and Lakeside Community on Oak Grove Road

A little sleep, a little slumber, a little folding of the hands to rest,
and poverty will come upon you like a robber, and want
like an armed warrior.
—Proverbs 24:33-34, NRSV

Charles Hall of Oak Grove Road is the millionaire next door in Monroe County. He was mopping the floor of the restaurant area of his grocery-gas station when I went to interview him. Hall's Store is at the intersection of Oak Grove Road and the Sweetwater Road. Gas, essential groceries, and country cooking are available. The grill heats up for early breakfast, and lunch is served until mid-afternoon. Forty-four can be seated at tablecloth-covered tables, and a dozen stools in front of the cooking area serve folks in a big hurry. A menu is posted for the week and features a different main dish and vegetables for each day, or a sandwich will be made for you. The business is several miles from the Vonore industrial complex, so piles of carryout dinners are picked up. The Hall family provides vending machines in the industries. A grill and hot meal around the clock is provided at TRW industry and at Merrimac. Johnson Control in Athens has his vending machines, and cooks keep the grill and ovens busy twenty-four hours a day.

Charles Hall of Oak Grove Road grew up in the community near his store. He went to the old Lakeside Grade School and graduated from Vonore High School about 1960. The Halls and the Giles are pioneer families in the area. His mother was a Giles, and her children are in process of selling the part of her farm the Tennessee Valley Authority left her in the Ball Play community near Vonore. About fifteen acres were in the Tellico River bottom and had deep soil. TVA bought that, but it did not flood and lies fallow and in ruin.

The Giles family acquired the farm in 1850. An uncle raised her when her father died. It was a lifestyle of making every asset count and never wasting their meager resources. His mother steadfastly refused to sell her property saying, "God is making no more land." From her $300-a-month social security she saved $100 a month and instructed her three children that the property tax was taken care of for about ten years. She walked, and her mind remained clear until about two weeks before she went to be with the Lord at age ninety-six.

When she was growing up, many sawmills operated in the Ball Play area. A loud whistle blew to call the men to work or meals. One of her favorite stories was awakening to the whistle and thinking Gabriel was blowing his horn and the world was ending. She remembered a big cave on the farm where people gathered to have singings.

"When Dale and I explored it, we tied a string at the entrance so we could follow it out. It is possible to go in one side of the hill and out the other side. We saw no need to venture that far into the darkness and mud. We did find the huge gathering room that Mama described."

Charles said, "Mrs. John Lackey (the family called her Ms. Johnnie Bell), was my mama's niece. Ms. Johnnie Bell's mother, Mrs. Dr. McCollum, and my mama were sisters. So family visits were frequent, but I did not pay any mind to their stories. Now if I had paid attention, I could know family history."

"I was raised in my daddy's store, which was about a mile from where we visit. Local folks called it the edge of Vonore and Lakeside. My grandfather, Nick Hall, died when I was three months old. They tell he weighed three hundred pounds and liked to walk to Vonore. He had two geese that always followed him to town and back. He lost his farm during the depression. Later, my daddy had a chance to buy it back for $5,000. It was two hundred acres, but Daddy did not have the cash and feared debt," Charles said.

"A cave on Grandpa's farm was called the Nick Hall cave. It had Indian writing on the walls and lots of worked stones on the floor. As a kid I never went far into that cave, but Dale and I found a huge room down a muddy passageway. The cave is around the bend from where the Sea Ray plant is now, but the lake water is in it since the flooding of the valley," Charles recalls.

"My daddy was BB or Bart Hall. He had a general store and three rolling stores. The rolling stores were old buses or trucks that visited the farmwomen and men with basic necessities. Crates for chickens taken in trade were built into the vehicles. One of the routes was Allegany Mountain in Blount County (Highway 72 East). My memory floats back to the day the revenuers stopped Daddy and told him not to sell any more sugar to a certain family. Daddy told him that "this person, you don't want him to have sugar, then you be there to tell him he can't have it. I'll not tell him not to buy. I don't know what kind of fellow he is." Dad said that he kept on selling him sugar, but it wasn't too long before the revenuers busted up his still."

"Daddy went to Hiwassee College when it had high school. Daddy sold everything a farmer could need in his general store. A lot of people had little cash, so Daddy carried them. Their hope was to sell tobacco or soybeans and pay their debt. When Daddy went out of business, he had about $50,000 owed to him. Nowadays that would be worth about $300,000. He decided not to try to collect any of it. Daddy believed you would not suffer yourself when you keep a neighbor from going hungry. He did his benevolence by putting it on the book so a man kept his dignity. People always intended to pay him."

Charles's memories of Vonore High School are fond and pleasant. He claims, "I only missed about three days of high school because there was nothing to do in Vonore to encourage truancy."

Charles remembers that Charles Niles, his old teacher, came to their high school reunion in June 2003. Mr. Niles can play almost every musical instrument and still sings at church, and he told how he wanted to get to WYXI and be a professional musician. But his daddy saw no profit in music and said, "No, take the scholarship to Maryville College and be a teacher, and you'll always have a job and a living."

This is how Charles remembers his senior-class trip. "Charles Niles and Margaret Evelyn Johnson Sheets were the Vonore school senior-class sponsors. Mr. Niles broke his leg that month but went on the senior trip to Charleston, South Carolina anyway. One night some of us boys thought we would slip out after everyone was asleep. From behind a big oak tree, Charles Niles, broken leg and about seven feet tall, stepped out and asked, 'Where are you going, boys?' We failed to see the city nightlife."

"Mr. Niles has only one eye, but he saw everything. He has a mischievous and witty personality. Sometimes, while we waited for lunch, he would remove his glass eye. The girls screamed and acted silly, and we enjoyed a good laugh."

"My senior year, I was the co-captain of my football team, and the team won nine games and lost two. The basketball team was fun, but the win's nothing to brag about. I swam in Fork Creek with the other boys in the neighborhood almost every summer day. The water was often muddy, but we carried a bar of soap along in order to say we were bathing. A couple of times a summer we would walk to Citico Beach, which was about sixteen miles east toward the Cherokee National Forest. The Citico Creek water was clear, cold, and clean but warmer than the Little Tennessee River or the Tellico River. The narrow gravel road had little traffic, so we ran and walked without fear."

"I coached little league baseball for my two sons, and I'm grateful I was able to do it. I am helping my wife put on the Bible school at the Vonore Missionary Baptist Church this week. I am proud that 230-250 children are coming each night. I only obey orders, as I am not a teacher or church leader."

Charles recalls, "My daddy said little about the flooding of the valley until TVA took the best land on the Ball Play Farm. It really upset him to lose that prime farmland and see it abandoned to briars and brush. Water never covered it. Daddy always said the dam could not be successfully opposed, so he never worked to prevent it."

Mr. Hall recognizes the puzzle of his communities' hopes and changes and the phony promises of the fighting years. He states, "No industry in the industrial park uses the lake water or barge transportation; however, my service businesses prospered in the last thirty-eight years. I started in 1965 with two employees. At peak employment levels, I have about fifty employees. At present I have thirty people working for me. The thing about vending machines is they don't talk back to you, and they don't lay out of work. People must eat, and I serve the best food. One of my sons manages the vending machines, and one son takes care of the paperwork and hiring and firing. They both graduated from college. They have given me two granddaughters and one grandson. I'm proud to say that both serve as deacons in the Vonore Missionary Baptist Church. I could never accept such an honor because I believe a deacon must serve the people in his church. My business keeps me so close and tied down that I never thought I could do the job. I do believe Jesus Christ is Lord. Sometimes, I get so tired and busy that I lose my temper, but I mean to lead a Christian life."

He directs, "I want you to put something in the book about my uncle John Hall. He ran the hardware store in Vonore, and it was a hub of the town. He never married but took care of his two maiden sisters, Lois and Anna Ruth. When I think of Aunt Anna Ruth, I remember the whipping she gave me in second grade. She was a strict teacher and made you learn."

"Uncle John Hall sold coal as well as general farm needs. He never refused to make a coal delivery, even when he knew they could never pay. Only the Lord knows how many people he kept warm during their hard times. John would carry farmers with seed and fertilizer, but my daddy said he didn't hurt from what some would call questionable business practices. My brother, Dale, managed Uncle John's dairy farm. As Uncle John and his sisters grew old, my brother took care of them."

"My daddy was a jolly, good-natured man. He frequently told Betty, my sister, and Dale and me, "Nobody is no better than you are. You are no better than anybody else.' One of daddy's jokes was, 'I never saw an ugly woman. Some just look better than others.'"

Charles Hall of Oak Grove/Sweetwater Road has used his dad's advice as he knows every face that comes into his store. He treats them all fair and square and smiles a greeting. He laments, "I once knew the name of at least one member of every family between Loudon and Citico. I can't do that now as they put houses up too fast."

One area of his store has many homemade signs from a computer. One sums up how he lives his life. It says, "Worldly wisdom is a dead-end street."[445]

Part Four

Looking Back at
Progress and Change

Introduction

Remembering

Valuing a community's natural resources while recognizing the need for progress, improvement, and change is revealed in these memories of living in the area as a teenager and working adult (Don Keeble), as a mature adult (Bill Keithley), and as an authority on the lumber industry, growing paper trees and management of Hiwassee Land Company, now Bowaters Woodlands (Louis Camisa).

Almost all of the people who told their stories recognize positive changes, but with no exceptions explain that the distribution centers, industry, and the utility company could have been located in Vonore or Monroe County without the forced buying or land grab of 42,999 acres of land and the removal of many families.[446] While a water-treatment system and improved roads are assets, private wells would not have been muddied (making water treatment necessary) or the relocation of roads would not have been required if the valley had not been flooded.

Don Keeble Says We Fail to See What We Had

"As a teenager the Little Tennessee River was my joy, but I failed to see the destruction of the river and community as a loss. I'm a big, tall man and was always the tallest in my class. My mother had Snyder's General Store to order my Converse shoes, especially for my large feet. They were $9.99 and outgrown before I could wear them out. The standing tease in Vonore High School was, 'Let's steal one of Keeble's shoes and float the Little T.'[447]

"An important part of growing up in Vonore was floating the Little Tennessee River. Chris Hughes, Claude Simmerly, and I rented an aluminum johnboat and floated the river as often as we could. The three of us set tobacco, handed tobacco, and put up hay and saved our money. The boat we wanted was in the Sears, Roebuck catalog, and cost $100. We ordered it, and my daddy took the three of us to the Knoxville Sears store and picked it up along with two oars. Each of us paid one-third. That boat put us on the river anytime. We floated and fished, swam or waded, and fished," Don said.[448]

"We waded in the fifty-degree water in our shorts and were quickly numb. Once I crawled into the boat and found my shoe full of blood. I had cut my ankle real deep. I still have a large rough scar. Chris grabbed my shirt and wrapped it up, and we elevated it. That was the only accident we ever had."[449]

"Claude was an active person. He was always casting or talking while Chris and I were contemplative. When I studied Cherokee legend and myth at the University of Tennessee, I learned about a rock bluff that often aroused our curiosity. It was on the Blount County side of the river and unusual. It was black chert rock with a vertical formation of white flint. At the foot of the bluff was a fierce whirlpool or suckhole."[450]

"The legend was that an eagle lived on top of that bluff, and the white flint was the eagle's droppings. The eagle guarded the whirlpool. If a bad Indian canoes by, the eagle would swoop down and eat him, but if a real bad man came down the river, he would be sucked into the hole to die. It is a strange and creepy feeling to know exactly where a Cherokee myth originated."[451]

"In November 1979, we three made our final trip down the former Little T. We were in our twenties, married and working. My daddy didn't have to carry us up to the Caulderwood Dam, and we left a car at our takeout spot at the mouth of the Tellico River. The water was backing up, and our last trip was a sad, quiet one. The fish, ducks, and even the water snakes were upset and confused. We paddled much of the way because the free-flowing river was backed up, still, and stagnant. Pride kept us from weeping, but we said a silent good-bye. Chris has the boat, a twelve-foot aluminum johnboat that never needed a motor to float the swift, white water. Our friend Claude is dead like the river we loved so dearly."[452]

"I majored in history at the University of Tennessee, so I can take a long view of the loss of the land and the Little Tennessee River, which the local folks called the Little T. I collected worked stones from the Mississippi cultures who were here for two thousand years,[453] and from the Cherokee who were here for at least 320 years. The white men took the land from the Cherokees in 1830, so the white men had the valley for 130 years. The farmers were displaced by their own government and by greedy white people. In terms of history, our displacement is a bump on the pages of history. I regret it because I lived through that troubling, unhappy time. My personal protest is to stay off the lake and to try to never speak the name of that falsely named body of water."[454]

"As a child the promises of our government sounded so exciting to me. Timberlake would have new houses, a movie theatre, big department stores and all city amenities. Timberlake never materialized, but the farmer's land was sold to rich, retired people from up north. Where I earned $34 for our johnboat by the sweat of my brow, costly homes and yachts are now."[455]

"I've been invited to the Rarity Bay Club to speak. The interlopers in the gated community don't understand the feeling of the native people. One lady scolded, 'The people were paid for their land'."

"My reply, 'They were forced to sell and forced to take whatever the Tennessee Valley Authority wished to pay. There was no fairness or justice in the land deals. You people in Rarity Bay paid many times what the farmers were paid in the forced sales, and their living came from the soil and their cattle'."[456]

Don continues, "I am now forty-five years old. My father was allowed to keep half of his farm, thirty-nine acres. The Tennessee Valley Authority leased back their purchased land for him to farm for a while. After graduating from the University of Tennessee I might have gone far away, but I'm glad that I chose to come home to work for the State of Tennessee Employment Agency at Vonore."[457]

Don's thoughts float to a historical overview, and he says, "It is thirty years since the people were moved out. The Tennessee Valley Authority promised jobs for the area. All of the industries could be here without the destruction of the farmland and river. As people became too old to farm, the land could be bought for building factories. For that reason I feel the citizens of the United States, especially Tennessee, paid too high a price for the forced industrialization of Vonore."[458]

"At this time, summer 2003, the Niles Ferry and the Tellico West industrial parks employ seven thousand people in a twenty-four-hour cycle. The Sweetwater industries employ five hundred to six hundred people in a twenty-four-hour cycle. Madisonville's industrial park employs several hundred. I reap the benefits of the Tennessee Valley Authority's socialist plan for fixing our area. My soul is in a quandary, however, for I do feel remorse about the area's losses."[459]

Keeble argues, "The Monroe county schools do not prepare their students as well as the surrounding counties. Our local people are harder to place in good jobs because of the educational deficiencies. Many of the people born and raised here do not value our schools. The commuters to Knoxville have little interest in their bedroom community, and the rich retired people came because of lower taxes and no income tax in Tennessee, so better schools are not a priority. A positive community attitude toward upgrading our school system is a need that I see in my work, which is placing people in jobs."[460]

Keeble explained the industrial development, "In order to manage the land that was not flooded, TVA created a stepchild agency, the Tennessee Reservoir Development Agency, TRDA. Their purpose is to avoid having it look like TVA is in charge of the selling or leasing of the TVA land. TRDA's mission is to manage the land for the good of the people. TRDA is a separate entity from TVA and is managed by a professional staff. At present, Ron Hammontree is the director; however, a nine-member board of directors sets policy. The county executives of Monroe, Loudon, and Blount counties, three persons appointed by the Tennessee governor, one TVA representative, one State of Tennessee person, and one person from the Game and Fish Agency comprise the board of directors."[461]

Keeble stated, "The Tennessee Reservoir Development Agency's first project was to sell Alfred Davis's family farm for Tellico Village, an expensive housing subdivision near Loudon. All that land is leased. Rarity Bay housing and golf area is about full also. Little land is available for new industrial development for the next ten to twenty years because it is now leased for housing or business. TRDA has completed its mission to manage the land taken under the law of eminent domain; that is, to manage the land for the good of the people. It remains to be seen whether free enterprise will be encouraged in the Tennessee Valley, or if the bureaucracy will continue to control what businesses can locate in the area."[462]

"History is my interest," Keeble admits, "I served on the Fort Loudoun Historical Association for about ten years. One of our dreams was to connect Fort Loudoun with a park in Loudon County with a 150-foot-wide pathway. The original Fort Loudoun is underwater, but TVA made dikes and rebuilt it. The community can thank Mrs. Alice Milton for that. She put up a hard battle, and they finally did what we have there now. In 1997, a rider for Fort Loudoun for $400,000 was attached to a bill for wetland in West Tennessee for duck hunting. $125,000 went for a feasibility study, $300,000 came from the Interior Department, and the Fort Loudoun Association raised $25,000. Eight hundred sixty acres of the McGhee-McClung-Carson farms became a state park. It is a beautiful place and used in the summer for swimming and picnics."[463]

"One of the few times I have ridden on the lake was in my work as a part of the TRDA and as a volunteer for the Fort Loudoun Association. The plan was to attract an English company to lease land in the industrial park. We rode on the Tennessee Valley Authority's barge from Loudon. We had men in red-coat uniforms, fired cannon, and flew the Union Jack. We served a dinner of roast beef and Yorkshire pudding, and tried to talk business with them. Unfortunately, this particular company did not invest in this area."[464]

"As a historian, public servant, and one emotionally involved in seeing the destruction of the Little Tennessee Valley, I know that proper leadership could have stopped the unneeded and unwanted damming project. The farmers did not have the money or education to deal with Washington. The fishermen and outdoor lovers knew it was a pity to destroy a unique fishery and tourist attraction, but they lacked organization and funding. The environmentalists recognized the snail darter (fish) and special plants and animals, but in the sixties and seventies, some people wanted manufacturing. The voice for the environment was too weak to stop the Tennessee Valley Authority from buying land."[465]

"I grew up in a family where politics were talked daily because my daddy was on the county court, now called the County Commission. The politics of Tennessee hallows and honors TVA and their vast power. Elected officials fear to criticize a TVA project. That is why Congressman John Duncan Sr. got the final bill approved in a late-afternoon session and why Carter signed it into law."[466]

"I hope the community will not forget the brave, foresighted people, who knew business and farming and tourist development could thrive without another lake: people such as my father, Cory Keeble, John Lackey, Claude Hammontree, Bob Dorward, Alice Milton, Beryl Moser, C. Griffin Martin, Judges Sue K. Hicks and Bennie Simpson, and so many others. I think of the fishery men like Bob Burch, Price Wilkins, and Dave Dickey of the Knoxville Chamber of Commerce." [467]

Keeble concludes, "I'm proud to work in this area and to try in every way to make it a better community. My roots go back to my great-grandmother, a full-blooded Cherokee, who was hidden during that removal. My grandfather, Keeble, was moved out from his farm at Friendsville, Blount County for the Fort Loudoun Dam and Lake. My father gave much of his time in the Monroe County government as an unpaid public servant. Discussions about local issues and budgets taught them to see and think about the many sides of issues and money problems in Monroe County. I try to work with the newcomers to explain the need for better educational opportunities, clean water, and to encourage respect of the farmers. Sometimes, I think that my voice of reason is heard." [468]

Bill Keithley Sees Society Change

Bill and Bruce Keithley and their three children, Richard, Carol, and Ginger moved from Memphis to Maryville in 1957. The nursery at Vonore on Rose Island was being developed. Bill's experience as a horticulturist and in plant science was needed. His friends Johnny and Marice, who traveled for the Federal Housing Association, FHA, heard about the starting of a pine-seedling nursery and urged him to write a letter. It sounded like the perfect job for his talents and interests. When an airline ticket arrived for him to come for an interview, he met Bob Edgar, Dick Dyer, Jim Hill, and Louis Camisa in the log building on the hilltop near the new paper mill.[469]

Bill was forty-two years old and the older man in the young company. In fact, he recalls that it was company policy to exclude anyone over forty-five for management jobs. His solid experience counted with his boss, Bob Dorward, who was sixteen years his junior. They developed a working relationship, so when the fight with TVA boiled, Bill covered the nursery work. He freed Bob to guide float trips of politicians and outdoor writers down the Little Tennessee River. Bill says, "That's about all I did, except write letters and go to the meetings"[470]

Bill has vivid memories of the meeting at Greenback School when Aubrey Wagner asked for community support. Bill realized the small maneuvers of Judge Sue K. Hicks, Bob Dorward, and John Lackey were no match against the sprawling bureaucracy.[471]

Bill was part of the tremendous societal change that flooded the Little Tennessee Valley and a little bit of the Tellico River Area. When he arrived in the summer of 1957, the job of leveling the lower end toward Loudon of the island was underway. Raised beds and irrigation lines were put in place. To his and Bob Dorward's amazement, several of the men had plumbing aptitude. It was the policy of the federal prison system to teach every prisoner a trade during the time they served for bootlegging. These master plumbers were an asset to the work.[472]

Bob Dorward wanted the dozer men to save the topsoil and replace it in the beds. As Bill remembers, the dozer operators would not do this. Bill says, "The top soil was about twenty inches deep, so it was still a superior nursery site."[473]

In 1957 the water level on the slack side of the island was determined by how much water TVA allowed from the several dams up the Little Tennessee. Sometimes, large trucks and bulldozers could drive through the river, but the first years, the seedlings were taken out in a johnboat along a towline. The workers went to work by boat also.[474]

In time, the Hiwassee Land Company built a two hundred-foot bridge out of west-coast Douglas fir. Tom Walbridge, Hiwassee forest engineer, construction superintendent, Gene Pendegraph, six men, a crane, and a bulldozer built the thirty-ton-capacity Little Golden Gate Bridge in six weeks. Rose Island was then ready to supply seedlings to the South. One of the first tests was a huge truck loaded with all the steel for the equipment building, packing shed, and offices. The bridge held up.[475]

"The bridge was threatened by heavy rains one spring. Up both the Tellico River, which flowed into the Little Tennessee and from up the Little Tennessee, trees and brush were swept into a raging torrent. All the regular employees, Bob Dorward, and I and a few people from the central office at Calhoun were there all night. Jim Hill and Louis Camisa had brought in cranes, and the men worked diligently," Bill said.[476]

Bill says, "I remember reaching down to free some vines that were acting as a dam and catching brush. I had rolled up my sleeves and later came down with a disastrous outbreak of poison ivy that sent me to the Vonore Drugstore where I found Dr. Troy Bagwell having his afternoon Coke. All the communities were aware of the danger to the bridge, for some of the men lived at Citico and at Toqua."[477]

Bob Dorward was responsible for planting and growing the seedlings. My style of work was more laid-back and accepting of what came. Bob measured the rainfall and kept records of the temperature. He had to decide whether the weather permitted the men to lift the trees. If extreme cold threatened, he would have trees pulled ahead so his crew could work inside packing the seedlings for shipping. That way he kept his crew working.[478]

"The seed orchard was my responsibility. In cooperation with Dr. Bruce Zoebel at NC State University, the company hoped to improve the quality of the pulpwood, get more wood per tree, and develop trees that reached optimum growth in a shorter time. Bill remembers Bob Edgar, company president, walking the seed orchard and saying, "If we could grow pulpwood in two or three years less, it would mean millions of dollars profit for the company." I believe this can be done in two or three hundred years. District foresters would search for superior trees when they bought land. Bob and I would grade the tree again and shoot sprigs or scions from the tree. The sprigs were grafted to an established rootstock to speed up the flowering and production of superior seed."[479]

Bill says, "I taught Henderson King to graft, and he had an outstanding ability to achieve a successful take. I had fifteen trees planted in a random pattern so trees could cross-pollinate. The crosses were put in a test area. Some would have superior growth rates and some would not. We controlled the pollination by putting a bag around the female flower and applying the pollen of a known tree. The record keeping was a job, but the men knew where the trees were and understood the importance of the project."[480]

"After it became certain TVA would destroy the river and valley. My crew and I moved about a hundred seed trees to Loudon County. In the horticulture and nursery business, I had supervised the moving and balling in burlap of many trees. Moving such large trees was a challenge, but the company had millions of dollars invested in producing seed for the nursery. A machine went four feet to cut the taproots, which were twelve inches in diameter. I have a proud memory that 85 percent of the seed trees lived. Crews with water trucks kept watering the big old trees all summer until they developed a new set of roots," Bill remembers how they labored.[481]

"Foresters, especially Jim Hill, started searching for a new site for growing pine seedlings. A suitable acreage was found in North Georgia, several hundred miles south on Highway 411. It was a sad time for the community, but the men had a philosophy that if a thing was going to hurt just go ahead and get it over with. Their attitude stood them in good stead," Bill stated.[482]

Bill remembers when Ross Bernhardt came and asked, "Can I offer Junior Melson a management job in the Etowah District. Earl was his name, but his friends called him Junior. Junior took on a lot of responsibility for the work. He was so dependable and understood what needed to be done and how to move the crews. I knew he could do the new job, so I told Ross to ask him. Melson stayed at the Etowah District until he retired because he was hired for the nursery while in his teens."[483]

"Another employee I greatly admired was Charlie West. He was my field foreman and would take the crew to the proper bed and lot number for digging. A lot of care must be taken in handling the tender seedlings, and he was so reliable in seeing that every man knew how to do it right. One of Charlie's hobbies was rescuing abandoned dogs and finding homes for them so that tells you a lot about him." Bill smiled.[484]

"For weeks, Bob and I heard the men talking about "Big Eye" coming home. "Big Eye" had a job in a factory in Michigan where he stood at a machine and stamped out metal parts. When he came, he allowed as how he could drive a truck, an eighteen-wheeler. Bob sent him to practice, and the nursery had the badly needed truck driver. His name was Carson Williams from Citico, and he made sure the trucks were loaded according to his planned route. When he returned he cleaned his truck and did routine maintenance on his truck. Carson moved to Georgia with the nursery and was foreman until he retired," Bill remembered.[485]

Many of the nursery workers had a limited education because of a belief that it was not important for their way of life. An example was blood brothers who spelled their name differently. It was a strict rule that a man could not sign another man's time card, but to avoid shaming them, Bob and I allowed one of their sons to sign for one man."[486]

"The workers knew how to do many hard jobs. One time, a half-dead tree was leaning toward the seed orchard. Homer Duncan was recommended as the man who could fell the tree without damaging the seed orchard. Bill remembers how he walked around the tree and then start chopping with a single-bit ax. The tree fell toward the river exactly where Homer planned. I am certain that no other man on the crew could have done this." Bill thinks back to that day.[487]

"As the dark cloud of removal loomed over the nursery, the crews moved eighty to one hundred of the seed trees to Loudon County. A hole about four feet deep was left. So Jeff Chapman, the archaeologist, made the holes about seventeen-feet deep with a toothless backhoe that he had developed. The diggers used ladders to examine what they found. It turned out people had lived on the island eight thousand to ten thousand years ago. The men and I liked to look at the excavations. I suppose the site was not an island then, and everyone wondered about the changes the river had made over time," Bill told me.[488]

"The remaining seed trees were cut off about chest high, and the tops were left for fishery development. I and most of my crew were so busy developing the new nursery that I can't remember if the buildings were moved away or are under the thirty-five feet of water of the lake. It was a long drive for us until some of the men found housing and others continued driving until retirement," Bill remembers.[489]

"In 2004, Bill and his Maryville Rotary Club visited Rarity Bay, a high-cost gated community. Bill is impressed that such rich people would agree to build their homes so much alike. No cute, little cottages, old farmhouses, or woods mar the barren hillsides where families once earned a living from the soil. It is a playground for the idle to play golf and to have a handy place to tie up their boats," Bill observes.[490]

"Bill takes advantage of trips provided by his independent living home, Shannondale in Maryville. On a recent trip, the residents thought it was a funny sight to see silos in the lake. He said few of the folks knew about the old Foute mansion and hard work that Frances and Ben Clark did to provide employment for several families. Bill said that these folks from outside the valley cannot believe the farmers and lumbermen believed they had a good life before TVA moved them out," Bill told me.[491]

Louis Camisa Says Values Have Changed in East Tennessee

"Values have changed for the better when I think of the environment," Louis Camisa muses. Louis Camisa thought back over his time of planting and harvesting trees in the Tennessee Valley. The outdoors, the water, land, and forests are valued more now. At the time of the flooding of the Little Tennessee Valley, farms and forests were discounted in favor of factories and the acquisition of land for resale for housing development.

"I was born in West Virginia and came to Tennessee in 1952 when Bowater organized a subsidiary company, Hiwassee Land Company. My forestry job was to buy land, which could supply pulpwood for the paper mill. I recall buying one thousand surface acres in Fentress County for $10 an acre. It was rolling, wooded country with clear, rushing creeks; however, the steep hillsides were rocky and the soil thin from subsistence farming and overgrazing. The mining company retained the mineral rights, and during the Carter energy crunch stripped mined a million dollars worth of coal from that tract," Camisa said.

"The need for reforestation of the areas cut for pulpwood became apparent. Forestry people plan for the next generation. By 1956, I had moved from my district forestry job to administration in the Calhoun, Tennessee office. Al Swayne and Jim Hill found a perfect site for a nursery on the Little Tennessee River at Rose Island near Vonore, Tennessee."

"Bob Edgar and I had hired several men with no definite assignments for them. Bob Dorward was selected to develop the nursery on Rose Island. I remember the cable across the slack side of the crystal-clear river. The nursery got off to a start, and the seedlings were ferried across the river, and trucks hauled them to the districts in Mississippi, Alabama, Georgia, and Tennessee. The island soil was deep and rich, and Bob Edgar, Jim Hill, and I loved the perfect site. The nursery became a showplace for college groups and visitors. Even Sir Eric Bowater, who was in charge of paper companies all over the world, was treated to a tour."

"Tom Walbridge and Gene Pendergraft were the forest engineers for Hiwassee Land Company. The corporation decided to build a bridge to their nursery, for the need for reforestation was growing. The district foresters were buying abandoned farms that were perfect for growing pine. I remember the western fir used to build the bridge as eighteen-feet long. I have a picture of Tom Walbridge, now a retired professor at Virginia Technological, Blacksburg, Virginia, and Gene Pendergraft admiring the project."

"With several dams on the Little Tennessee River, the area seldom flooded. One spring, sudden heavy rains for days caused the water to rise quickly. Tom Walbridge, Bill Keithley, and Bob Dorward and his local crews and I stayed up all night. Entire trees were uprooted and hurled toward the million-dollar bridge. Tractors and crawlers kept working all night. Although water covered the low, flat island area and seeped into the sorting and bundling building, little damage was done. The large pumps used for irrigation came through safely," Camisa said.

"Millions of trees were shipped out of the nursery. Hiwassee Land Company and Bowater in cooperation with North Carolina State University started a superior tree program. Several seed orchards were developed to provide seed for the nursery. Foresters all over the southeast searched for superior trees and Dorward and Keithley graded the trees. Luckily, Bob Dorward was a superior marksman, for the project required shooting scions from the tall, straight trees then grafting one to established root stock. I appreciated Bill Keithley who kept meticulous records and made the project outstanding enough for college students from Clemson, Georgia, and North Carolina to visit."

"I liked to joke with my workers. Earl Melson would come to the Calhoun mill to pick up the payroll checks for the Etowah district. I would ask, 'What are you doing here, boy?'"

"He would tell me that he came to pick up the pay checks, I would shake my head and walk away saying, 'and I hope there is enough money in the bank to pay you.'"

"One of my trademarks was my love for delicious fresh pies. From South Georgia to Calhoun, Tennessee, I knew the little restaurants which made fresh apple or peach pie in season. This made me unpopular with my younger employees who traveled with me and didn't care for between-meal sweets and wanted to be home near quitting time," Camisa laughed.

"I remember promoting a protest hike of twenty-eight miles to try to prevent a road that would destroy virgin timber. Bob Dorward, Gene Hill, and other foresters participated with me," he said.

"For my eighty-first birthday my granddaughter bought me a computer. I compiled a book on changes in logging practices in the Appalachian Mountains. I got pictures and stories from forestry friends from all over the southeast and scanned them into my computer," he said.

Unfortunately, Mr. Camisa died at eighty-eight before completing the project to his satisfaction. His views on the changing values toward the water, forests, and fish were respected by all who enjoyed talking to him. He and his kind are unique, but they completed projects that renewed the forests and protected the water sheds in the southeast.[492]

Part Five

Dam the Little T

Introduction

Wanting Change

A significant segment of the population believed destroying the rivers would allow the Tennessee Valley Authority to bring in industrial development in a way the people living in the tri-county area of Blount, Monroe, and Loudon could not or would not allow because they preferred their present way of life. Mr. Charles Hall of Tellico Plains, business man and politician, imagined that the advantages of steady factory work for young people would make out-migration of youth unnecessary.

Mr. Hall worked as CEO of the Tellico Telephone Company, was mayor of Tellico Plains, and was a Monroe County commissioner. He influenced public opinion and worked closely with TVA to promote their forum that the county would be wealthier without the farmers, small businesses, the scenic rivers, and trout fishery.

Wild rivers, scenic rivers, the fisheries, and endangered species in the area were of no value to Mr. Hall, Violet Wolfe, and the Griffith sisters. No land that they owned was flooded or condemned for industrial development, so they hoped the flooding of the valley would result in prosperity for the communities.

Charles Hall of Tellico Plains Speaks from TVA's Pocket

Charles Hall of Tellico Plains says, "I keep an overwhelming passion to see my community grow and prosper. The needs of my community prompted me to spend ten years making trips to Washington for TVA and speaking to as many clubs and groups as I could in favor of building the Tellico Dam."[493]

"I graduated from Tellico Plains High School, and was deferred from military service because of severe asthma. I migrated to Arizona where I worked as a tool and die maker building B29 airplanes. After World War II ended, the Tellico Mountains called me home and to my childhood sweetheart, Billie."[494]

"I owned and operated a furniture and appliance store. One of the irritating problems for me and the town was poor long-distance telephone service. Two lines served the town, but often it would take me two days to call to Nashville. Calling to Nashville to order furniture and appliances was essential. After my order was in, it took two days to get the furniture delivered to Tellico Plains."[495]

"In 1954 my years of pestering and nagging Mr. L. G. Hicks paid off, and I was able to buy the Tellico Plains Telephone Company, which also served Vonore and Niota. I paid $6,000 for 180 magneto[496] stations. My first step was to secure a government loan from the REA, the Rural Electric Administration, for $200,000. I used this to expand service in every direction possible and paid the loan off in ten years. The Tellico Telephone Company began converting all 267 of its stations to dial and cut them over on October 10, 1956. Thirty-one years later, in 1985, I sold the company. Four of my original employees were still with me. I employed twenty-three people when Telephone Data Systems, TDS, bought the company, a four-and-a half-million-dollar value. Under my ownership the decrepit systems had been replaced to serve four thousand subscribers on six hundred miles of line throughout Monroe and McMinn counties."[497]

"I read as much as I can and subscribe to twenty or more magazines and have hundreds of reference books. My lifelong reading habit paid off in 1961 when I read in the Knoxville newspaper that TVA was reviving the Fort Loudoun Extension project that World War II halted. I saw the Tellico Project as a way to speed industrial development in Monroe County."[498]

"I was the mayor of Tellico Plains and on the Monroe County Court, now called the County Commission. I went to all the civic clubs and TVA meetings to promote the building of the Tellico Dam. I placed advertisements in the county newspapers urging people to write letter supporting TVA's fund-raising efforts in Washington."[499]

"I traveled to Washington to appear before at least four committees: the appropriations, the fisheries, public works, and the environment committees. Some years TVA would get funding for two years, but for about ten years I went to Washington to help TVA get funding for the dam. I was the business and county government representative in a group of forty-two persons who testified in July 16, 1965, and at other hearings before both House and Senate."[500]

"When President Carter signed the final appropriation bill into law, I got a telephone call from an aide on Air Force One. It was a moment to be proud of my years of work to flood the valley. My hope was that TVA would quickly bring a large industry to the Tellico Plains or Monroe County area."[501]

"I was born in Reagan Valley on the northeast side of the Tellico River. When I was three the family moved to Ghorley Way Station west of Tellico Plains. Ghorley Way Station was established in 1860 and ran until 1895 and was owned by my great-grandfather. The stagecoach started in Sweetwater, and the travelers spent the night at the Way Station and the next day proceeded to Murphy, North Carolina. In 1927, my family moved to the log house to care for my grandparents. After the grandparents died, my family moved to the town of Tellico Plains where I met Billie in the primer class. We were sweethearts all the way through high school and celebrate our marriage every day."[502]

"I come to my private museum about seven each morning and work and study until the gift-shop staff comes to work at nine. The museum has the history of the telephone and area items of interest. Through the years, I collected many guns and coins. Some local people have placed their Indian artifacts in my protection. The effigies, stone pipes, tools, and arrow points are of superior quality for any museum. Admission to the museum is free, and it is becoming and developing rather than finished."[503]

"I treat my asthma twice each day, but I do not allow my lungs to keep me from caring for several horses and my farm. I try to stay strong and fit, both physically and mentally"[504]

"My current project is preparing a video for visitors to the museum. The visitor can touch an icon to delve as deeply into the history as interested. All visitors to the museum are photographed, and I can see who enters from the TV set on my desk."[505]

"In 1991, I shared my notes with writers, Jim Thompson and Cynthia Brooks, who wrote *Tellico Dam and the Snail Darter*. I published the book, and it is available in area libraries. The large black-and-white photographs tell the story of the development of the area after the closing of the dam. My book presents the horror and disgust of businesspeople and TVA over the Endangered Species Act. Nowadays, I read about sustainable development, a fishery unique for east of the Mississippi River, and the protection of the soil and the free-flowing river, but those issues were unimportant because men needed factory jobs. Hindsight prompts me to question why the land and history of the area had to be flooded in order for TVA to allow private individuals to slowly or speedily support economic development,[506] Mr. Hall said.

"The flooding did not affect Tellico Plains or the Tellico River near the town. I am proud that several hundred people in Tellico Plains drive to the industrial park at Vonore to work."[507]

"I can't believe that fishermen lost much by losing the river fishing. Trout fishing below the Chilhowee Dam, the former Little Tennessee River, is available except that a boat must be used. Many folks race up and down the lake in speedboats. I never fished the Little Tennessee River or the new lake, and I never floated in one of those beat-up aluminum boats."[508]

"I give credit to the local opponents of the dam for fighting the project in a civilized manner. Judge Sue K. Hicks and John Lackey were in meetings that I attended, so I observed their behavior firsthand. When I think about that troubled time, I am grateful there was no bloodshed, for I know the Tellico Dam project is both loss and gain to the three county areas. I hold that the gain is the greater. The Tennessee Valley Authority did bring industrial development to the area."[509]

Violet and Estel Wolfe Push Upward

I know of no more encouraging fact
than the unquestionable ability of man
to elevate his life by conscious endeavor.
—Henry David Thoreau

Violet Wolfe said, "I stick up for TVA. Nobody bad-mouths the Tennessee Valley Authority around me. I agree with the government that this area needed sweeping out."

"Estel and I fell in love in ninth grade and courted our four years of high school. As soon as I graduated in 1951, we married and moved into a house on the J. R. "Junior" Pugh farm where Estel and his parents sharecropped."

"My parents farmed in the Lakeside community near the Lutheran Church, which is still in use. Estel farmed about the same as my daddy. We lived a happy, contented life, similar to our parents. The Wolfe's grew corn, wheat, hay, tobacco, soybeans, and had some beef cattle and a milk cow."

"Estel ran water from his dad's well, but I had to heat water for my wringer washer, and we had an outdoor toilet. Our way was like hundreds of other sharecroppers. The profit on the tobacco was divided half-and-half of the expenses and profit. The farmer got half of the profit on the sale of cattle and hay. On the small grains the landowner got three fourths of the money of the sale. The landowner furnished land, seed, and fertilizer."

"Nowadays, more people lease the land and pay a flat fee. My son Neil paid $40 an acre this year and paid for seed, fertilizer, and furnished the farm machinery and the gas and oil. If it rains or insects eat your crop, the farmer owes the lease fee anyway. It is a gambler's way to make a living, but a man does have the freedom to work when he wants."

"Estel and I started out better than his parents or my parents. Junior Pugh, the landowner furnished a tractor. Our parents turned the soil walking behind mules. The labor is less backbreaking with machinery. We got on good with Junior and Tina, his sister, but having a payday only a few times a year is a hard way to live. I wanted better for us than sharecropping on three hundred acres. Estel worked some for Hiwassee Land Company pulling pine seedling for a few winter months. They paid regularly and let us use their bridge to drive to the other end of the island. Freedom to drive to the island fields without watching the depth of the river let us get to work when we needed."

"After we had sharecropped for five years, my grandfather Floyd offered Estel work at the Dixie Roller Mill in Madisonville. That was in 1957. Grandfather Floyd was on my mama's side. I was a Kirkpatrick. Then Estel got on at the Aluminum County of America (Alcoa) and drove many miles each day from 1967 until he retired in 1993."

"My brother Richie got out of the navy and entered Hiwassee College near Madisonville. My mama and daddy offered to tend to Neil, who was five years old, and Shelia when she got off the school bus. We both finished at Hiwassee, and we graduated from the University of Tennessee, Knoxville, with our degrees."

"Our home is on six acres in Loudon County on Trigonia Road, so I applied in Greenback. Hank McGhee offered me first grade. At first, I hesitated because I felt first grade was too important for a beginning teacher. Mr. McGhee insisted I would do fine. I taught first grade for almost thirty years from 1967 until 1995 when I retired. Like the women at Vonore, Ms. Johnnie Bell Lackey and Ms. Kidd, I stayed in first grade and loved the beginners until retirement."

"I remember the day Lakeside community got electricity in 1945. When the family returned from the Lutheran Church graveyard from burying Grandmother Floyd, the men were placing the electric pole in the front yard. It was my ninth birthday. I thank TVA when I turn on a light or the range. It was a day to celebrate when the farmers got electricity. Vonore, only two miles away, had electricity, but the farmers couldn't get it."

"Like electricity, the Vonore Community and Monroe County could not bring industry here. It took a washing out of the landowners like TVA did with the lake. The farm owners and the tenant farmers held to their land like a tick on a hound. I know many people hated to see their life's work destroyed and be forced to give up the only work they knew how to do. The community in the sixties until the nineties declined and businesses closed because TVA moved so many families out. Then TVA started some of the things they promised when they politicked to flood the area."

"TVA brought millions of dollars worth of industries in on the land they bought up for factories. The local people were moved out for about thirty miles along the Little Tennessee River, and a little of the Tellico River, in all 42,999 acres were bought. [510] TVA had gated communities built for rich retired people. They started at Loudon, then two developments at Vonore, and recently TVA has a developer building houses on the Greenback or Loudon County side."

"My son Neil doesn't see it my way and manages a living by farming. I think he should bury his pride and anger about the community's losses and get a factory job."

"I think this area is lucky the government moved the old families away. My home is on Trigonia Road, a piece from the former river, but I know the river from our experience driving the tractor or mules across to plant and harvest. My opinion is that tourists would not have visited the river to float or trout fish, so why speculate about what could have been?

"Anyone who lived as a sharecropper rejoices to live with TVA in charge. Factory work for Estel and a career in education beats the old ways of not knowing what sort of paycheck a family might get a few times a year. I'll argue with anyone on it."

Betty Griffith Wolfe is a Vonore Museum Docent

Let your speech always be with grace,
seasoned with salt,
that you may know how you ought to answer each one.
—Colossians 4:6, NKJV

Betty Griffith Wolfe contributes to the Vonore Museum with her artistic hand-printed signs and displays. She showed me many displays and said, "I think people have a greater interest in local history now because of the changes in our society."

"I started teaching at the Vonore school when I was nineteen years old in 1959 and taught forty years, except for a year when each of my sons was born. Third grade was my choice, but I taught five years in the seventh and eighth for a federal title program for reading."

"When I started teaching all the parents knew me and I knew them. When I retired it was hard to teach because of all the testing and mountains of reports. Early on, all the Vonore teachers worked together and shared materials and helped each other."

"I didn't try to save the Little T. I tried to be neutral, not for or against the flooding of the valley. It brought a lump to my throat and a few tears when that lake destroyed the bottomland. I watched the Tellico River rise day after day as I drove along Niles Ferry Road to school. A fence measured it, and I knew not only farmland, but farmers were also drowning."

"Our family farm was on Old Niles Ferry Road. Our great-great-grandfather had four hundred acres after the Cherokees were removed. None of our land was bought by the Tennessee Valley Authority, but in 1982 the family sold the last acreage after the dam was closed."

"I live with my son near where the Brakebill School stood on my family's land. My husband was Buddy Thomas Wolfe. Yes, his given name was Buddy. He was Estel's brother, and Violet is my sister-in-law."

"As I said I was not for or against the dam and did nothing to help TVA or the farmers who stood to lose their lifestyle or the fishermen who loved the river. Both rivers were beautiful, but I was on it only once. About five of my friends found a wooden boat tied to a tree near the mouth of the Tellico River where it flows into the Little Tennessee River. We thought a boat ride would be exciting. All five of us got in, and I pushed the boat off with the oar. It soaked up the water like a sponge. We sat on the sandy bottom in our wet dresses and screamed a minute before we waded ashore."

"I see both ways to study the economic situation. The factories could close and move away, and the fertile, deep soil could not be reclaimed. The soil was nurtured for thousands of years and produced food and meat. I remember when the sewing factories moved to Central America, and I know the fancy huge houses will age, the retired people will die, and my community will change."

"I love Vonore: our museum, library, schools, and churches. I recognize the old families and my many students who are now adults. It is the place that I want to live near, and I try to welcome all the new people who chose to be here."[511]

Kathleen Griffith Garren Miller
Observes Progress

Kathleen Griffith Garren Miller volunteers as a docent at the Vonore Museum. She grew up on the Griffith land grant on Old Niles Ferry Road about half way between Madisonville and Vonore. The land was in the Griffith family for 150 years.

"I did nothing to support the flooding of the valley. I graduated from Madisonville High School, and my husband worked as an undertaker in Madisonville. Madisonville expected the Tennessee Valley Authority to bring in big business, so it was exciting to expect the progress, but I personally took no part in it. My land was not touched by the dam," Kathleen said.

About this moment in our talk, a husky man, Matthew Cathcart, entered the museum and sat down with us. After introductions of the Vonore fireman, Mrs. Miller asked, "Do you give a damn about the damn dam?"

Fireman Cathcart looked bewildered and shook his head, "No,"

"What have you heard?" I asked.

"It was before I was born," Cathcart explained.

Mrs. Miller warned, "You will have a hard time finding anyone in Vonore who wanted that dam."

"Do you know anyone in Madisonville who worked to get the dam?"

"No, it was a sad time for the valley, but TVA did bring in industry by leasing the land they forced the farmers to give up. I know farmers who felt cheated because they had a time finding farmland to buy."

"My family sold the family estate in 1982, but Betty and I live on our share. My son is a pharmacist in Madisonville and leases pasture for cattle. He makes a profit on his hobby, so I guess he can't get the country out of his blood.

"I think the flooding has aroused interest in the history of this area. We always knew about the Cherokee Americans from the place-names and mounds. An example is Corntassel Road or Community. Corntassle was a chief, and his name is in the history books. I knew where Ice House Bottoms were before the excavations by the University of Tennessee. Today, people who have roots here appreciate their heritage more than my parents who gave it little thought. My parents and grandparents worked all the time at hard physical labor."

"One of my ancestors was Rebecca Jane White, who is buried in the front yard of Earl and Betty Moser Black's old house. Betty's mother was a White, who married a Moser. Most people think the graveyard stopped the TVA from tearing down the old mansion and buying that farm."

"It is both sad and good to remember the deep, rich soil. Many families like the Griffith, White, Moser, and Black are sad to remember the destruction of our community. My sister Betty and Violet Wolfe agree our community would have rocked along for fifty years with slow change. The Tennessee Valley Authority moved the area along in thirty years with their advertising and pushing. They moved the rich people onto the land the agency took with the law of eminent domain and moved in business from foreign countries."

"I love Monroe County as is it now, but our past deserves respect. I don't want the people who tried to save the Little T and soil, water, and forest forgotten. I am glad that I can volunteer in our museum and tell people about the way folks lived in bygone times."

October 24, 2007

Part Six

The Cherokee Bloodline

Introduction

The Cherokee Connection

The Cherokee connection to the Little Tennessee River and the Tellico River valleys is evident in place-names that survive, such as Toqua ('toe co'), Chota, Tellico (a corruption of Tahlequah), Ball Play, Chilhowee, Hiwassee, Ducktown, and Turtletown (from the duck and turtle clans), and Tallassee changed to Tennessee.

Many people living in the seven Southern states of the Carolinas, Virginia, Kentucky, Tennessee, Georgia, and Alabama know from family stories and racial characteristics about their Cherokee ancestry. Some like Bill Land and Lydia Borden Salvador, Maynard and Linda Kirkland Thompson have revived local interest in their Cherokee connection. Bill Land says that the group has permission from the Eastern Band to name their organization the Chota Nation.

Until about the last thirty years, their grandmother's background was a family secret or at least not broadcast. A notable exception to connection through a grandmother is the Matoy family. A Matoy chief married a white woman who chose to stay with her sons and farm, but her daughters went West with the removal to care for their father. Several Matoy families remain in the area; one is Elder Matoy of Vonore. Chief Matoy, who is referred to as emperor of Tellico in 1730, was elected by other chiefs and appointed men to visit the King and Queen of England, and a Matoy of Great Tellico is reported killed in battle in 1741.[512]

Elder Matoy farmed and worked at Rose Island Nursery, Vonore, and at the Hiwassee Land Company nursery in North Georgia near Fairmont until his retirement. Other persons who reported Cherokee connections are the Mildred Lane family and Don Keeble. Books are available at the Sequoyah Museum, and libraries that list families who claim Cherokee blood, but Mildred Lane and Don Keeble say their folks did not list.[513]

White Buck "Bill Land" Says Don't Forget the Cherokees

White Buck (Bill Land) was born in 1962 to Judith Annette Tucker and her third husband Billy Land. Bill has two sisters who have dark skin and eyes, high cheekbones, and Cherokee noses. With bright, clear, blue eyes, blond hair, and fair skin Bill looks 100 percent Scots-Irish.[514]

At eight years of age, the children watched western movies on television, and Bill, later named White Buck, would imagine Indian life. That spring he found an arrowhead in the family garden. He treasured it for years and made up adventures about a Cherokee lad of long ago. Later, he learned his arrowhead was from a time long before the Cherokee peoples moved into the Little Tennessee and Tellico River valleys.[515]

At fourteen (1976), his older sister took him to Chota and told him Cherokee history and explained the threat to the former Indian villages. Bill walked the bottoms with his sister at Chota and found some worked stones. They examined the anthropology digs that Dr. Jefferson Chapman[516] and the University of Tennessee had done. Bill was stirred to know more about how the ancient people had lived. Although only fourteen, Bill knew he was helpless to stop the flooding of the land and the damming of the river. He knew the promises in the Madisonville newspaper of instant prosperity to the town by the closing of the Tellico Dam. To this day, he puzzles that the dam is at Loudon, nearly a hundred miles from Tellico Plains or the Tellico Mountains.[517]

Bill's knowledge of anthropology was enriched by Fred Snyder, who grew up in Etowah in a railroad family. Fred would ride the train with his father over the mountain possibly to Copperhill or to Tellico Plains. His dad would let Fred off the train at a likely spot where he could spend his day searching for artifacts, and his dad would pick him up on the return trip.[518]

Bill says that his friend was listed in *Who's Who* in anthropology and that he donated some of his best relics to the Smithsonian Museum in Washington DC. In later life, Fred opened a museum at Ten Mile in Meigs County on Watts Bar Lake, and Bill was able to buy some special and rare artifacts from him. Bill's imagination and interest was really fired up, and by 1998 he burned to know more about the Cherokee Nation.[519]

Bill joined the Chota Nation Clan and started going to the events to learn and to keep the Cherokee tradition known to this generation. He traveled to the Qualla Boundaries in North Carolina (also known as the Eastern Band Cherokees) to learn the ceremonies and to be able to pass the knowledge to the next generation. The Monroe County group received permission to name their group the Chota nation.[520]

A principal chief and seven chiefs, one for each clan were elected. Bill Land (White Buck) is now the head warrior, and before that, he served as fire tender. The head warrior is elected for seven years and can be re-elected or voted out. In 2006, the principal chief is Maynard Thompson, and his wife is Linda Kirkland Thompson, who also has a Cherokee heritage from the Citico Creek and Chota area. They live on a farm near Sweetwater, Tennessee, and the Chota nation holds their ceremonies on their property.[521]

White Buck explains, "We have learned four of the seven ceremonies from the North Carolina Cherokees (also called the Eastern Band Cherokees). We do the purification ceremony at the full moon in the spring: sometimes referred to as the water ceremony. In May we hold the planting of corn ceremony, in August we hold the green corn ceremony, and in September we hold the harvest of corn ceremony."[522]

Bill advises, "The ceremonies of the Chota nation are open to anyone who wishes to attend, but they are not shows for the public. The purpose is to keep the traditions; therefore, three participations at ceremonies are required for membership." Bill frowns, "We have to discourage people who only want to dress up and show off. We don't require any written documentation of Indian blood."[523]

Bill explains, "My grandmother is not sure of my great-great-grandmother's name but thinks it was Matilla Grommett. She was from the Qualla reservation in North Carolina and married a white man who took her to Kentucky. She was fourteen years old when they married, and she had five children by the age of twenty-one. She wanted to go back to her Cherokee family, but her husband could not take her. She hung herself at age twenty-one, so we don't know any details beyond these bare facts."[524]

Bill states, "My great-grandmother was Beecola, and she was married to Billy Rose. As I said, we are not sure of her birth name. My grandmother is Helen Rose, who married Hestes Tucker. Grandma Helen was married first to Charles Cecil Felts, and they had one child, Charles William Felts, before divorcing."[525]

Bill says, "My mother is Judith Annette Tucker, and her third husband was my father, Land. My mother has married four times." White Buck or Bill Land lives alone in Madisonville, Tennessee, with his vast collections of pressed glass, milk glass, Indian memorabilia, and a room of genuine artifacts of ancient times. He dresses in his Indian costume and speaks to many groups and demonstrates authentic crafts to children, such as the Camp Etowah after-school program at the Little Children of the World near Etowah, Tennessee.[526]

Lydia Borden Salvador Explains Her Cherokee Indian Connection

Lydia Borden Salvador wishes to explain her Cherokee Indian connection and why she supports the ceremonies of the local Chota nation, which meets on the Maynard and Linda Kirkland Thompson farm near Sweetwater, Tennessee in Monroe County.[527]

Lydia points to her tee shirt, which has a photo of her daughter imprinted on it. "My daughter looks like a princess and will graduate from Sequoyah High School this year and is accepted at Hiwassee College. I'm proud of her, but I'm proud of the hard way her ancestors came. I'm telling you my stories so the family that comes after me will know. Maybe they will learn the ceremonies and carry on Cherokee traditions."[528]

"Chief Ninrod Jarrett Smith, who was the third principal chief in the Qualla boundaries or the Eastern Cherokee Tribe, was the brother of my great-great-grandmother, Louella. They had a white father, but I don't know his given name.[529] Great great Louella Elizabeth Smith was 50 percent Indian and was subject to the removal. She was married to a white man, John Henry Freeman, who hid his family out on Freeman Top Mountain. I think that it is east of the Reliance Road and west of the Coker Creek area of Monroe County. Anyway, there are a lot of Freemans buried in DeHart Cemetery, which is in that area. It is a narrow road along one of the most beautiful creeks in the world. Towee Falls and Towee Falls Church is in that somewhat remote area. My eyes fill with tears when I think of a family surviving on a mountaintop where the soil is so rocky, thin, and erodes."[530]

"One of great-great-grandmother's sons was Mentor Freeman, who is a bit notorious. He went to the civil war and was captured by the Yankees but escaped the prison and returned to the Tellico area. He was arrested, but we don't know the charges. While waiting to go to trail, he jumped from the second story of the Monroe County courthouse. Someone was waiting with a horse, and they escaped. He returned to the confederate army and was honorably discharged and given a medal for bravery. Someone in the family used to have his papers and the medal. Mentor is buried in the DeHart Cemetery."[531]

"Grandfather was Otis Freeman, and   my grandmother was Elizabeth Waldrup, but I don't know much about her. A noteworthy, but sad, fact about grandfather, Otis, is that he was functionally illiterate with only a few months of schooling to the fourth grade, probably about ten years of age. The inability of the family to send the children to school tells me a lot about their poverty and limited knowledge of the wider world."[532]

"My mother is Sylvia Freeman, and she married my father, Harry Borden."[533]

"My family was powerless to stop the removal of the Cherokee Indians, who lived in the Little Tennessee and Tellico River area for two hundred years. When the long struggle to stop the flooding of the valleys and the removal of the white people, who farmed here for two hundred years, dragged on and on, my family was unable to change the course of events. Nevertheless, I'm proud to live in Monroe County, and my patient Indian blood says to watch and wait to learn how long the rich outlanders and foreign industrial investors hang around."[534]

Maynard and Linda Kirkland Thompson Support Chota Nation

The ineluctable coda to any discussion of American Indians
is that they are largely gone,
and that their disappearance owes, directly or indirectly,
to the coming of Europeans.[535]
Travis Kavulla in National Review magazine

Maynard Thompson stated firmly, "I got mad, Indian-temper mad, when the UT (University of Tennessee) people would dig up the bones and relics and sell them at night. Chota bottoms were a sacred place." [536]

I asked, "Who were the customers?"

"The sorry, disrespectful local people who lived nearby."

"A bunch of us Native Americans got it in mind to burn up their trailers one night. Fortunately, for UT they moved their trailers that day to another site before we did it."

"I want respect for Indian graves," Thompson declared.

"Linda and I lost on preventing the flooding of the Little Tennessee Valley, but we helped with one success. The state of Tennessee was widening a road through an Indian gravesite at Townsend. The Overhill Band and the Chota Band camped up there. The state concreted over the graves and did not disturb them. We wanted the government not to move the graves," Thompson explained.[537]

"I went to about three meetings at Fort Loudoun near Vonore. The lawyers from the University of Tennessee were there. About four of them spoke about a lawsuit and took up a collection. Mrs. Alice Milton and Wanda Shirk Franklin set it up. I guess about twenty-five or thirty farmers and Cherokees were there, a roomful as I remember."[538]

"My daddy moved to the old Highway 68 area, the road from Madisonville to Sweetwater after the Thompson family or clan lost three thousand acres in Cherokee County in North Carolina for the Cherokee National Forest. The Snowbird Mountain clan regarded living on the Qualla Reservation or Eastern Band property as being in a penitentiary. I was born at Hanging Dog, North Carolina in Cherokee County. Hanging Dog is now a campsite and near the impoundment of the Hiwassee Dam. I was six years old when the government forced us out. Several families moved here with us."[539]

Maynard said, "When I remember back, every family in our church, Pisgah Baptist, was Indian or part. It was a family secret about being a Snowbird Indian. I didn't understand I was Cherokee until I was grown because I was told nothing. Chief Robert Bushyhead was the preacher."[540]

"My daddy had a blacksmith shop, a sawmill, and a dairy herd. When I was twelve years old, a slab threw off and cut his head. He was fixing a chain. He lived six weeks, but with burying him, I buried my boyhood. I had nightmares for two years and still do sometimes. It was a terrible thing to see."[541]

"Mama sold the farm and bought a house in Sweetwater and rented two farms because she kept one hundred dairy cows. I got up at 4 AM every morning, rode my bicycle to milk the cows, and put the milk in a cooler for Pet Milk Company truck to pick up. I would finish one farm and bike to the other, then home to eat and dress for school. That was my seventh—and my eighth-grade years, and my last schooling. Besides milking our cows by hand, I worked building houses, and Mama and I kept the family together. When I was thirteen, I rented one hundred acres and moved our cattle to one farm. Mama had only me and my younger brother to make a living."[542]

"When I was seventeen, Mama married again, and I met the love of my life, fifteen-year-old Linda Kirkland. Linda and I have been married forty-seven years this year and raised four children. That is a picture of my grandson who is a marine in Iraq. I built this house on my fifty-acre farm ten years ago, and this is a place for the sacred ceremonies of the Chota nation.[543]

"I am Chief White Hawk. The Snowbird Clan gave me and Linda and others permission to form our own group. We travel there to learn the ceremonies. Several groups of Cherokee descent are active in the area, but we felt a separate group was needed to observe the sacred ceremonies. We observe Corn Planting, the seven days of corn planting, Green Corn, thanking the Great Spirit for growth, Gathering Ceremony for harvest. In April, we observe the cleansing ceremony before the planting ceremony. The Chota nation has participated in a few public ceremonies at the Sequoyah Museum near Vonore and at the Red Clay Park in Bradley County. I believe our ceremonies should be private and sacred, and not shows."[544]

"Bill Land, White Buck, is head warrior now. In the past, he has served as fire tender and had other jobs. My neighbor is our spiritual leader, White Raven, Craig Fairall. Craig works a job and is the pastor of the Wilson Station Presbyterian Church in McMinn County near Englewood."[545]

"Remember that my Indian name is White Hawk, but I had never seen one. The White Hawk is sacred to Cherokee lore. My daughter Sharon was helping me build a house near Englewood and saw the white hawk first. We watched it fly to a rotten tree, so when we broke to rest and eat, I walked up the hill to look for a feather. I did find three feathers.[546]

"Three days later I saw the first white hawk on my farm. This spring she has three babies who are learning to fly. It was a scary thing to see her here the first time. I think it was Spirit that brought them here. I put out food and protect them from shooters.[547]

"When Linda and I got interested in our heritage, we took a seven-thousand-mile trip to visit every reservation we could. We went to Washington State, Utah, Arizona, and Mississippi, and I don't know where all. We learned all we could and watched ceremonies and ended up wanting to learn more. We spent the longest time in Oklahoma."[548]

"We joined the Overhill Band and then got permission to start our own band. We learned the ceremonies from traveling to Snowbird where the traditions are kept in the purest form. Native Americans believe in a Creator God, and we praise and thank him. We don't worship wooden or clay effigies or idols. We call God, the Great Spirit, but we believe one God is over all," Chief White Hawk explained.[549]

Linda Kirkland Thompson said, "It is work to have the Chota Nation meet here every first Saturday night. Lydia Salvador is my right hand. We have to get the yard ready, and I cook a roast of beef, pork, or deer, make tea, and bake hot bread. It wears me out, but I'm glad that I can do it. I don't want my children to forget the ancient Cherokee ceremonies and where they came from."[550]

"My daddy was John H. Kirkland (b. 1913-d. 1957), and he and Mama, who was a Shirk, had only two children. My grandfathers had ten, twelve, or even fifteen, and mostly boys, but the land at Chota and Citico was crowded by 1945 when I was born. When I was six years old, my daddy moved us to Pine Island, New York where he worked farming. They grew onions in black dirt and cut the tops off to make them large."[551]

"When I was eight, Daddy wanted to move back home, so we settled in Loudon. He worked for Ray Purdy in a sawmill and ran a still and sold his whiskey to a man in Vonore. Dad had a profitable deal, but he fell dead of a heart attack. I was twelve years old, and Daddy was forty-four. He left ten children, seven still at home when he died. He hadn't paid into social security, and we got no welfare. Mama cleaned houses and ironed for people. The youngest two got Aid to Dependent Children after the rest of us were grown," Linda remembers that troubled time.[552]

"I met Maynard at a rodeo in Sweetwater where he was riding a bull. It threw him and I grabbed his hat. He found me to get his hat and asked me out. Soon, we wanted to marry. I was barely fifteen, but Mama signed for me. He was seventeen. We had our first baby two years later, so I tell people that it was not a shotgun wedding. Chester Millsaps married us, and that was forty-seven years ago," Linda brags about her long-term marriage. [553]

"I go back four grandfathers to Nathan Kirkland, a Snowbird Cherokee chief, who is noted for hiding his people during the removal. One family tale is he hid a thousand in a cave near Robbinsville to escape the soldiers. Nathan or Ne-Di-Sny-Ge-Gi-Li-Sni was never charged with a crime or arrested. My family says that he murdered Bob Stratton, who kept Native Americans as slaves and who told the soldiers where to find families. A monument marks the Stratton homestead at Stratton Gap. Bob's Bald and Stratton Bald are on the maps, and there are hiking trails up there where the family kept cattle from spring until fall. It is about on the Tennessee and North Carolina line and in the Nantahala National Forest. That is more land that the government forced whites and Cherokees to give up, so nobody can make a living on it now," Linda explained.[554]

Maynard interrupted her story with, "The Kirklands were a gang of thugs way back there."[555]

Linda doesn't take a breath or pause but continues, "They were called bushwhackers. Anyone who passed through the Tellico Mountains risked a chance of being robbed and murdered. It is hard for me to figure out how they spread over all those miles. This was before Highway 129 was built with sleds and mules and picks and sledgehammers. The Kirkland gang used the road now called the Cheohala Parkway, Highway 165 in Tennessee, and 143 and 129 to Robbinsville, North Carolina. It runs ridges, but it must have been a slow horseback ride."[556]

"At some time my ancestors were forced to leave Snowbird Mountain or go to the Qualla Reservation or Eastern Band. They settled in the Citico

Creek bottoms and Little Tennessee River bottoms. That's where my daddy, John H. Kirkland, was born (b. 1913-d. 1956). His daddy was Warren D., and Warren's father was James (b. 1814-d. 1893), and James's father was Nathan (b. 1755-d. 1851), and James's mother was Lily Berry. Both were full-blooded Cherokee. It is hard to believe those dates because I thought Native American died young. My mama claims the Kirklands had it no harder than the Scots and Irish with whom they intermarried at Chota, Citico, and the Mountain Settlement. Cash money was scarce because getting tobacco and corn out was a rough trip. I can't imagine how they survived to raise large families. They did earn some money by making whiskey or white lightning," Linda declared.[557]

"A search of the *Monroe County Deed Book Q* on page 167 lists John Kirkland as being deeded land on January 3, 1859 as heir of Thomas Giles. I guess this was John Jackson Kirkland. My great, great-great-grandfather without a doubt! Mrs. Sarah G. Cox Sands lists from a census report, 'Camp Graves, Tennessee, April 19, 1871, Big Jim Kirkland, Head Cone Creek, four miles East of North.' My guess is that Cone Creek flowed into Citico Creek. The following entry excites me for it is Bill Thompson next to Kirkland. However, my Internet search with Google reports six thousand Thompsons. I remember when Mrs. Sands went to every store on Main Street in Sweetwater, and the most information on the Kirklands is in her Sweetwater book, volume 2."[558]

Maynard turned the subject back to the Chota nation, "I allow no whiskey or beer at our ceremonies. I throw out anybody who comes after drinking and make them leave my farm. Alcohol has ruined too many Native Americans and white Cherokees. I will say the part Cherokee or white Cherokees in Monroe County and in North Carolina are better off economically than the reservation Indians that Linda and I visited out West."[559]

"I've made and sold a lot of corn whiskey. When the sheriff's election was close was the best time for me to make some money. The candidates would order it, and I put the fruit jars in the back of my pickup truck and put stovewood around it. It looked like I was delivering stovewood to the poor section of Sweetwater or Madisonville where they cooked on a wood range. The candidates gave the liquor away for the promise of a vote."[560]

"I set up my still in a cave, but eventually the law busted it up. Linda and I visited the Lost Sea caves and when I saw the still set up there, I suspected it was my old still. My cave was not near the Lost Sea tourist attraction, and even my kids don't know where it is," Maynard laughed and enjoyed his secret.[561]

Linda says, "I have the bone structure of my Native American ancestors, but my skin is not as dark as Maynard's who has spent his life farming and working in building trades. Maynard built this spacious home with all the amenities of our neighbors. I have collected family pictures and relics. I do research on my computer and keep in touch with musicians and western peoples. My studying continues to expand my horizons, and I invite folks to come, who wonder about great-great-grandmother, who looks Cherokee in an old picture. I can explain the family connections by studying my books and the Internet. My mother was a Shirk, and other family names were the Grays, Shells, Millsaps, Hunts, Giles, and others."[562]

Maynard said, "Anyone who thinks they have Cherokee blood is welcome to come to the ceremonies. I expect a person to attend three meetings before I consider them a member and will let them take part in the ceremonies. Our ceremonies are sacred, and as Chief of Chota Nation, I demand respect for the Great Spirit or God the Creator."[563]

Part Seven

The In-Migrants Today

Introduction

Folks Move In

When arguments for building the impoundment or keeping what the valley folks had were hot, the problem of out-migration was an issue. Young men graduated from high school and joined relatives in industrial cities, such as Detroit or Cleveland, Ohio. Young people who graduated from college took jobs out of the tri-county area. Families and politicians wanted people to remain in the area. Some folks rejoiced that TVA promised wealth to the area by bringing in factories and businesses.

However, instead of the light industry and businesses that were promised, the government contracted with developers to lease or sell some land for upscale housing. Several large housing developments have now been built, most with gates to protect the privacy and quiet of the wealthy landowners. These gates also clearly mark the distinction between the local people and those who have benefited from the land grab. Most of these people simply don't think about the history of the land they live on or don't feel they, as individuals, have wronged anyone.

The people that I interviewed see promise for a better lifestyle in their enclosed retirement communities. Both families are happy that they found rural East Tennessee and want to stay here. They report making friends outside their gated housing development by serving as volunteers and feel accepted by some "old-timers." Both families are assets to their country and are useful to the local communities.

Larry and Susan Miller Come as Rejoicing Saints

O Lord, you are our Father,
We are the clay and you are our potter;
We are the work of your hand.

—Isaiah 64:8 NIV

Larry and Susan Miller live in Tellico Village. They learned about Tellico Village while living in a Cooper development near Hot Springs, Arkansas and investigated East Tennessee. They liked the climate and found a suitable home.

The Millers were high school sweethearts and celebrate forty-eight years of marriage. Larry is now retired from Dow Chemical Company, but during their working years they lived in Michigan, Ohio, Illinois, Arkansas, South Florida, and Indiana.

Wherever the Millers lived their hearts turned toward a church. Sometimes they served in a Lutheran church and sometimes a United Methodist church. Susan served in woman's groups and children's ministries. She found her special blessing in teaching Bible studies and in leading women to grow in their knowledge of Jesus Christ. She and Larry trained in the Stephen Ministry and serve their church by helping people.

The Millers have three children and two grandchildren. Their daughter worked for ACT (Adult Community Training). The government agency is charged with aiding adults with handicapping problems. She asked her mother to find a place for the group to share a luncheon and program. Susan and the church family in Central United Methodist Church in Lenoir City organized an event for the adult handicapped persons.

When Susan saw people with handicapping conditions, God spoke to her. She taught and prayed to be an empty vessel for God to use as He saw fit. In 2006, she was led with others in her church to start a Tuesday worship service and luncheon, and later, a Sunday afternoon worship service. The ministry is named rejoicing saints and is patterned after a similar ministry in Pennsylvania.

I met Larry and Susan when they came to McMinn County United Methodist Ministry to share the Rejoicing Saints Ministry and to help the McMinn County Methodists organize a program for adults, who have special needs. The goal is to help those who receive and those who give to express their joy and to serve according to their gifts.

The Millers moved to East Tennessee as god's servants and have blessed their new community in many ways.

George Smith Is Retired, but Not Sleeping

We have more dams to impound water,
but of equal potential in unseating our way of life
and of adversely affecting the ingredients of what
I think of as the good life is the population potential.
—Harvey Broome, *Earth Man*

George and Sandy Smith searched for ten to twelve years for the ideal place to retire before finding Monroe County. When visiting relatives in South Carolina or Western North Carolina, they looked at property. In 1995, they found Rarity Bay. Rarity Bay had the amenities they wanted: water, golf, low county property tax compared to Illinois, no state income tax, pleasant year-around temperatures, and few long-lasting snows. Recently, they moved to a new home in a similar retirement community, Kahite, which is also in Vonore.

Sandy feared they would not be able to assimilate into the wider community. The Rarity Bay community is a closed community, which Sandy appreciated after observing the way a Southern open community in Mobile, Alabama made it difficult for her family to be accepted into social activities. She and George found a welcome and a place of service at the Cora Veal Senior Citizen Center in Madisonville.

George says, "I chop vegetables, wash pots and pans or give whatever help the paid staff asks. The Center provides meals for home-bound seniors, and volunteers take them to their homes or serve folks who come to the Center."

George laughs, "Reynelda Gentry's Southern hospitality tied me into the library club. Reynelda, our librarian, calls it Friends of the Library. It's an Appalachian way of welcome."

"I kept a book out way too long, so I am working off my carelessness by delivering books. Reynelda joked that it was too great a debt for a cash fine.

So I take milk crates of books to the preschool at Vonore Elementary, the Tellico West Day Care at the industrial park, and the day care at Greenback on Highway 411. Every five or six weeks I pick up the ones they have read and give them different books. I like to see the little children and enjoy paying off my never-ending library fine," George explained.

"The Friends of the Library are having a fund-raiser starting today. I've got a load of stuff to bring over from our recent move. We want to help the library keep up to date and for the children to find the computer programs they need," George said.

"I can understand the cheated feeling that so many local people experience. When I worked for Caterpillar Inc. (equipment company), we sold machinery for road building. The law of eminent domain was enforced to get the right of way. People want roads, but not in my backyard. Some people here wanted immediate industrial development, and the Tennessee Valley Authority's use of the law of eminent domain was a shortcut to avoid private development. The decision to sell the land condemned for industrial development for gated housing development is questionable when the purpose of the Tennessee Valley Authority is studied. In preparation for this interview, I read the book *TVA and the Tellico Dam 1936-1979* by history professors William Bruce Wheeler and Michael J. McDonald. It is not easy to read about the politics that destroyed the valley and displaced the people who had lived here for generations."

"I think the thousand or so new people that TVA or Mr. Michael Ross moved into Monroe County are already an asset. We are a retired class of educated people who have time, talent, and a willingness to help the community by going to government and community meetings. Our work experiences give us a broad, even international, view of the county's possibilities," George thinks.

"I think Monroe County will continue to improve as more retirement communities, like Rarity Bay are built. I see sustainable economic growth with more people moving here, for this is a wonderful place to live. I am glad that Sandy and I picked Vonore for our home," George concluded.[564]

Part Eight

The Pastors

Introduction

Men of Faith and How They Ministered

The lay people and the clergy revealed faith and courage as they faced the loss of their land and the unknown societal changes their futures promised.

Dennis Moore, now in his late forties, and James Patton, now in his late eighties, reveal their personal experiences. The two preachers are an extreme cultural contrast, and their stories provide insight into the range of responses to the changes that took place.

Robert Denny Moore, A Missionary Baptist Preacher, Shares Jesus

Go and make disciples of all nations.
—Matthew 28:19

A map of the world covers a long wall in the Madisonville, Tennessee, office of the Sweetwater Baptist Association, which the Reverend Robert Denny Moore directs. The Reverend Moore works with many Baptist Churches in Monroe County to organize mission trips. Their slogan is "Churches Working Together Sharing Jesus." From his many trips to the Holy Land, he has collected pieces of wood, a cross, and an icon, which are framed in a shadowbox in his office. At home, he has artifacts of ancient peoples who once lived in the area of the Little Tennessee and Tellico River Valleys.

Denny's first job was with the Fort Loudoun Association, a private historical preservation society at Vonore. He worked for Mrs. Alice Milton and Wanda Shirk Franklin when they wanted the grass mowed or sawdust hauled to mulch trees and flowers. Even today, when he stumbles across an artifact in his garden, he is compelled to pick it up.

Preacher Moore wishes boys could grow up as he did near Vonore. He and some friends would go to the Steele's boat dock on the Little Tennessee River and rent a flat-bottom aluminum boat to float and fish or just drift and think. His daddy would meet the boys at the confluence of the Tellico and Little T and return the boat.

Mr. Moore remembers, "You can't describe the beauty of that clear, clean water, wooded islands and banks, cultivated fields of corn and soybeans and cattle on pastures. I miss the river."

"Griffin Martin organized a Boy Scout troop and turned over McGhee Island to the scouts. One time, he had five hundred boys for a camporee. The

Game and Fish Commission stocked the area with rainbow trout. Griff and I were close friends, so he picked me to sleep over on the island with him, so no one could start fishing before the fish got acclimated to their new habitat. I woke up at dawn and started fishing. Before Griff caught me, I had caught about seventy fish, which was way more than the legal limit. Griff was so upset with his fish guard. He forgot that I was only a kid, who was excited to throw his spoon and every time catch a fish."

"J. D. Galyon and Burl McCollum were also my scout leaders. Sometimes, Johnny Galyon and I camped on JD's farm and fished from the bank. Johnny and I floated the river often."

"The Little League baseball team impressed me so much that I still have my uniform hanging beside my Boy Scout uniform. Families were moving out, but Ollie Williams, who owned a grocery story in Vonore bought our equipment and uniforms. Finally, so many families moved away Ollie had to close his store. The Galyons and the McCollums moved to Greenback in Blount County, and Griff to Signal Mountain, Chattanooga. Gene Curtis was our baseball coach. People in Vonore were generous with the community children. Now I know Mr. Ollie Williams wasn't rich but gave us the baseball equipment and uniforms anyway."

"My daddy and my brother got a contract from the Tennessee Valley Authority to make thousands of concrete fish-habitat boxes to put in the new lake. The fish needed places to hide, mate, and shade. The fish boxes are still stacked in the lake. Dad and my brother also worked for two years building the new railroad bridge."

"As a teenager I worked hauling bales of hay for twenty-five cents a bale. We furnished the wagon and tractor. Griffin Martin and Dr. Troy Bagwell's bottoms looked like a hundred miles, but we lifted bales every day and felt strong and rich."

"The death of the river in 1980 fascinated me. Every day, I went to the Citico Creek Bridge where I took out my stick and measured how much the water had risen. After days, the bridge was covered by water. Everyone teased that the water would cover Vonore. The engineers were precise however, and the water stopped at the brass markers placed on the land in 1937."

"One day, I knew I had a fever and was miserably sick. Somebody advised me to go to the drugstore and let Dr. Bagwell give me a shot. Several old men sat around the table, but a dreadfully sick woman was first. Dr. Bagwell gave her a shot, and she left the store. He asked me what was wrong and offered to give me a shot. I noticed that he put his syringe in a tray of alcohol after each use, and then he filled it up out of the same bottle. Nobody had throw-away syringes, but I refused the shot. I had an idea I might catch a worse ailment from the sick woman. Anyway, I was scared of the idea of a shot."

"Dr. Bagwell operated successfully on my daddy for back trouble, but he did operations in Knoxville. I know he hated losing his fertile land and the old Indian mound that he protected. He was an old man and moved to Knoxville where he had practiced medicine before retiring to his farm at Toqua."

"The thing about Vonore was everybody knew everybody and where to find them. Dr. Bagwell was too old to operate or practice in a big, busy way, but he would listen and tell people where to go. Braver souls than I got a shot. That day, I remember everyone got the same medicine from the same little bottle. Thinking about it, I guess we all had the same germ. When he died, I worked for Biereley-Hale Funeral Home in Madisonville and drove to Knoxville for his body. We buried him in Madisonville Memorial Gardens."

"When I answered the call to preach, I went to Clear Creek Baptist College in Campbell, Kentucky. My first pastorate was Lakeside Baptist, not far from where I now live. In that first church most of the 'moved-out' people were gone, but three families waited and prepared to leave."

"One of my families who suffered was Bert Rogers and his two maiden sisters. Bert served twenty years in the navy and never expected his farm would be taken for industry. The Rogers had their land for four generations, so they hurt. I guess a single man and maiden ladies take it harder than a large family. Their farm was near the Cory Keeble farm. As their pastor, all I could do was urge them to accept their loss and trust the Lord, but it was hard. They did not live too long after moving to Greenback in Loudon County."

"Later, I served for fourteen years as pastor of Vonore Missionary Baptist Church. People were slow healing because they felt so cheated. It was a lifestyle we lost. We lost our community and knew it was never going to be the quiet, friendly rural area we had."

"I remember going to watch the bulldozers flattening Beryl Moser's house and barns and the federal marshals serving him with papers to appear before the TVA judges. That night he was on television."

"No one could envision the changes these twenty-five years have brought. The dead, sad years are behind us. Most people went on to fairly decent lives. A few grieved to death over their loss."

"I was probably away at college, so I don't remember the talk about industrial development without flooding the area. No industry in Vonore or Loudon uses the lake. It is the destruction of fertile soil and free-flowing water that hurts the most. After all, the Bible says the earth is the Lord, take care of it."[565]

James Patton Is a Man Called to Preach

"And he (Jesus) said, "Follow me,
and I will make you fish for people."."
—Matthew 4:19 NSV

James Patton is a man molded and shaped by God to preach the Word. I asked him to tell me how he ministered to his people during the struggle to save the land from the Tennessee Valley Authority's buyouts.

"I was not happy about that awful time. Berthie and me owned ten acres on the Tellico River. We had a house, barn, and smokehouse and had lived there for eighteen years. The Tennessee Valley Authority man walked up to me and declared, 'I'll pay you for nine acres. Your deed ain't right. You get $7,600, and no talking back to me.'"

"It was bitter to swallow. Some claimed it was for progress. I had to wait three years for my money. The government was slow, but Berthie and me found a place on old Highway 68. I went to the TVA office. I complained, 'You took my property, but me and the Lord will make it.'

The TVA man nodded, "I don't doubt it.'"

"I knowed the scripture, 'Do anything in anger. You will be sorry.' That scripture hepped me take it."

"My old land is only three-tenth covered by water, less than three acres. Geraldine Williams still lives near my old homeplace. One lot of it sold recently, so she went over to speak to the newcomer who paid $250,000 for it. Geraldine said she told the woman to be careful what you do here. This land is holy. They took it from a preacher so they could sell it to you."

"Mr. Patton pauses to explain some scripture to me. 'You remember when Moses was at the burning bush God told him to take off his shoes because he was standing on holy ground. God tells me all the land is holy because he made it for us to use wisely.'"

James Patton was born May 2, 1920, in Ground Hog Cove near Notchey Creek and Hopewell Springs of the Mountain Settlement in Monroe County, Tennessee, into a family of eleven children. The family moved to Nickels Cove, a fertile level area but even more isolated than the Mountain Settlement, and past Farr Gap and east of Big Slick Rock Creek. The job was to herd cattle, but Daddy and Mummie grew a garden of corn, beans, and taters, picked wild blackberries and blueberries. His daddy walked or led a loaded horse over to Topoca where the Aluminum Company of America (ALCOA) had a dam. The workers were hungry for fresh food and bought everything his dad could carry four miles over the steep and rough trail.

"My oldest brother got kicked by a horse and died. Word went to the Mountain Settlement where we was kin to everybody. About twenty men came. They made a stretcher out of two stout poles and quilts. Four men at a time carried his body to Mountain Pleasant Church. When one team gave out, four more taked a turn. It was at least twenty miles and only a sled road. The grave was hand-dug, and either Dallas Stratton, Nelson Borrows, or Robert Bain made the narrow coffin. The body was buried within one day because all Mummie had was comfort oil and spices to keep the odor down. All funerals and burials were times to renew with the kinfolk and to meet new babies. The community hurted and grieved with my family."

James said, "I want to tell you about that house in Nickel's cove. The floors were puncheon, which means the log was dressed on one side to be smooth. I think Dodsons built it, but they had only an ax, crosscut saw, and hammer. The poplar logs were wider than that cabinet, pointing to the plywood doors on a cabinet, which were about thirty inches in width. They used an ax to smooth the log until it was as level and even as lumber from a sawmill. It was a sturdy, warm log house."

"My mummie put up every vegetable and fruit she could gather. She pickled corn on the cob, cabbage (kraut), and cucumbers in wooden barrels. We ate well. Besides the canned and dried food, we ate eggs from the chickens and milk from our cow. Daddy and my older brothers hunted squirrel, rabbit, coon, and turkey. We never lacked for good eatin'. Mummie made blackberry wine in case anybody got croup or chills."

"When I was eight, Daddy moved us back to Tallassee to the head of Jake Creek in the Mountain Settlement. Alvin and me started the first grade, and we went to school for three years. The Mountain Settlement School was one room with no electricity or plumbing, but none of us kids had indoor toilets or electric lights at home. We were happy to get to go to school. At home work was waiting for each of us. I learned to read, and today I read with my magnifying glass with the light. Not a day goes by that I don't read my Bible."

"When I was eleven years old Daddy said I must stay home and work the farm with Mummie. He was cutting logs and pulling them out with draft horses. When the lumber company moved out, my daddy took day jobs. My dad worked on a farm for Mr. Dave Garner down on the Little Tennessee River for fifty cents a day. Some days Mr. Dave had no money, so he paid Dad with meat. It was a ten—to twelve-hour day for ten pounds of meat or a bushel of corn. The cured side meat was old, but it was good to eat after Mummy soaked it. At times Dad couldn't get a job that paid anything, and the family needed cash for shoes, clothes, and coal oil for the lantern. Coal oil cost five cents a gallon, so when we had no coal oil, we would gather pine butts to make torches to use for lighting. We skinned the rabbits, coons, and squirrels we caught and dried them to sell to a man who would come up and buy the hides. Mummie cooked the game for our supper. Our family worked to survive and used everything, and wasted nothing."

"In 1933, Daddy lost our farm because he could not make the cash payments. It was sad to lose the twenty-three acres. Mr. Tom Dodson, the original owner, felt sorry for us and gave us a milk cow. In 1937, I was sixteen years old and I worked with my dad on his last timber job for the Conasauga River Lumber Company on the Jack River. We worked each side and up the hollows using big draft horses to drag the logs out. The government had a Civilian Conservation Corp (CCC) camp on Citico Creek. Alvin joined and later worked as a fire lookout for the Forest Service for nine years."

"The economic depression hung over Appalachia until World War II began. Mummie could earn only five cents a dozen for eggs. The roads were so rutted that travel was slow, even if a market would buy our corn, vegetables, and fruit. The depression taught my family to take care of what we had, not to waste, and to think ahead about what might happen. Berthie and I tried to teach our children about managing their money and never to buy foolishly."

"My daddy played the banjo, and Dale Hooper the fiddle. So the neighbors would gather, and we would pop corn (dance) and play games. We children had a happy childhood, and we were no poorer than our neighbors and kin."

"When I was nineteen, I spied a beautiful girl, my Bertha. We have been married for sixty-six years now. She was sixteen, and I was nineteen. When we were first married, we lived with my family at Rocky Springs east of

Madisonville, Tennessee. One morning my brother Alvin and I went up on Soft Spring Mountain to pray and talk. We were close in age and thinking.

"'If you promised not to tell anyone, I have something to tell you,' Alvin confided to me.

"I said, 'I promise.'

"Alvin confessed, 'Since I was fourteen years old, God has been calling me to preach.'

"I said, 'If you promise not to tell, I have a secret to tell you.'

"Alvin promised.

"I said, 'God is calling me to preach, and it is laying heavy on me.'"

James said, "We prayed for the Lord to have his way with us and went back to work with our daddy and Johnny our brother."

"We were topping corn when the Holy Ghost knocked me down. Daddy and my brothers carried me to a little spring and washed my face until I come to. Daddy said to go to the house, and Johnny could walk with me.

"I said, 'I can walk by myself.'

"When I got to the house, I told Bertha, 'Get Connor Cline to preach my funeral. I am going to bed to die.'

"I didn't stay in bed too long before I regained my strength, but I still hadn't told my dear little wife about the rough, hard road ahead of her as a preacher's wife. Instead of telling Berthie what I was scared and worried about, I told her I was going to Citico Missionary Baptist Church where they were having a day-and-night revival meeting. No way how you travel it: it's twenty to thirty miles. I knew that Berthie couldn't make it, so I started out walking alone.

"I aimed to tell Berthie, but I couldn't. It was crazy. I had three years of schoolin', talked country, penniless, and scared to death. And by any standards, God could not want me to speak"

"I stayed the night with Lon Dodson, who was married to my first cousin, Laurie Patton. I got to Citico the next day, but I sat outside with her daddy, Henderson King, who I judged wasn't living right. But Henderson suspected something was up.

"Henderson questioned me, 'Ain't you goin' into the preachin'?'

"I shook my head. 'I'll stay out here with you. We can hear the singin'.'

"Her daddy stood up and said, 'We're going in. Get up.'

"They had singin' and preachin', but the meeting was as cold as a rock.

"Frank Mayfield, the pastor, said, 'Somebody here needs to say something.'"

James remembers, "I was hurtin' and cryin'.

"The pastor repeated, 'Somebody needs to say something.' About the fourth time, I gave up and said through my tears, 'I have a word to say. The Lord has called me to preach.'

"Everybody got happy and started shouting and praising God. It was a sight that I can never forget.

"This August 2006, it will be sixty-six years since I confessed my call to preach at the revival at Citico. The Lord has held me up all these years.

"For about two years I fought the call to preach, but I preached revivals when asked. Then I was called by my childhood church, Mountain Pleasant, to be ordained and to be their pastor."

Berthie put in a word to say, "I could have hunted the world over and not found a better husband than my James, and the life of a preacher's wife blessed me.

"I preached at the Bethlehem Missionary Baptist Church near Tellico Plains on June 11, 2006. It is the twenty-fourth year that Pastor Frank Hicks has invited me to preach at their homecoming. With diabetes and blindness due to glaucoma, I only preached about twenty minutes. I will preach anytime folks come and get me, but I'm not in physical shape to pastor a church.

"One of the healing miracles the Lord did was at that Bethlehem Church. Aunt Fannie Duggan, Bob's wife, was told that she was 'eat up' inside and should have surgery on Tuesday. We had a special prayer service for her on Sunday, and when Doctors Young and Huer opened her up, she was healthy inside. She lived thirteen years after that.

"The Lord blessed my obedience to preach by giving me a good memory. I can't read fast, but I can memorize scripture. When I preach, the Bible comes to me, and the Holy Ghost gives me a message. I'm what some folks call an oral preacher because I can't write a sermon. I only tell what the Bible says.

"Another time Deacon Eudy came to me and told me, 'The Lord told me to go get you to pray for the church song leader's wife, and the Lord will heal her.'

"When I got to the house, it was full of all her kinfolks, for everyone loved that old lady. The Lord did heal her, and she lived several years. The people at Carrenth in Loudon County had faith.

"Another healing miracle was Troy Williams's baby. It was the third revival I ever preached because I was still dodging being ordained, so I remember it well. It was the Old Middlin Church, a Methodist Church with only two members, but it was packed for their revival. The log building had no windows. Their boy was sickly baby, but the Lord healed him, and he grew up healthy. However, he was killed in a car wreck when he was in his twenties.

"I have baptized a lot of people, but the first time was when I pastored Mount Pleasant in the Mountain Settlement of Monroe County. The men dug a hole out in Jake Creek and Alvin was to help me. Several were baptized that day, but one young woman was big and stout. She came up out of the water shouting. Alvin let go of her and went to the house. I only weighed 128 pounds, but I got her out of the pool. When I got home I asked Alvin, 'Why didn't you help me?'

"Alvin claimed, 'I thought she was puttin' on.'

"I explained, 'The Holy Ghost had a holt of her in a mighty way, and she couldn't stop it.'"

James and Bertha have happy feelings about all the churches they served. Hopewell, Notchey Creek, Mount Zion, and Mount Pleasant are all in Monroe County. They also served in Graham County, North Carolina, at Lone Oak, and at Tuskeegee. The rural people love their preachers but did not expect to be their sole financial support. Bertha remembers the poundin' the churches gave them. Their people might give them a live chicken, corn to grind, or five pound of sugar, which cost twenty-five cents. James remembers the gift of a barrel of flour from Johnny Stevens, who owned a store.

As a young husband, Mr. Patton worked for ten cents an hour, ten hours a day. The year was 1939. "I worked for George Kiel, who owned a rockcrusher," James remembers. "I knew my church people could not give me cash, but as the years passed the churches supported us."

Bertha and James never received public assistance or welfare. James recalls applying for a Work Progress Administration (WPA) job. He answered many questions and admitted he owned thirty chickens, two hogs, two cows, a mule, and made fifteen gallons of sog molasses. The clerk took the application form and tore it up saying, "Mister, you have too much molasses."

James says, "Remember that old schoolhouse where I learned to read. My son Ralph Patton bought it and uses it as a hunting retreat. He built two bedrooms, a kitchen, and two bathrooms onto the one old room. Hunting bear is his favorite sport, and he has several trophies on the wall. Berthie and I remind Ralph how special he is to God. Berthie's labor was not straightforward, so I got Dr. Sharp to come. He said, 'I cannot save both the mother and the baby, and your girls need their mother. I have to cut the baby out.'

"Dr. Sharp put his instruments on the woodstove to boil. A neighbor, old man Jessie Tallent and Berthie's daddy, Henderson King, were there. The three of us went up the hillside to pray. When we prayed out, we returned to hear a newborn's sweet cries. Ralph was bruised and swollen, but he grew up big and healthy. Today, he builds houses, and we think of him as our miracle baby."

Berthie says, "We had one boy, who died at four months. He needed an operation because he could not keep food down, but we had no car to take him to Knoxville to a hospital or money to pay a doctor.

"We tell our firstborn, Climera, about her home delivery. It was at my daddy's house. The custom was for the baby to be born between the daddy's knees; however, I was so exhausted that James had to lift me out of bed onto my daddy's knees. Climera was beautiful and healthy, and my daddy knew how to help me.

"Once in the fall of the year, Climera, our daughter, got it into her head to visit Nickels Cove. From the nearest road in the Mountain Settlement, it's about a seven-mile hike and nearly five thousand feet. We climbed along the old sled road. Bertha carried six pound of ham, and I carried a tent. Climera and George, Hank and Dovie Millsaps, and Douglas and Viola made the overnight. The young people brought hammocks for sleeping, and all sorts of dried backpacking dinners.

"I knowed it would be chilly as soon as the sun went down, so I roused myself up to put wood on the fire about two in the morning. Out of those hammocks that bunch rolled because they were frozen.

"Bertha cooked that ham and several dozen eggs. They forgot all about that dried dinner mix and ate like pioneers in from the field.

"The old house had rotten down, but I found John Dodson's and another grave. I said some scripture, and we had a prayer. The beauty of the place demanded thanking God for letting us be in a place where He is so close and real.

"Looking after cemeteries is a way I reminded my people where they came from and where they will end up, at least their bodies. I never went to a new church without finding sassafras in their graveyards. I would insist the men bring their mattocks, and we would set any tilted gravestone and root out the saw briars and thistles. I preached if you forget the dead, you won't do right by the living.

"My four sons and my daughters turned out well and bless me every day. They visit Bertha and me here at the Woods Presbyterian Nursing Home in Sweetwater, Tennessee where the staff takes excellent care of us. Bertha and I are happy that we took the rough, hard road of serving as a country preacher and preacher's wife. God did it because no man or church congregation would pick a near-illiterate young couple with zero experience to speak and live as an example of Jesus to their community."[566]

Part Nine

The Future

Introduction

Concluding Hopes

The broken treaties, bloody and cruel treatment of the Cherokee, who were removed by the U.S. Army and herded West, is a contrast to the bloodless but equally ruthless removal, 130-150 years later, of the farmers and landowners, who fought legal battles to preserve the land, water, and fishery. Persons who owned no land but respected the wild and scenic rivers were hurt along with the farmers and small landowners who were paid minimum prices and forced to take it or lose money by going to the TVA court.

Nearly fifty years later, thoughtful people look to the future. As scripture says, we see through a glass darkly. Our hope is that honesty and justice will prevail over greed, whether that of government or an individual.

Dr. Elaine Jay Dorward-King Sees Lessons from the Little T

Background

Growing up on the banks of the Little T and spending my childhood fishing, boat riding, and playing on or near the River was a rare privilege. Those experiences, including observing as a child the early battle to save the River and then witnessing the emotional aftershocks on individuals who lost so much of themselves in the fight, were pivotal in my life. I continue to reach back to those days for inspiration and strength and seek to learn from the people I knew and from what took place.

It would be a shame if we as a society do not learn from events such as the damming of the Little T. This was a tragedy and waste of the earth's resources that did not have to happen. It took nearly four decades for the death of the Little T to be final. There was plenty of time for individuals in power to have had the courage to change the course of events and deliver a different final outcome. That final outcome could easily have been one that delivered economic opportunity to the Little Tennessee Valley without the adverse environmental and social effects.

To best learn the lessons from the event, then we have to understand what happened and the root causes. There is a great need for a scholarly analysis of the Tellico Dam project, which assesses the original purpose of the project against what has been achieved and analyzes the political processes used to achieve the end result in the context of the socioeconomic situation.

Observations

In the absence of a recent scholarly analysis are the following observations.

As has been told in other places in this book, the Tellico Dam was conceived in the thirties, and one of the reasons that it took so long to get approved and built was that it was a project without a purpose. It was not needed for electricity, for flood control, or to propel the economy to another level in a short period of time. It was however needed if the TVA was to remain a power center for construction and employment. This political driver, and the greed of a few individuals, ultimately was the dominant forces in achieving the end result.

What happened to the Little T was largely a failure of government to do what was right for both people and the environment. Economic gain was seen as the only value worth having, and the economic benefits of the dam as portrayed were based on inaccurate or misrepresented information. Just when the battle to save the River appeared lost politically, based on the accepted economic justification, there was a reprieve under the Endangered Species Act. But once again, government (meaning individuals in power) failed its people and the environment. Even after the Supreme Court ruled in favor of the Little T, those with career or personal interests at heart (who did not live in the affected area), had the law of the land changed to allow the dam to be built.

If one looks as a dispassionate outsider at what has taken place in the twenty-eight years since Tellico Lake began to fill, one might at first not see any problems. There is a long narrow lake with large expanses of pastoral countryside around it, some evidence of light industry, and a growing number of affluent suburban developments springing up on the lakeshores. A large number of the homes in these rural suburbs are being purchased by people who are retiring from northern states or states where the cost of living, including taxes, are much higher. This could be regarded as a good thing—these should be well-educated people who will spend money in the local economy and possibly become involved in the local community.

But if one looks more closely, one discovers that these in-migrants often have no interest in the local community or are more interested in creating a new community—one that remains isolated from the people who have lived there the longest and whose lives were disrupted by the Tellico Dam and the land acquisition that went with it. They often leave their investments in place back home, and because their tastes differ from those of the local people, spend their money fifty to sixty miles away. If one looks at the types of businesses that have been developed, then one can see that while people are employed, the jobs are not ones that build transferable and sustainable skills.

What happened to the Little T is antithesis of sustainable development—the concept that we should use the resources of today in a way that leaves resources for future generations. More directly put, it means treating the earth as if we mean to stay.

The main tenet of sustainable development is the balancing of economic opportunity, environmental protection, and community/social values and opportunity. One would hope that if another such project was proposed in the United States of America, not only would the laws and regulations better protect both innocent people and the environment, but people would better understand what is required to fight illegal uses of power and would have better tools for the fight.

Perhaps one lesson from the Tellico Dam experience is the importance of getting the right knowledge to enough people in time to make a difference, and understanding that knowledge in and of itself is not enough—that political decisions require information to be framed for the public and for politicians again and again in ways that have meaning.

Can we learn?

Much has changed in the world since the final decision on the dam. Are there reasons to believe that in the future, better decisions will be made in situations like this? Is it unreasonable or not pragmatic for decisions to be based on consideration of environmental and social priorities, as well as economic ones?

I think there are reasons to hope. I also believe that the most pragmatic approach for sustained economic prosperity, both in the United States and globally, is in balanced-development decision-making.

Awareness

Firstly, I see hope in the increased environmental awareness of people and in their access to information. Although most people today are further removed from the natural world in their everyday life than thirty years ago, most of the public (in the developed world) say they want to protect the environment. There is broad recognition that the world's natural resources and green spaces are dwindling.

This greater public appreciation is reflected in the growth and evolution of the conservation movement, as well as in government. In the late fifties and sixties, the environmental movement was only getting started, and most people were much more trusting of the government and those in authority, and much less likely to speak out in opposition. It was also more difficult for information to move around—there was no Internet, television was much less accessible to many people, and newspapers were fewer and more influential.

There was no U.S. EPA, there were only a few environmental organizations, and most of them were locally focused and lacked very much broad influence. There were few activist NGOs, such as National Resources Defense Council or the Environmental Defense Fund, who may have been able to mount a more sophisticated early defense and possibly flushed out and made public the financial deceptions.

Not only is this shift in public interest and involvement and the increased visibility of the issues reflected in the growth of NGOs. It is also reflected in government and in pressure on business. There are more public agencies and resources devoted to the environment, and politicians are keenly aware of the importance of the issue to voters. Corporations are under increasing pressure to state and to demonstrate a commitment to social and environmental responsibility.

Again, the public has a role to play here. Those who are seeking to "do good while doing well" must be rewarded in the marketplace for their leadership. This is beginning to happen in some places; social and environment performance is an increasingly important and mainstream consideration for large pension funds, such as CalPERS. Large investment banks and some analysts are starting to take notice, but still often on the periphery rather than as a central aspect of investment decision making.

Procurement policies of governments and large manufacturing and retail corporations are beginning to shift to require certain standards in performance from suppliers of goods and services. This has the potential to be a strong driver for corporate decision making. Strong social and environmental performance need to be better understood as fundamental aspects of managing business risk, and become a mainstream investment and decision-making consideration.

The private sector

A second reason for hope is the change in the power of the multinational corporation and in their response to society's demands for a different level of public engagement and social and environmental performance from the past. Many large publicly held corporations today have a great deal of influence over environmental and social outcomes in some parts of the world. Governments may be weak, inexperienced and/or corrupt, and not able or interested in protecting the natural environment or in securing the best opportunities for individuals. However, corporations are increasingly under scrutiny not only for their social and environmental policies, but also for their implementation on the ground. They have learned from bitter experience that not only is resource extraction or industrial development without the consent and support of those most affected inconsistent with their stated values, it is not tenable financially.

This conundrum requires these corporations to play a role that is often uncomfortable but increasingly important—insisting on higher standards for project development than might be legally required of them, and seeking to influence others to recognize the importance of taking the long-term view of economic development. Sometimes, this may mean that they could be put at a competitive disadvantage to other less scrupulous developers. Both the public and government have roles in ensuring that there is a reward in the marketplace for good performers.

Climate change and ecosystem services

A third reason for hope is the recent increase in public understanding and political acceptance of the threat that global-climate change poses to environments, and consequently to people. Whether directly linked to climate change or not, the dependence of people on the environment has been recently brought home by devastating hurricane damage in the United States, droughts or cyclones in Australasia, loss of shoreline and shifting of seasonal transitions in Europe, and the irrefutable evidence that large ice sheets are melting at a much faster rate than in the past or than was predicted. There is increasing recognition that the earth is one small planet, and since we can't go anywhere else, we had better take care of it.

Perhaps this recognition will translate not only into investment, into cleaner, less carbon-intensive ways for us to live and move ourselves and goods around, but also in more questioning about all sorts of decisions that impact on the "common." Until we value something, there is little incentive to protect it.

There is increasing understanding of our reliance on the services ecosystems provide, which are essential for human well-being. These services include delivery of environmental goods, such as food, fuel, and fiber; regulating services such as water purification and climate regulation; and supporting services such as nutrient cycling and soil formation. [567] Ecosystem services also include aesthetic, spiritual, educational, and recreational benefits. Progress is made in developing approaches for defining the value of these ecosystem services in quantifiable economic terms that can be used to influence investment in conservation, preservation, restoration, and maintenance. [568]

A better understanding of the value of the ecosystem services to be lost would have contributed greatly to an honest and holistic analysis of the Tellico Dam project. The irreplaceable assets to be lost—a free-flowing cold-water river, rich bottomland topsoil, cultural artifacts, and sites—were not valued at the time. The losses were often seen as financial and emotional losses of a few families and fishermen. What should have been better stated was the magnitude of the irreversible loss to future generations of a unique and irreplaceable resource that belonged to and had value for far more people than the displaced locals. The Little Tennessee watershed with the rivers provided a resource not of just cultural and aesthetic values, but real tangible benefits to the Tennessee Valley ecoregion. Instead, future generations have inherited yet another warm and stagnant man-made lake.

Conclusions

Could things have been done differently and achieved the same or better outcomes? My belief is yes, and we have the opportunity if not to make things right, then to ensure that such a tragedy does not happen again.

If the premise of the project had truly been to better the lives of the local people, then an honest assessment of all the options for that would have been done. Building a hydroelectric project might have been one of the options, but not the only one. It is clear in hindsight that the Tellico Dam project was an answer that needed a problem, not the other way around.

Most of those who were opposed to the dam would likely have agreed with the need for better economic opportunity in the area and the advantages that it could bring. However, they did disagree with the means to achieve it and understood, sometimes intuitively, that much of this development could and would occur without the dam project.

It would be an interesting and important research project to analyze whether Tellico Dam has been good for Monroe and surrounding counties in all the aspect of sustainable development. Has the economy become more diverse, more stable? Has it presented more people with better jobs? Has the community become more sustainable and have people benefited from improved infrastructure and social support services? Have natural resources been protected for future generations, and have the ecosystem values and services that the local community valued been protected or enhanced? An analysis could also examine whether benefits from the dam could have been achieved in another way.

My current work for one of the world's largest mining companies often involves developing new mineral resources in areas of great natural beauty. Often these areas are economically depressed and communities are vulnerable because of the lack of economic opportunity. Corporations must deliver financial value to shareholders but do so in a socially responsible manner. This requires working with all stakeholders to clarify values and objectives for the project, striking a balance between economic opportunity, ecological protection, and social benefits. It sometimes means walking away from projects or designing projects that produce less short-term economic return in order to protect or enhance environment or social outcomes in the long term.

It is regretful that the U.S. government was unwilling to do the same in 1960. It would be unforgivable if they, or any other public or private entity, are allowed to do the same again.

We as individuals must pay attention and be willing to take action. The ability to take meaningful action is enhanced by the improved ability to access information, to enlist the help of powerful organizations, and to insist on the reasonable rule of law. But in the end, it is up to all of us to leave the world a place of beauty and opportunities for future generations.

Bill Sloan Jr. Sees a Good Future

Bill Sloan was kneeling in the isle of his hardware store, copying reorder numbers onto a note pad. Maybe his computer inventory told him to buy bug spray, and he was checking his computer.

The Sloan family has lived in the Monroe and Blount county areas since Archibald Sloan returned from the Revolutionary War to settle on the north side of the Little Tennessee water shed at Nine Mile in Blount County. Archibald Sloan migrated from England, and he and Rebecca Guy had seven sons and three daughters.

William Henderson Sloan Sr. was Bill Sloan Jr.'s great-great-grandfather and a union soldier in the civil war. He and Susan Snider had eight sons and one daughter.

Bill's grandfather was William Henderson Sloan Jr. He and Saphrona Elizabeth Mason had eight sons and one daughter and lived in the Gudger community of Monroe County. He was the father of William Wallace Sloan (1911-1975). William Wallace had two wives, Ida Mae Williams and Viola Atkins. William Wallace Sloan Jr., born 1937, is the owner of the Sloan Center on Highway 411 in Madisonville, Tennessee. His partner is his first cousin, Steve, who was the son of Kenneth Sloan in insurance and politics.

The Sloan tradition is to work as merchants, storekeepers, and businessmen. The Sloan descendents had community stores in Vonore, Tellico Plains, and Gudger. William Wallace Sloan Sr. decided the time of community stores was in decline and moved his business from Gudger to Madisonville, Tennessee. Aware of the need for telephone service, he built a telephone line from Madisonville to Gudger so he could order by telephone.

The successes of the Sloan connections in business may be summed up in an old editorial concerning the death of Paul "Mutt" Sloan, who owned a furniture and hardware store in Madisonville. "His word was his bond. If he told you something you could bank on it," the editor wrote.

The promise of a four-lane bypass away from the downtown of Madisonville spurred Bill Jr. and his cousin Steve to buy four acres on Highway 411. The Sloan Center looks toward a Wal-Mart superstore and an Ingles Supermarket, plus other shops. The Sloan Center has a bright-green roof with lines to attract attention and was designed by Mrs. Steve Sloan. Bill Sloan Jr. states, "My success with the Sloan Center is not directly related to the building of the Tellico Dam."

"I did profit by the recession of the early nineteen-eighties after the flooding. Credit was hard to get. Business got sour, and things were really dead. My cousin Ben Snyder had a boat business and general store in Vonore. Thelma, my daddy's first cousin, and Darrell and Ben Snyder decided to move the general store from downtown Vonore to the Highway 411. Darrell died of diabetes at forty-seven years of age, and Thelma was killed in an automobile wreck at the intersection of 411 and 360 near the store."

"My cousin Ben could get no credit because of the national recession, and only about four hundred people left in the Vonore area. It was a sad time. The location was perfect for a store, so Ben sold it to me and paid off the estate and business debts. You might say his hard luck benefited me."

"The first day I ran the Vonore store, the net receipts were $800 in 1982 or thereabouts. Now the average daily sales are $30,000 each day, and I don't carry diesel for big rigs. The business is a BP gas station, general groceries, fresh meat and vegetables, cow and horse feed, a few clothes, and hardware items. My only failure at Vonore was the lumber business. Now I let Mr. Tate sell the lumber: he knows how to make a profit on it," Mr. Bill Sloan explained.

"I'm proud of the success of the Sloan Center here in Madisonville," Mr. Sloan told me. "Steve Sloan takes care of the gas station and convenience store. An area is leased for a roasted chicken take-out restaurant and a variety of side dishes. Another leased area is for cellular phones. People line up three deep to sign for cell phones. The other end of my building is a Taco Bell and Kristal Restaurant. Travelers want gas, food, and clean restrooms. Steve and I make sure our restrooms are clean and neat. Outside this building there is a private employment agency, a loan company, and a pizza restaurant."

When I entered the building, I noticed zinc buckets of varying sizes, Radio-Flier tricycles and wagons, fireplace inserts, stacks of five-gallon cans of paint, and rows of hardware needs. On the west side of the building, a glass wall revealed lawn mowers and lawn tractors.

Mr. Sloan told me, "I've got the most complete hardware store in East Tennessee. People come in for gas and the rest room and look about. A man drove here all the way from Cartersville, Georgia to buy a Radio Flyer bicycle for his granddaughter. His wife and he saw them, talked and searched their area, and drove back to buy it."

"Another item people off the road buy is fireplace inserts. I had one go to Mobile, Alabama, and another one to northern Virginia. Most of my business is local people who come often. I try to have enough help so people can get exactly that they need."

Mr. Sloan reflects on the growth of the area. "I think my business is sustainable as long as people drive to Vonore to work. At 8 AM each day, the traffic is bumper to bumper as far as the eyes can see. In the eighties if the price of gas was $2.85 a gallon, there would be little traffic. Then people did not have credit cards or much reserve when money trouble hit."

"I think the four-laning of 411 was twenty to thirty years too late. The trip to Atlanta and Maryville-Knoxville is easier nowadays. The new folks at Vonore want to drive to airports. The Monroe County Airport serves Madisonville and Sweetwater but accommodates only private planes or helicopters. Tellico Plains has a similar-size airport, and it probably helps tourism."

"Some of the Sloan family supported Dan Hicks, the newspaper editor, in his push to flood the valley. When the dam closed, I was forty-two years old, so I never went to Washington or wrote letters. I did visit with John Duncan Sr. to show support for the dam," Mr. Sloan stated.

"Some of my family suffers by the flooding of the area. My opinion is the Tennessee Valley Authority's use of the law of eminent domain is rotten. They paid the people too little to buy a farm of comparable value. Many of my close relatives were upset and hurt by their loss of land," Mr. Sloan explains the other side of the dam controversy. "I do not remember plans to bring industry to the county without flooding the valley, but people in Madisonville were unaware of the value of the soil and the free-flowing river for the most part," Mr. Sloan declared.

Mr. Sloan gives TVA credit for development at Vonore. "TVA has brought many investors to Vonore. As long as these industries are working, my business at Vonore and Madisonville will continue to profit. As far as I can see, economic growth should continue in Monroe County," Mr. Sloan of a longtime business family believes.[569]

Frank Isbill on TVA and Eminent Domain

Frank Isbill gets hot, red-fire hot and blue-fire angry, when he reflects on the use of the law of eminent domain by the Tennessee Valley Authority on the Little T and Tellico River valleys. Frank is a graduate of Vonore High School and the University of Tennessee. As a management engineer, he traveled from Texas to California from Illinois to North Carolina and to other jobs. Drafted into the army during the Vietnam Conflict, he served two years.

When his mother, Sina Mae Webb Isbill, needed care in her final years, he returned to Vonore. He found the old unincorporated village struggling to maintain its identify because the now-incorporated town is wedged between the Monroe County Industrial Park, controlled by Monroe County, and the Tellico West Industrial Park controlled by Tellico Reservoir Development Agency (TRDA).

Tellico Reservoir Development Agency was created in April 1982 to develop the land the Tennessee Valley Authority seized by their use of the law of eminent domain. This body was given the authority to develop the land inside TVA's taking line. On August 25, 1982, the TVA Board approved a contract, which would transfer roughly eleven thousand acres to TRDA. TVA retained an equal amount of land for recreational and historical uses. TVA would provide money for promotion of industrial and residential development.[570]

Local residents complain that the town of Vonore has no member on the Tellico Reservoir Development Agency (TRDA) board. Frank Isbill says, "The nine-member board is composed of the county executives of Blount, Loudon and Monroe counties and two people selected from each county by their respective county commissions."[571]

Frank said, "The Tennessee Valley Authority has changed for the better. During their struggle in the sixties and seventies with the landowners, fishermen, historians, environmentalists, and lawyers, TVA was secretive. Information about the taking lines and how the cost-benefit ratio was determined was impossible to obtain. If John Lackey, Griffin Martin, Judge Sue K. Hicks, or any of that early bunch of fighters had understood the lies about the benefits and costs of the project, the outcome of TVA's destructive scheme could be different. Our county could have a white-water rafting and float river that equals the White River of Arkansas and other western rivers. It is a pity so much was destroyed. The valley did not have to be flooded in order for industries to be here."[572]

Isbill continued, "In 2006, the Tennessee Valley Authority opened and reopened the public comment period on its plan for selling protected shoreline along the Tennessee River system to private residential developments, like Rarity Bay and older Tellico Village. The board voted to ban the sale or transfer of public land for residential and commercial development. This openness is the new TVA."[573]

Isbill said, "I am interested in the Tennessee Conservation League. In this clipping from the *Atlanta Journal-Constitution*, Mike Butler, the executive director says TVA has three hundred thousand acres of public land that it is expected to protect for public use for the benefit of current and future generations. In that same write-up, William Minser of the University of Tennessee Department of Forestry, Wildlife, and Fisheries says these land deals betray the farmers whose land was seized years ago. The land developers, like Michael Ross, want to build gated housing developments and golf courses."[574]

Isbill argues, "The Tennessee Valley Authority took the land for industry and to provide jobs for ordinary people. Building these monster castles provides temporary construction jobs, but not the permanent work with health benefits and better wages."[575]

"When TVA asked for public opinion input regarding selling public land for gated communities and golf courses on the shores of its many lakes, Mayor Fred Tallent and I drafted several e-mails to reply," Frank remembers. "Our comments have merit and are honest. Fizz Tallent and I see truth and honesty as straight: white as white and dark as dark. The documents were sent on August 22, 2006 and on November 27, 2006."[576]

"A few of the points I want remembered are that Vonore is the only municipality directly affected by Tellico Dam but is not represented on the Tellico Reservoir Development Agency board. TRDA was approved by the Tennessee legislature as an agency for transferring land taken by the law of eminent domain to private development agencies and to persons for the purpose of bringing industry to the Little Tennessee and Tellico River valleys. They have fulfilled that purpose, so thoughtful people think private enterprise or the Vonore or Monroe County Commissions and the planning board can do the job. TRDA costs plenty to operate, so the time is here to say good-bye. It should not become a self-perpetuating agency," Isbill emphatically stated.[577]

"Many thousand acres of prime farmland and timbered areas are either underwater or being turned into asphalt and shopping centers. The original residents of the area had their lives changed and their plans for their future thrown on the trash heap of TVA policies and national politics. Some of the distribution businesses brought in operate largely on the basis of temporary workers, who get no health benefits or company retirement. In other words, some businesses operate on the blood of their employees," Frank complained.[578]

"I feel strongly that TVA should get out of the land swaps. They will bring it up again and again. I call it greed. The persons adversely affected by the TVA social engineering and land-use policies should be heard regarding the shoreline sales for housing. TVA, via TRDA, has created a monstrosity in allowing developers to run over the local government and the local residents. The land not used to protect the lake and for economics development should be returned to the heirs or the original owners or at least to Vonore city government."[579]

Frank thinks, "The folks whose land was taken under the threat of the law of eminent domain should be reimbursed 10 to 20 percent of the price the developers received for the property. Money could buy goodwill and heal the hurt the arrogant socialist bureaucrats, pork-barrel congressmen, greedy promoters, and corporation-housing developers have inflicted on the tri-counties area. It is time for the public lands to be open to the local people for camping, fishing, and hunting. I hope to see private companies develop industries and businesses and TRDA disbanded and the TVA make amends for the mistakes made in the sixties, seventies, and eighties and until this day in 2007."[580]

Frank talks to me in the Vonore Historical Society's museum. Genealogy and history are interests, and he explains that Vonore was named for a Mr. Vaughn, who mined iron ore in the area. "His first name is lost to history as far as I know," Frank explained. "A road in Vonore is named Slag Road, so I think that goes back to ore brought here by mule-drawn wagons."

"I do agree with people who ask why a dam, about sixty miles from the little town of Tellico Plains, is named Tellico Lake. The misnamed lake confuses tourists, and I hope to live to see this disgusting name changed. Perhaps to a Cherokee word that reveals the greed of the land grabs of the twentieth century and reflects ninetieth century greed of our ancestors and our nation."[581]

Appendix

(documents and photographs)

Map of a section of the lower Little Tennessee River valley prepared by British Lt. Henry Timberlake in 1762 (from Williams 1927). The locations of the 18th century Overhill Cherokee towns assisted archaeologists in relocating the sites 200 years later.

The Henry Timberlake Draught of the Cherokee Country, March, 1762, accurately shows the site of the Cherokee and older civilization villages until destroyed by the Tellico Dam.

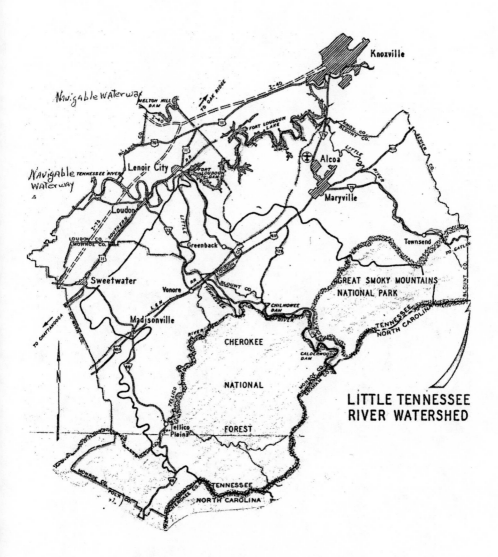

Map of the Little Tennessee River watershed

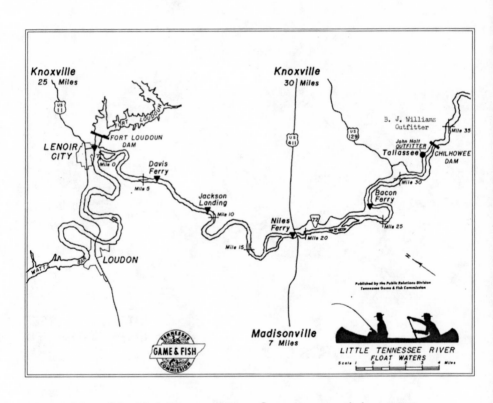

Map of the Little Tennessee River float waters until about 1979

SPORTSMAN'S NEWS
should there be a Tellico Dam?

ATTENTION FISHERMEN
Last Call To Save Tennessee's Greatest Trout River

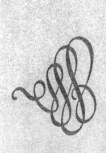

YOU CAN HELP KEEP THIS GREAT FISHING ON THE LITTLE TENNESSEE RIVER BY WRITING THE CONGRESSMEN LISTED BELOW.

WHEN WRITING YOUR LETTER TO CONGRESS, SIMPLY WRITE ONE LETTER TO TENNESSEE'S REP. JOE L. EVINS AND SEND CARBON COPIES TO THE OTHER SIX CONGRESSMEN LISTED BELOW.

Democrats	JOE L. EVINS (Tenn.)	Republicans
Michael J. Kirwan (Ohio), Chairman	address	John J. Rhodes (Ariz.)
Jamie L. Whitten (Miss.)	HOUSE OFFICE BLDG.	Glenn R. Davis (Wis.)
Edward P. Boland (Mass.)	WASHINGTON, D. C.	Howard W. Robinson (N. Y.)

HOUSE APPROPRIATION SUBCOMMITTEE ON PUBLIC WORKS

This power Subcommittee handles funds for civil functions of the Army Engineers, Bureau of Reclamation, Atomic Energy Commission, TVA, and power-distributing agencies of the Department of the Interior.

A protest flier urging letters to Congress protesting the flooding of the valley

The Knoxville Journal
Feb. 2, 1965

THE TVA TELLICO DAM PROJECT
WOULD DESTROY THESE EXISTING
RESOURCES

ROSE ISLAND FOREST TREE NURSERY

----the second largest commercial nursery
in the South

----a $1,000,000 investment by Hiwassee Land Co.

----nine years of genetic experimentation in
breeding superior trees

RICH FARMLAND

----over 14,000 acres of productive bottomland

----a $3,000,000 annual yield in agricultural
products

----over 250 prosperous farms

UNIQUE INDUSTRIAL ADVANTAGES

----level, riverfront sites

----cold, clean processing water

HISTORIC VALUES

----Fort Loudoun, built 20 years prior to the
American Revolution (now being restored)

----seven town sites of the Overhill Cherokees

----many village sites of pre-Indian cultures

SPORT FISHING POTENTIAL

----20 miles of scenic river providing
near-perfect habitat for trout

----productive capacity for raising fingerling
trout comparable to the total natural
stream mileage of the Tenn. Appalachians

----a foreseeable $5,000,000 float fishing
industry serving the 8 million people now
visiting the area

Organizations Actively Opposed To Tellico Dam

American Forestry Association
National Audubon Society
Trout Unlimited
Tennessee Game and Fish Commission
Tennessee Conservation League
Tennessee Outdoor Writers Association
Tennessee Farm Bureau Federation
Tennessee Livestock Association
Southeastern Outdoor Writers Association
Association for Preservation of Little Tennessee River
The Eastern Band of Cherokee Indians
Fort Loudoun Association
National Capital Chapter, Trout Unlimited
Monroe County Farm Bureau
Monroe County Farmers Cooperative
Monroe County Livestock Association
McMinn County Farm Bureau
Blount County Livestock Association
Greenback Farmers Cooperative
Vonore Lions Club
Chilhowee Rod and Gun Club - Athens
Chattanooga Trout Association
Chattanooga YMCA
Highland Sportsman's Club - Chattanooga
Cherokee Sportsman's Conservation Assoc. - Chattanooga
East Tennessee Historical Assoc., McMinn Chapter
East Tennessee Duck Hunters Association
Sweetwater Valley Feeder Pig Assoc. (10 counties)
Knox County Young Republican Club
Southern Field and Creel Club - Knoxville
West Knoxville Sertoma Club
Knoxville Men's Garden Club
Knoxville Retreiver Club
Cherokee Rifle and Pistol Club, Inc. - Morristown
Onsoli Circle - Knoxville
Middle Tennessee Conservancy Council

The cartoon was in the Knoxville Journal and is used by permission
of Mr. Daniels, a list of organizations who protested the Tellico
Dam, and facts from the Association for the Preservation of the
Little Tennessee River.

Raj. Burma & Deanna Kennedy home - Venore
TVA took for Tellico dam.

The Roy and Burma Kennedy house is similar to others in the valley, such as Billie Curtis, Roy Gentry, and Wade Swafford's. The Kennedy home was bought, but was not on flooded land.

Mr. and Mrs. Att Millsaps and their daughter Burma celebrate. Alfred Davis relates Mr. Att's story of dealing with a Tennessee Valley Authority land buyer.

ROSE IS. FOREST TREE NURSERY.tif

Rose Island Nursery sign about 1959 from Louis Camisa files.

STUDIES INDIAN HOMELAND — Associate Justice William O. Douglas, of the US Supreme Court, learns of the historical significance of Little Tennessee River Valley from Mrs. Alice Milton, Chattanooga, and Dr. Alfred Guthe, of University of Tennessee's archaeology department. Mrs. Milton is executive director of Fort Loudoun Association.

A newspaper clipping shows Mrs. Alice Milton, executive director of Fort Loudoun Association, Associate Justice William O. Douglas of the U S Supreme Court, and Dr. Alfred Guthe, of the University of Tennessee Knoxville's Archaeology department and says they are studying the historical significance of the Little Tennessee River Valley.

The fort area is now under water, but a similar fort is rebuilt and is a Tennessee State Park.

Maryville-Alcoa Daily Times

The Best Little Metropolitan Newspaper In The South

!2, No. 3   Single Copy 5c   Monday, April 5, 1965   Maryville, Tenn. 37803   Home Delivery 30 Cents A W

Douglas Presented Cherokee Indian Protest

U. S. Supreme Court Justice William O. Douglas accepts petition from Cherokee Indians protesting TVA's proposal to build a dam on the Little Tennessee River. The petition was presented at Chota, once the sacred city of the Cherokee nation, near Vonore. From left are Alva Crowe, Richard Crowe, Charles Crowe, Douglas. Richard Crowe represented principal Chief Jarrett Blythe, ruler at Qualla Indian Reservation near Cherokee, N. C. Douglas was in the area to write an article for National Geographic Society Magazine on the Cherokee Indian.

— AP Wirephoto

U S Supreme Court Justice William O. Douglas accepts a petition from Cherokee Indians protesting TVA's proposal to build a dam on the Little Tennessee River. The petition was presented at Chota once the sacred city of the Cherokee nation. From left are Alva Crowe, Richard Crowe, Charles Crowe, and Douglas. Richard Crowe represented Principal Chief Jarrett Blythe, ruler at Qualla Indian Reservation near Cherokee, N. C.

Maynard Thompson, Chief of Chota Nation, welcomes Cherokee descendants to his farm to learn Cherokee ceremonies. The monthly meetings are open to anyone who claims Cherokee descent. The farm is near Sweetwater, Tennessee.

Alfred Davis is at home after work at his tractor garage and sales business. The family fought a long legal battle with TVA. His home is at Philadelphia. Tennessee.

Dr. David Etnier identified the snail darter.

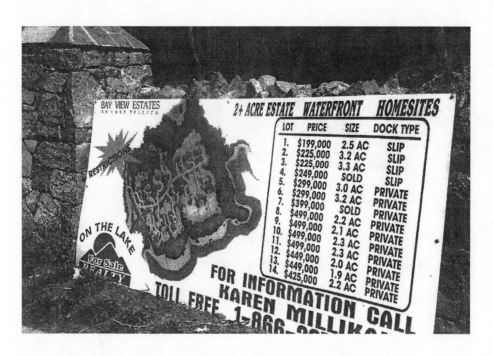

The land bought by TVA for an average price of $356 an acre, but up to $800 an acre, is offered for sale for a housing development, not the industry promised. The picture was made about 2007 by Fran Dorward.

The Knoxville Journal/GARY HAMILTON

Thomas Beryl Moser looks at the ruins of the house in which he was born 47 years ago after Tennessee Valley Authority bulldozers destroyed the house. Moser, a Monroe County rural mailman, was evicted by federal marshals less than two hours before TVA wrecked the home to prepare for the flooding of the Little Tennessee Valley. The picture was in the *Knoxville Journal* on November 14, 1979, and is credited to Gary Hamilton.

Thomas Beryl Moser looks at the ruins of his house after Tennessee Valley Authority bulldozers destroyed his home, where he was born 47 years ago. Moser, a Monroe County rural mailman, was evicted by federal marshals less than two hours before TVA wrecked the home to prepare for the flooding of the Little Tennessee Valley. This picture was in the Knoxville Journal on November 14, 1979, and is credited to Gary Hamilton.

Beryl Moser has been re-elected as Vonore City Judge for many years, and now lives on a high ridge.

A BUMPER CROP OF PINE TREES — 18 million seedlings to be exact — is growing in the Bowaters nursery this summer. Bob Dorward, Hiwassee forester in charge, is proud as can be as he displays the baby pines, above. These future pulpwood logs, now only six inches tall, are growing in the nursery beds at the rate of one million seedlings per acre. The beds have been irrigated as required and carefully weeded. After heavy frost falls in November the seedlings will be lifted from the soil, bundled, and moved to Tree Farm planting sites to begin growing into the trees that will be part of the pulpwood at Catawba and Calhoun beginning around 1985.

Bibliography

Books

Bartlett, Richard A., *Troubled Waters: Champion International and the Pigeon River Controvers*. Knoxville, Tennessee: The University of Tennessee Press, 1995.

Beacham, Walter, Frank V. Castronova, Suzanne Sessine, Editors, *Guide to the Endangered Species of North America*. Vol 2:1086. Detroit, Michigan: Gale Group, 2001.

Bolick, Clint, *Leviathan: The Growth of Local Government and the Erosion of Liberty*. Stanford, California: Hoover Institution Press, 2004.

Brewer, Alberta and Carson, *Valley So Wild: a Folk History*. Knoxville, Tennessee: East Tennessee Historical Society, 1977.

Broome, Harvey, *Harvey Broome: Earth Man*. Knoxville, Tennessee: Greenbrier Press, 1970.

Brown, Louise, Robert Clemons, Mike Hicks, *Telephones for Tennessee*. Nashville, Tennessee: Telephone Association, 1995.

Callahan, North, *TVA: Bridge Over Troubled Waters, A History of the Tennessee Valley Authority*: London, UK, A. S. Barnes, 1980.

Chapman, Jefferson, *Tellico Archaeology: 12,000 Years of Native American History*. Knoxville, Tennessee: Tennessee Valley Authority, 1985.

Conley, Robert J, *Sequoyah: A Novel of the Real People*. New York, NY: St. Martin's Press, 2002.

Cothran, Helen, editor., *Opposing Viewpoints: Endangered Species*, San Diego, California: Greenhaven Press Inc., 2001.

Corkran, David H, *The Cherokee Frontier: Conflict and Survival, 1740-62*. Norman, Oklahoma Press: University of Oklahoma Press, 1963.

Douglas, William O, *My Wilderness: East to Katahdin*. Garden City, New York: Doubleday and Company, 1961.

Drake, Richard B, *A History of Appalachia*. Frankfort, Kentucky: University of Kentucky, 2003.

Duncan, Barbara R. editor, *Living Stories of the Cherokee*. Chapel Hill, North Carolina: University of North Carolina Press, 1988.

Ehle, John, *Trail of Tears: The Rise and Fall of the Cherokee Nation*. New York, N Y: Anchor Books Doubleday, 1988.

Fundaburk, Emma Lila and Mary Douglass Foreman, *Sun Circles and Human Hands: The Southern Indians Art and Industry.* Kingport, Tennessee: Kingsport Press, 1957, 1965.

Grove, Doris, *50 Hikes in the Tennessee Mountains*. Woodstock, Vermont: Back Country Press, 2001.

Holy Bible, Revised Standard Version. Grand Rapids, Michigan: Zondervan Bible Publishers, 1952.

Howell, Benita J., *Culture, Environment, and Conservation in the Appalachian South*. Champaign, Illinois: University of Illinois Press, 2002.

Jenkins, Ray H., *The Terror of Tellico Plains*. Knoxville, Tennessee: East Tennessee Historical Society, 1978.

Jones, Loyal, *Faith and Meaning in the Southern Uplands*. Chicago, Illinois: University of Illinois, 1999.

Kelly, Paul, *Fort Loudoun: The After-Years, 1760-1960*. Knoxville, Tennessee: Historical Quarterly, Volume XX, Number 4. December 1961.

King, Duane H, *The Cherokee Nation: A Troubled History*. Knoxville, Tennessee: University of Tennessee Press, 1979.

Lisagor, Peter. The *World Book Encyclopedia*. Vol 11. Chicago, Illinois: Field Enterprises, 1974. article on Lyndon Baines Johnson.

Mazo, Earl, *World Book Encyclopedia. Richard M. Nixon*. Chicago, Illinois: Field Enterprise, 1974. vol. 14 p 36.

Montgomery, Michael B. and Joseph S. Hall, *Dictionary of Smokey Mountain English*. Knoxville, Tennessee: University of Tennessee, 2004.

Montrie, Chad, *To Save the Land and the People: A History of Opposition to Surface Coal Mining in Appalachia*. Chapel Hill, North Carolina: University of North Carolina, 2003.

Moorehead, Warren K., *Prehistoric Implements*. Union City, Georgia: Charley G. Drake Publisher, 1900, 1968, 1972.

Owen, Marguerite, *The Tennessee Valley Authority*. New York, New York: Praeger Publisher, 1973.

Ramsey, J. G. M., *The Annual of Tennessee to the End of the Eighteenth Century*. Originally printed Charleston, South Carolina, Walker and James, 1853. Reprinted Kingsport, Tennessee: Kingsport Press, 1926.

Sands, Sarah Cox. *History of Monroe County, Tennessee*, Volumes 1, 2, and 3. Altimore, Maryland: Gateway Press, 1982.

Thompson, Jim and Cynthia Brooks, *Tellico Dam and the Snail Darter*. Tellico Plains, Tennessee: Tellico Publications, 1991.

Witmore, Alexander, *Water, Prey, and Game Birds of North America*. Washington, DC: National Geographic, 1965.

Wheeler, William Bruce and Michael J. McDonald, *TVA and the Tellico Dam 1936-1979: A Bureaucratic Crisis in Post-Industrial America.* Knoxville, Tennessee: University of Tennessee Press, 1986.

Wolfe, Violet, Frank Isbill and others, *Vonore: Yesterday and Today. Vonore, Tennessee.* Vonore, Tennessee: Vonore Historical Society, 1991, 1996.

Congressional Documents and Manuscripts

Hearings before the Subcommittee of the Committee on Appropriations on HR 9220. Washington DC., 1965, pp. 44-50.

Hearings before the Senate Subcommittee 89th Congress, 2nd session, pt 4, p. 68. 1965.

Hearings House Public Works Appropriations Committee, 1966.

Tennessee Valley Authority. Annual report for 1960, released 1961.

Tennessee Valley Authority Alternative Report #1, Division of Water Resources. August 18, 1976.

Zygmunt J. B. Plater. *Reflected in a River: Agency Accountability and the Tennessee Valley Authority Tellico Dam Case.* Tennessee Law Review 49, 1982. pp. 747-787.

Thesis

Dickey, David. *The Little Tennessee River as an Economic Resource: A Study of Its Potential Best Use.* Norman Oklahoma: University of Oklahoma, 1964.

Etnier, David A. *Percina tanasi, a New Percid Fish from the Little Tennessee River, Tennessee. Proceeds of the Biological Society* 88 (44): 469-645, 1976.

Starnes, W. C. The *Ecology of Life History of the Endangered Snail Darter.* Ph. D. Dissertation University of Tennessee, 1977. 144 pages

Unpublished Material

Robert E. Dorward. Papers, letters, and material of the Association for the Preservation of the Little Tennessee River, Vonore, Tennessee, 1962-1979.

Newspapers and Periodicals

Maryville Alcoa Daily Times, 1961-1999
Atlanta Journal-Constitution, 2003
Bowater World, 1961
Charlotte Observer, 1965
Chattanooga News-Free Press, 1972-2004
Chattanooga Times, 1960-1965
Daily Post Athenian, 1965-2006
East Tennessee Citizen, 1964
East Tennessee Journal, 1964
Field and Stream Magazine, 1964, 1965
Knoxville Journal, 1963-1979
Knoxville News Sentinel, 1961-2006
Lenoir City News Banner, 1963

Madisonville Democrat, 1964
Madisonville Citizen-Democrat, 1965
Maryville Enterprise, 1963-1969
Maryville Journal, 1964-1969
Nashville Banner, 1971-1978
National Review Magazine, 2007
Nation's Business, 1965
News Week Magazine, 1978
Oak Ridge Newspaper, 1978
Saint Louis Post Dispatch, 1978
Skyway News, 2006
Tennessee Law Review, 1982

Interviews, Correspondence, and Telephone Conversations

Peter Allemon
Barbara Bell
Beatrice Duncan Bivens
Sarah Simpson Bivens
Betty and Earl "Red" Black
Beuna Frank Black
Shirley McCollum Brown
Louis Camisa
Jefferson Chapman
Billie Curtis
Tom Curtis
Alfred Davis
David Dickey

Bob and Fran Dorward
David Etnier
Gail Galyon
J. D. and Elizabeth Galyon
Reynelda Gentry
Charles Hall of Tellico Plains
Charles R. Hall of Lakeside and Vonore
Hiram "Hank" Hill
Frank Isbill
Don Keeble
Bill Keithley
Roy and Burma Kennedy
Elaine Dorward-King

Lib and Homer Kirkland
John Lackey
Bill Land
Mildred, Richard, Judy, Debbie Lane
Elder Matoy
Muriel Mayfield
Mary Fay Maynard
Ricky Maynard
Earl Melson
Edith and Herbert Millsaps
Alice Milton
Beryl Moser
Mabel and Charles Niles
James Riley "Junior" Pugh
James and Bertha King Patton

Zygmunt J. B. Plater
Linda Borden Salvador
Melvin Sheets
Ben Snyder
Billie Jo Steele
Joey Steele
Margie and Wade Swafford
Fred "Fizz" Tallent
Maynard and Linda Kirkland Thompson
Cap and Shirley Watson
Dick and Camille Williams
Violet Wolfe
George Smith
Bill Sloan

Museum and Libraries

Etowah Carnegie Library
Fisher Public Library, Athens, TN
Fort Loudoun State Park and Museum
Junaluska Museum, Robinsville. N. C.
Madisonville Public Library
McClung Museum, Knoxville, TN
Sequoyah Museum, Vonore, TN
Vonore Historical Museum
Vonore Public Library

Notes

1   *Maryville-Alcoa Daily Times.* Wednesday, December 9, 1964.
    Wheeler, William Bruce, and Michael J. McDonald, *TVA and the Tellico Dam1936-1979: A Bureaucratic Crisis in Post-Industrial America.* (Knoxville, University of Tennessee Press. 1986) p. ix

2   Tennessee Valley Authority. Annual Report for 1960, released January 1, 1961 on Future Multiple-Use Projects. Knoxville News-Sentinel. January 1, 1961.

3   *Ibid.*

4   *Ibid.*
    Maryville-Alcoa Daily Times. December 9, 1964

5   *Ibid.*, January 25, 1965.

6   *Maryville-Alcoa Daily Times,* January 19, 1965.

7   *Knoxville News-Sentinel,* January 1, 1961.

8   *Ibid.* January 25, 1965.
    The *Maryvile-Alcoa Daily Times,* December 8, 1964.

9   Maryville-Alcoa Times. December 9, 1964.
    Knoxville New-Sentinel, January 19, 1965.

10 Personal interviews: Burl Moser, Earl Black, Herbert Millsaps, others

11 Lisagor, Peter, "Lyndon Baines Johnson", *The World Book Encyclopedia.* Vol 11. (Chicago, Ill. Field Enterprises. 1974) 120.

12 *Ibid.*

13 Jenkins, Ray H. *The Terror of Tellico Plains.* (Knoxville, East Tennessee Historical Society. 1978)

14 *Ibid.*

15 Personal interviews: David Dickey, John Lackey, Jr., Louis Camisa.

16 *Maryville-Alcoa Daily Times.* October 14, 1964. *Maryville Journal,* October 1, 1964. *East Tennessee Citizen,* October 23, 1964.

17 *Ibid.*

[18]   William Bruce Wheeler and Michael J. McDonald, *TVA and the Tellico Project 1936-1979: A Bureaucratic Crisis in Post-Industrial America.* (Knoxville, University of Tennessee Press, 1986), 89-100.

[19]   William Morris, editor, *Dictionary of the English Language,* (New York, American Heritage Pulishing Company, 1969) 427.

[20]   Wheeler, *op. cit.* 10-12, 142, 221-224.

      Bolick, Clint. Leviathan: *The Growth of Local Government and the Erosion of Liberty.* (Stanford University, California. Hoover Institution Press. 2004) 88-97.

      The Knoxville Journal. April 12, 1965. P. D. Cate-on the commission system vs. jury trial.

[21]   Interview with John Lackey, Jr., June, 2005.

[22]   *Ibid.*

[23]   *Maryville-Alcoa Daily Times.* October 14, 1964.

      Knoxville Journal. December 18. 1964.

[24]   *Knoxville News-Sentinel,* September 11, 1964 and September 23, 1964.

      Knoxville Journal, October 17, 1964.

[25]   Conservation News. (Washington, DC, National Wildlife Federation) January 11, 1965.11)

      William Bruce Wheeler and Michael J. McDonald. *TVA and the Tellico Dam 1936-1979: A Bureaucratic Crisis in Post-Industrial America.* (Knoxville, Tennessee, University of Tennessee Press, 1986) 87-110.

[26]   *Ibid.* 93-100, 103-105.

      Interview with John Lackey, Jr., June, 2005.

[27]   Wheeler. *op.cit.* 103-105.

      Interview with John Lackey, Jr., June, 2005.

[28]   *Knoxville News-Sentinel.* October 12, 1965

      Alberta and Carson Brewer. *Valley So Wild: A Folk History.* (Knoxville, Tennessee, East Tennessee Historical Society, 1975) xiii, 227-278.

[29]   Jefferson Chapman. *Tellico Archaeology.* (Knoxville, Tennessee, The Tennessee Valley Authority, 1985)

      Warren K. Moorehead. *Prehistoric Implements: A Reference Book.* (Charley G. Drake, 1900 and 1972)

[30]   Interview with John Lackey, Jr., June, 2005.

[31]   *Ibid.*

[32]   *Ibid.*

[33]   *Ibid.*

      The Monroe County Citizen Democrat, January 24, 1965.

Clint Bolick. *Leviathan: The Growth of Local Government and the Erosion of Liberty.* (Stanford University 108 Interview with Sarah Simpson Bivens, January, 2004)

34 Interview with John Lackey, Jr., June, 2005.
    Hamilton County Herald, November 6, 1964.
    Knoxville Journal, January 29, 1965 Walter Amann

35 Wheeler. *op. cit.* p. 108. *Knoxville Journal,* March 26, 1965

36 Personal interview with John Lackey, Jr., June, 2005.

37 *Ibid.*

38 *Knoxville Journal,* March 26, 1965.

39 *Ibid.*

40 Wheeler. *op. cit.* 67-77.
    Jim Thompson and Cynthia Brooks. *Tellico Dam and the Snail Darter.* (Tellico Plains, Tennessee, Tellico Publications, 1991). 24, 30.

41 Wheeler. *op. cit* 79.
    Personal interview with John Lackey, Jr., June, 2005.

42 Personal interview with John Lackey, Jr., June, 2005.
    Wheeler, *op. cit.* 108.

43 *Chattanooga Times.* October 6, 1960.
    William Bruce Wheeler, and Michael J. McDonald. *TVA and the Tellico Dam 1936-1979: A Bureaucratic Crisis in Post-industrial America.* (Knoxville, Tennessee, University of Tennessee Press, 1986). 78.

44 *Bowaters World.* April 1961.
    Daily Post Athenian. October 3, 1963.

45 *Bowaters World.* April 1961
    Chattanooga Times. October 6, 1960.

46 Personal interview: Bill Keithley, Louis Camisa, November 2004.

47 *Ibid.*

48 Personal interview: Mildred Lane, Don Keeble

49 Personal interview with Ben Snider, July, 2005.

50 *The Lenoir City News-Banner.* April 25, 1963.
    East Tennessee Citizen. October 23, 1964.
    The Knoxville Journal. December 29, 1964.

51 Carson and Alberta Brewer. *Valley So Wild: A Folk History.* (Knoxville, Tennessee, East Tennessee Historical Society, 1977) 271-276

52 *Ibid.* 271-272.
    Wheeler, *op. cit.* 74
    Monroe Citizen Democrat. September 23, 1964.

53 Personal account of writer

54 *Ibid.*
55 *Maryville-Alcoa Times*, September 6, 1963.
    Maryville Enterprise, September 13, 1963 and September 30, 1964. by Joe Halburnt.
56 *Maryville-Alcoa Times*, August 7, 1964, September 24, 1964.
    Madisonville Democrat, September 24, 1964.
57 *Knoxville Journal*, November 17,1963, October 17, 1964.
    Maryville-Alcoa Times, September 13, 1963, October 14, 1964.
58 *Maryville Enterprise,* November 18, 1964.
    Charlotte Observer, January 19, 1965, by Tom Higgins.
59 *Knoxville News Sentinel*, October 12, 1963
    Ibid. November 17, 1963, by Carson Brewer. *Tennessee Citizen*, October 23, 1964.
60 *Maryville-Alcoa Times*, October 14, 1964.
    Knoxville Journal, October 17, 1964.
61 *Maryville-Alcoa Times*, September 24, 1964.
    Madisonville Democrat, September 24, 1964.
    Knoxville News-Sentinel, March 30, 1965.
62 Hearing attended by John M. Lackey, Burl Moser, others many times.
    House Public Works Appropriations Committee, 1966.
    Hearings before the Senate Subcommittee, 89th Congress, 1965.
    And others, but no newspaper accounts of their visits to Washington DC. through the years of the struggle to save the Little T.
63 *Chattanooga Free-Press*, December 18, 1964.
    Ibid. August 6, 1964. by Bob Burch.
    William Bruce Wheeelr and Michael J. McDonald. *TVA and the Tellico Dam 1936-1979: A Bureaucratic Crisis in Post-Industrial America.* (Knoxville, TN. University of Tennesee Press, 1986) 127-130.
64 Personal account of David D. Dickey. November 19, 2003.
65 *Ibid.*
    Maryville-Alcoa News, October 14, 1964. *The Knoxville Journal*, October 17, 1964.
66 *Knoxville Journal*, April 6, 1965.
    Knoxville News-Sentinel, March 30, 1965. *East Tennessee Citizen*, October 23, 1964.
67 *Ibid.*
68 *Chattanooga Times*, April 5, 1965 and April 6, 1965. Other area newspapers.
69 Personal account of David D. Dickey, November 19, 2003.
    Wheeler. *op. cit.* 71.

70   *Ibid.*

71   *Knoxville Journal*, April 5, 1965, by Walter Amann.
      Knoxville News-Sentinel, April 5, 1965.

72   *Ibid.*

73   Anne Broome. *Harvey Broome: Earth Man.* (Knoxville, TN, Greenbriar Press, 1970.) p. viii.
      William O. Douglas. *Points of Rebellion.* (Garden City, New York, Doubleday and Company, 1970.)

74   *Chattanooga Times*, April 5, 1965.
      Knoxville Journal, April 5, 1965.

75   Wheeler. *op. cit.* 130-131,83-84.
      Account of David D. Dickey, November 19, 2003.

76   Wheeler, *op. cit.*, 82, 85.
      Account of David D. Dickey, November 19, 2003

77   *The Chattanooga Times*, April 6, 1965.
      Account by David D. Dickey,November 19, 2003.

78   Paul Kelley, *Fort Loudoun: the After Years, 1760-1960.* Tennessee Historical Quarterly, December 1961. vol XX, no. 4, p. 1, 9-12.
      Alberta and Carson Brewer, *Valley So Wild: A Folk History.* East Tennessee Historical Society. 1975. 31-40.

79   Interview with Bill Selden, member Fort Loudoun Association in 1960 and before.
      Observation of Frances B. Dorward.

80   *Chattanooga Times*, Chattanooga, Tennessee. December 9, 1964.
      Conservation News. National Wildlife Federation Washington, D. C. January 1, 1965.

81   *Knoxville Journal*, October 17, 1964.
      Chattanooga News-Free Press, January 15, 1965.

82   Testimony of personal friends Sarah Simpson Bivens, Bill Seldon.
      Monroe Citizen-Democrat, Madisonville, Tennessee. February 3, 1965

83   *Knoxville Journal*, February 1, 1965.
      Knoxville News-Sentinel. February 6, 1965.

84   *Knoxville Journal*, April 5, 1965.
      Observation of Frances Brown Dorward

85   *Ibid.*
      Observation of C. Griffin Martin and Johnnie Bell Kirkland.

86   *Chattanooga Times*, June 17, 1965.
      Interview with Sarah Simpson Bivens, January 2004.

[87]   *Knoxville News-Sentinel*, April 13, 1965.

William Bruce Wheeler and Michael J. McDonald, *TVA and the Tellico Dam: 1936-1979.* (Knoxville, Tennessee. University of Tennessee Press, 1986) 191, 215.

[88]   Observation at Fort Loudoun State Park, by Frances Brown Dorward and Bill Selden.

[89]   Jefferson Chapman, *Tellico Archaeology: 12,000 Years of Native American History.* (Knoxville, Tennessee, Tennessee Valley Authority, 1985) iii

William Bruce Wheeler and Michael J. McDonald. *TVA and the Tellico Dam 1936-1979: A Bureaucratic Crisis in Post-Industrial America.* (Knoxville, TN. University of Tennessee Press, 1986). ix

[90]   *Ibid.*

[91]   *Ibid.*

[92]   Interview with Roy and Burma Kennedy, January 29, 2003.

[93]   Chapman, Jefferson. *Tellico Archaeology: 12,000 years of Native American History.* (Knoxville, Tennessee, The Tennessee Valley Authority, 1985), 121.

[94]   Diamond, Jared. *Collapse: How Societies Choose to Fail or Succeed.* (New York, New York, Viking Penguin, 2005

[95]   Interview with Sarah Ann Simpson, Bivens, January 2004.

[96]   *Ibid.*

J. G. M. Ramsey. *The Annals of Tennessee to the End of the Eighteenth Century.* (originally printed 1853, Charleston, South Carolina, Walker and James, 1853; reprinted Kingston, Tennessee, Kingston Press, 1926) 323, 389, 569, 588, 658, 659, 663, 666.

[97]   Interview with Sarah Ann Simpson Bivens, January 2004.

[98]   *Ibid.*

Earl Mazo. *World Book Encyclopedia,* (Chicago, USA. Field Enterprise, 1974) vol 14, 336h.

[99]   Clint Bolick, *Levathan: The Growth of Local Government and the Erosion of Liberty.* (Stanford, California, Hoover Institution Press, 2004), 88, 94.

William Bruce Wheeler and Michael J. McDonald. *TVA and the Tellico Project 1936-1979.* (Knoxville, Tennessee, University of Tennessee Press, 1986) 142.

[100] Maryville-Alcoa Daily Times, December 9, 1964.

Chattanooga Times, December 9, 1964.

[101] Wheeler, *op. cit.* 89-110.

Nation's Business. November 1965. pp. 47-48. by U. S. Chamber of Commerce.

[102] *Monroe Citizen Democrat*, February 17, 1965 by Judge Sue K. Hicks
Monroe Citizen Democrat, February 10, 1965 by Paul Evans, TVA Director of Information.

[103] *News-Sentinel*, October, 21, 1964.
News-Sentinel, January 18, 1965.

[104] *Nation's Business*, November 1965, vol 3, no.1,
Tennessee Perspective, October 23, 1983.
Maryville-Alcoa Daily Times, February 11, 1999.

[105] Ray H. Jenkins. *The Terror of Tellico Plains*. (Knoxville, Tennessee, East Tennessee Historical Society, 1978)
Wheeler, *op. cit* 126

[106] Edited by Walton Beacham, Frank V. Castronova, Suzanne Sessine. *Beacham's Guide to the Endangered Species of North America*. (Detroit, Michigan, Gale Group Publishers, 2001), Vol. 2, 1086-1088.
Helen Cothran, editor. *Opposing Viewpoints: Endangered Species*. (San Diego, California, Greenhaven Press, 2001)

[107] Wheeler, *op cit.* 144-145.
Knoxville News-Sentinel and Chattanooga News Free-Press, March 3, 1972.

[108] Interview with Sarah Simpson Bivens, January, 2004.

[109] *Ibid.*

[110] *Ibid.*

[111] *Ibid.*

[112] *Ibid.*

[113] *Ibid.*

[114] *Ibid.*

[115] *Ibid.*

[116] *Ibid.*

[117] *Ibid.*

[118] *Ibid.*

[119] *Ibid.*

[120] *Ibid.*

[121] *Ibid.*

[122] *Ibid.*

[123] *Ibid.*

[124] Conversation with Sarah Ann Sinpson Bivens, January 2007.

[125] *Ibid*

[120] Visit by Frances B. Dorward, May 1, 2006.

[121] Interview with Mabel and Charles Niles.

[122] *Ibid.*

Alberta and Carson Brewer. *Valley So Wild: A Folk History.* (Knoxville, Tennessee, East Tennessee Historical Society, 1975.) 88-91, 211.

[123] Interview with Mabel and Charles Niles, May, 2006.

[124] *Ibid.*

[125] *Ibid.*

Wheeler, *op cit.* 222.

[126] *Ibid.* 142.

Interview with Mabel and Charles Niles, May 2006.

[127] *Ibid.*

[128] *Ibid.*

[129] *Ibid.*

[130] *Ibid.*

[131] *Ibid.*

[132] *Ibid.*

[133] *Ibid.*

[134] *Ibid.*

[135] *Ibid.*

[136] *Ibid.*

[137] *Ibid.*

[138] *Ibid.*

[139] *Ibid.*

[140] *Ibid.*

[141] *Ibid.*

Atlanta Journal-Constitution, October 19, 2003 and *Chattanooga Times Free-Press,* February 8, 2004.

[142] Interview with Charles Niles, May, 2006.

[143] *Ibid.*

[144] *Ibid.*

[145] *Ibid.*

[146] *Ibid.*

[147] *Ibid.*

[148] *Ibid.*

[149] *Ibid.*

[150] Interview with Beryl Moser, February, 2004.

Knoxville Journal, November 14, 1979.

[151] *Ibid.*

[152] *Ibid.*

[153] *Ibid.*

William Bruce Wheeler and Michael J. McDonald. *TVA and the Tellico Project 1936-1979: A Bureaucratic Crisis In Post-Industrial America*. (Knoxville, Tennessee, University of Tennessee Press. 1986). 21-222, 142.

TVA land Branch Records, Chattanooga, Tennessee.

Atlanta Journal-Constitution, October 19, 2003.

154 *Ibid.*

Atlanta Journal-Constitution, October 19, 2003.

155 *Ibid.*

156 *Ibid.*

Interview with Alfred Davis, January 15, 2004

157 Interview with Beryl Moser, February, 2004.

Knoxville Journal, November 14, 1979. Knoxville News-Sentinel, June 5, 2001.

158 Interview with Beryl Moser, February, 2004.

159 *Ibid.*

Wheeler, *Op. cit.* 214-215.

160 Interview with Beryl Moser, February, 2004.

161 *Ibid.*

162 *Ibid.*

163 *Ibid.*

164 *Ibid.*

165 Interview with Alfred Davis, Loudon County, Tennessee. January 15, 2004.

166 *Ibid.*

167 *Ibid.*

168 *Ibid.*

169 *Ibid.*

170 *Ibid.*

171 *Ibid.*

172 *Ibid.*

William Bruce Wheeler and Michael J. McDonald. *TVA and the Tellico Project 1936-1979: A Bureaucratic Crisis in Post-Industrial America*. (Knoxville, Tennessee, University of Tennessee Press. 1986) 142.

173 Interview with Alfred Davis, January 15, 2004.

174 *Ibid.*

175 *Ibid.*

176 *Ibid.*

177 *Ibid.*

178 *Ibid.*

179 *Ibid.*

Wheeler, *op. cit. 194, 207, 73, 130.*
[180] Interview with Alfred Davis, January 15, 2004.
[181] *Ibid.*
Wheeler, *op.cit* 64-66.
Knoxville News-Sentinel, Knoxville Journal, and Chattanooga News-Free Press, September 23, 1964
[182] Wheeler, *op cit.* 210.
Alternative Report #1, division of Water Resources, August 18, 1976.
Zygmunt J. B. Plater. *Reflected in a River: Agency accountability and the TVA Tellico Dam Case,"*
Tennessee Law Review 49 (1982), 47-787.
[183] Wheeler, *op cit.* 212.
Knoxville News-Sentinel, July 18, 1979, *Kingsport Times,* July 18, 1979.
[184] *Knoxville News-Sentinel,* June 18, 1978
Wheeler, *op. cit. 156-157.*
[185] *Ibid.* 204-205.
Interview with Alfred Davis, January 15, 2004.
[186] *Ibid.*
[187] *Ibid.*
Wheeler, *op cit.* 189-190
[188] Interview with Alfred Davis, January 15, 2004.
[189] *Ibid.*
[190] *Ibid.*
[191] The Holy Bible. Revised Standard Version. (Grand Rapids, Michigan, Zondervan Bible Publishers, 1952) Ecclesiastes 3:1-8. 973.
[192] Interview with Margie Moser Swafford, March, 2004.
[193] *Ibid.*
[194] *Ibid.*
[195] *Ibid.*
[196] *Ibid.*
[197] Wiliam Bruce Wheeler and Michael J. McDonald. TVA and the Tellico Dam: 1936-1979: *A Bureaucratic Crisis in Post-Industrial America.* Knoxville, Tennessee, University of Tennessee Press. 1986. 127-128.
Tennessee Record, September 13, 1963.
[198] Interview with Margie Moser Swafford (Mrs. Wade), March, 2004.
Wheeler, *op. cit.* 126.
[199] Wheeler, *op. cit.* 12.
Interview with Margie Moser Swafford, March, 2004
[200] *Ibid.*

201   *Ibid.*
202   *Ibid.*
203   *Ibid.*
204   *Ibid.*
205   *Ibid.*
206   *Ibid.*
207   *Ibid.*
208   *Ibid.*
209   *Ibid.*
210   *Ibid.*
211   *Ibid.*
212   *Ibid.*
213   *Ibid.*
214   *Ibid.*
215   *Ibid.*
216   *Ibid.*
217   *Ibid.*
218   *Ibid.*
219   *Ibid.*
220   *Ibid.*
221   *Ibid.*
222   *Ibid.*
223   Interview with Fred Tallent, May, 2003.
224   *Ibid.*
225   *Ibid.*
226   *Ibid.*
227   *Ibid.*
228   *Ibid.*
229   *Ibid.*
230   William Bruce Wheeler and Michael J. McDonald. *TVA and the Tellico Project 1936-1979: A Bureaucratic Crisis in Post-Industrial America.* (Knoxville, Tennessee, University of Tennessee Press. 1986) 222.
          Knoxville Journal, November 14, 1979
231   Sam Venable. *Old Wounds Take a While to Heal. The News-Sentinel,* December 3, 2006.
          Skyway News, Spring, 2006
232   Wheeler, op. cit, 218 on TRDA, 212 Duncan violates House rules
          Chattanooga Times Free-Press, February 8, 2004. by Chris Joyner and Will Morris on TVA land changes along Tellico Reservoir

[233] Interview with Fred Tallent, May, 2003.

    The News-Sentinel, September 23, 1964. Letter by Aubrey Wagner.

    The News-Sentinel, October 7, 1964. Letter by Gilbert Stewart, TVA Informational Director

[234] Interview with Fred Tallent, May, 2003.

    Skyway News, Spring, 2006. by Melissa Kinton

[235] Interview with Fred Tallent, May, 2003

[236] *Ibid.*

[237] *Ibid.*

[238] *Ibid.*

[239] *Ibid.*

    Wheeler *op. cit.* 76. Wheeler names Mrs. James Carson of Vonore.

[240] Interview with Fred Tallent, May, 2003.

[241] *Ibid.*

[242] *Ibid.*

[243] *Ibid.*

[244] Interview with Herbert and Edith Millsaps, June, 2006.

[245] Interview with Ricky and Mary Fay Maynard, July, 2005.

[246] Interview with Earl Melson, March, 2003.

[247] Interview with Mrs. Billie Curtis and her son Tommy Curtis, July, 2005

[248] Interview with Muriel Shadow Mayfield (Mrs. Scott), July, 2004.

[249] *Ibid.*

[250] *Ibid.*

[251] *Ibid.*

[252] William Bruce Wheeler and Michael J McDonald. *TVA and the Tellico Project 1936-1979: A Bureaucratic Crisis in Post-Industrial America.* (Knoxville, Tennessee, University of Tennessee Press. 1986) 142.

    Sam Venable. *Old Wounds Take Awhile to Heal. The Knoxville News-Sentinel,* December 3, 2006.

[253] Interview with Muriel Shadow Mayfield, July, 2004.

[254] Wheeler, *op. cit.* 64-66

    Knoxville Journal, Chattanooga News-Free Press. September 23, 1964.

[255] *Knoxville Journal,* October 12, 1964 by John H. Murrian.

    Field and Stream Magazine, March, 1965 by Richard Starnes. 16.

[256] Interview with Muriel Shadow Mayfield.

[257] Wheeler, *op cit.* 131. *True Magazine,* May, 1969 *This Valley Waits to Die.*

    Wheeler, *op. cit.* 205. S. David Freeman, *Alternatives.*

[258] *Daily Post Athenian,* June 9, 1965.

    Field and Stream Magazine, Op. cit.

259   *Beacham's Guide to the Endangered Species of North America.* Edited by Walton
      Beacham, Frank V. Castronova, Suzanne Sessine. (Detroit, Michigan, Gale
      Group, 2001) vol. 2: 1086.

         W. C. Starnes. *The Ecology and Life History of the Endangered Snail Darter.*
      PhD Dissertation, (Knoxville, Tennessee, The University of Tennessee, 1977).

260   Interview with Muriel Shadow Mayfield and Zyg Plater
         Wheeler, *op. cit.* 188-189.

261   Wheeler, *op. cit.* 192 and 108.

         Hearings before the Subcommittee. Senate, 89th Congress, 2nd Session,
      pt. 4. 68.

262   Interview with Muriel Shadow Mayfield.

263   *Ibid.*

264   *Ibid.*

265   *Ibid.*

266   *Ibid.*

267   *Ibid.*

268   *Ibid.*

269   *Ibid.*

270   *Ibid.*

271   *Ibid.*

272   Interview with Ben Snyder

273   *Ibid.*

274   *Ibid.*

275   *Ibid.*

276   *Ibid.*

277   *Ibid.*

278   *Ibid.*

279   *Ibid.*

280   William Bruce Wheeler and Michael J McDonald. *TVA and the Tellico Dam.*
      (Knoxville, Tennessee The University of Tennessee, Knoxville. 1986) 222. TVA,
      Land Branch Records, Chattanooga.

281   Knoxville News Sentinel, June 5, 2001. Wheeler 60,61, 67, 68

282   Interview with Ben Snyder, August 12, 2004.

283   *Ibid.*

284   *Ibid.*

285 *Ibid.*

    Epigram: William O. Douglas. *My Wilderness East To Katahdin*. (Garden City, New York. Doubleday & Company. 1961.) 179

286 Interview with Juanita McCollum, February, 2003.

287 Interview with Shirley McCollum Brown, March, 2004.

288 *Ibid.*

289 *Ibid.*

290 *Maryville-Alcoa Daily Times*, October 14, 1964.
    Knoxville Journal, October 17, 1964.

291 Shirley McCollum Brown, March, 2004.

292 *Ibid.*

293 William Bruce Wheeler and Michael J. McDonald. *TVA and the Tellico Dam 1936-1979: A Bureaucratic Crisis in Post-Industrial America*. (Knoxville, Tennessee, the University of Tennessee Press, 1986) 212.
    Knoxville News-Sentinel, June 19, 1979. *Kingsport Times*, June 26, 1979.

294 Interview with Shirley McCollum Brown, March, 2004.

295 *Ibid.*

296 *Ibid.*

295 *Ibid..*

297 *Maryville Alcoa Times*, October 14, 1964
    Knoxville Journal, October 17, 1964

298 Interview with Shirley McCollum Brown

299 *Ibid.*

300 William Bruce Wheeler and Michael J. McDonald, *TVA and the Tellico Dam 1936-1979: A Bureaucratic Crisis in Post-Industrial America*. (Knoxville, Tennessee, University of Tennessee Press, 1986) 212. Knoxville News-Sentinel, June 19, 1979. Kingsport Times, June 26, 1979.

301 Interview with Shirley McCollum Brown

302 *Ibid.*

303 Interview with J. R. Pugh

304 Interview with Billie Jo Slatton Steele, October 1, 2006
    Knoxville Journal, February 16, 1965. Condemnation System.

305 Interview with Billie Jo Steel, October 1, 2006

306 Interview with Joey Steele, August 26, 2006

307 *Ibid.*

308 *Ibid.*

    Alberta and Carson Brewer, *Valley So Wild: A Folk History*. (Knoxville, TN, East Tennessee Historical Society, 1975) 128-129, and 153-154.

309 Interview with Joey Steele, August 26, 2006

310 *Ibid.*

311 *Ibid.*

312 *Ibid.*

313 *Ibid.*

314 *Ibid.*

315 *Ibid.*

316 *Ibid.*

317 *Ibid.*

318 *Ibid.*

319 William Bruce Wheeler and Michael J. McDonald. *TVA and the Tellico Dam 1936-1979: A Bureaucratic Crisis in Post-Industrial America.* (Knoxville, Tennessee, University of Tennessee Press, 1986) 219.
    Interview with Alfred Davis and Ben Snider.

320 Interview with Joey Steele, August 26, 2006
    Wheeler, *op. cit.* 215.

321 Interview with Joey Steele, August 26, 2006

322 *Chattanooga Times*, March 24, 1965. Wagner Argues for Dam Project.
    Knoxville Journal, April 7, 1965. Support Urged.

323 *Knoxville News-Sentinel*, April 3, 1965. Bert Vincent on land buying
    Daily Post-Athenian, November 17, 2006. Sale of TVA public lands

324 Interview with Joey Steele, August 26, 2006.

325 *Ibid.*

326 *Ibid.*

327 *Ibid.*

328 *Maryville-Alcoa Times*, September 6, 1963. by Joe Halburnt.
    Knoxville News-Sentinel, November 17, 1963, by Carson Brewer.

329 William Bruce Wheeler and Michael J. McDonald. *TVA and the Tellico Project 1936-1979: A Bureaucratic Crisis in Post-Industrial America.* (Knoxville, Tennessee, University of Tennessee Press. 1986), 156-157.
    Jim Thompson and Cynthia Brooks. *The Tellico Dam and the Snail Darter.*(Tellico Plains, Tennessee, Tellico Publications, 1991)
    Area newspapers: *Nashville Banner, Saint Louis Post-Dispatch and Knoxville News-Sentinel*, June 15, 1978.

330 Wheeler, *op cit*, 192.
    Area newspapers; Knoxville News-Sentinel, October 27 and December 4, 1974, Chattanooga Times, December 4, 1974.

331 Wheeler, *op. cit.* p. 208.
    Area newspapers: *Nashville Banner, Saint Louis Post-Dispatch and Knoxville-News-Sentinel, June 15, 1978.*

332　*Ibid.*

333　*Knoxville News-Sentinel,* March 14, 1975.
　　　Zygmunt J. B. Plater, "Reflected in a River: Agency Accountability and the TVA Tellico Dam Case," *Tennessee Law Review* 49 (1982), 747-787.

334　Wheeler, *op Cit,* 212.
　　　Knoxville News-Sentinel, June 19, 1979.
　　　Knoxville News-Sentinel, July 18, 1979 and September 11, 1979.

335　Interviews with Alfred Davis, Shirley McCollum Brown

336　Interview with Zygmnut Plater, May, 2004
　　　William Bruce Wheeler and Michael J. McDonald. *TVA and the Tellico Project 1936-1979: A Bureaucratic Crisis in Post-Industrial America.* (Knoxville, Tennessee, University of Tennessee Press. 1986) 188-189.

337　*Ibid.* 195.

338　Interviews with Hiram Hill, Peter Alliman, Zygmunt Plater.

339　*Ibid.*
　　　Wheeler, *op. cit.,* 194.

340　Clint Bolick. *Leviathan: The Growth of Local Government and the Erosion of Liberty.* (Stanford, California, Hoover Institution Press. 2004) 86. 169.
　　　Knoxville News-Sentinel, January 19, 1965.

341　Wheeler, *op. cit.,*195.
　　　Interview with Zygmunt Plater, May, 2004.

342　*Ibid.*

343　*Ibid.*

344　*Ibid.*

345　Wheeler, *op. cit.,* 91, 144.
　　　Walter Beacham, Frank V. Castronova, Suzanne Sessine, editors. *Beacham's Guide to the Endangered Species of North America.* (Detroit, Michigan. Gale Group, 2001) Vol. 2, 1088.

346　Interviews with Peter Alliman, Hiram Hill.

347　*Chattanooga Times, Knoxville Journal,* and *Oak Ridger,* October 16, 1978.

348　*Knoxville New-Sentinel,* June 19, 1978.
　　　Newsweek Magazine, June, 26, 1978.

349　Interview with Zygmunt Plater and Thomas Beryl Moser.
　　　Knoxville News-Sentinel, June 19, 1979.

350　Wheeler, *op. cit.,* 212.
　　　Knoxville News-Sentinel, June 19, 1979. *Kingsport Times.* June 26, 1979.

351　Interview with Zygmunt Plater, April, 2004.

[352] William Bruce Wheeler and Michael J. McDonald. *TVA and the Tellico Project 1936-1979: A Bureaucratic Crisis in Post-Industrial America.* (Knoxville, Tennessee, University of Tennessee Press, 1986) 192.
Knoxville News-Sentinel, October 27 and December 4, 1974.

[353] Interview with Peter Alliman, March, 2003.
David Dale Dickey. *The Little Tennessee River As an Economic Resource: A Study of Its Potential Best Use.* (Norman, Oklahoma, University of Oklahoma, 1964).

[354] Wheeler and McDonald, *op. cit.,* 156-157.
Knoxville News-Sentinel. June 18, 1978.

[355] Interview with Peter Alliman, March 13, 2003.

[356] *Ibid.*
Knoxville Journal, February 1, 1965.

[357] Wheeler and McDonald, *op. cit.,*108.
Jim Thompson and Cynthia Brooks. *Tellico Dam and the Snail Darter.* (Tellico Plains, Tennessee, Tellico Publications, 1991).

[358] Wheeler and McDonald. *op. cit.,*190-191.
Ibid. 138.

[359] *Ibid.* 190, 206.
Knoxville News-Sentinel, December 15, 1963. by Bill Felknor.

[360] Wheeler and McDonald, *Op. cit., 190,* 188, 193.
Zygmunt J. B. Plater. *Reflected in a River: Agency Accountability and the TVA Tellico Dam Case."* Tennessee Law Review 49 (1982). 747-787.

[361] Wheeler and McDonald, *op. cit.,* 297-208.
Chattanooga News-Free Press, July 20, 1965.

[362] Wheeler and McDonald, *op. cit.,*212.
Knoxville News-Sentinel, June 19, 1979.

[363] Wheeler and McDonald, *op. cit.,* 206.
Maryville-Alcoa Times, September 6, 1963 and September 13, 1963.

[364] Jefferson Chapman, *Tellico Archaeology.* (Knoxville, Tennessee, The Tennessee Valley Authority, 1985) 1-3.
Warren K. Moorehead. *Prehistoric Implements.* (Cincinnati, Ohio, Robert Clarke Company, 1900) 67, figure 78.

[365] Interview with Peter Alliman, August 13, 2003.
Interviews with Realtors Shirley McCollum Brown and Richard Lane.

[366] *Maryville-Alcoa Times,* September 6, 1963. *The Developing Trout Fishery.*
Field and Stream Magazine, January, 1964, Volume LXVIII N0. 9

[367] Interview with Hiram (Hank) Hill, August 13, 2004.

D. A. Etnier. "*Percina tancest, a New Percid Fish from the Little Tennessee River, Tennessee.*" Proceeds of the Biological Society 88 (44): 469-645. 1976.

[368] Walter Beacham, Frank V. Castronova, Suzanne Sessine, editors. Beacham's Guide to the Endangered Species of North America. (Detroit, Michigan. Gale Group. 2001) Vol. 2, 1086-1088.

Interview with Hiram Hill, August 13, 2004.

[369] Interview with Peter Alliman, Zyg Plater, and Hiram Hill.

[370] William Bruce Wheeler and Michael J. McDonald. *TVA and the Tellico Project 1936-1979: A Bureaucratic Crisis in Post-Industrial America.* (Knoxville, Tennessee, University of Tennessee Press, 1986) 196-197.

Knoxville News-Sentinel, October 15, 1976, and *Chattanooga Free-Press,* January 31, 1979.

[371] Wheeler and McDonald, *op. cit., 88.*

Interview with Hiram Hill, and with Dr. David Etnier.

[372] *Ibid.*

Wheeler and McDonald, *op. cit.,* 190-193.

[373] *Ibid.* 197.

Interview with Alfred Davis and with Thomas Beryl Moser

[374] Interview with Hiram Hill, August 13, 2004.

Wheeler and McDonald, *op. cit.,* 144-145.

[375] J. G. M Ramsey. *Annals of Tennessee to the End of the Eighteenth Century.* (originally printed by Walker and James, Charleston, S. C., 1853. reprinted Kingsport, Tennessee, Kingsport Press. 1926). Coyatee Treaty, p. 343, 679.

Alberta and Carson Brewer. *Valley So Wild: A Folk History.* (Knoxville, Tennessee. East Tennessee Historical Society. 1977.) 56.

[376] Wheeler and McDonald, *op. cit.,* 145.

Interview with Hiram Hill and with Alfred Davis.

[377] *Ibid.*

Clint Bolick. *Leviathan: The Growth of Local Government and the Erosion of Liberty.* (Stanford University, California. Hoover Institution Press. 2004) 87-91.

[378] Interview with Hiram Hill, August 13, 2004

Wheeler and McDonald. *Op. cit.,* 221-224.

[379] *Ibid.* 107.

Ray H. Jenkins. The Terror of Tellico Plains. (Knoxville, Tennessee, East Tennessee Historical Society, 1978) 190.

[380] Wheeler and McDonald. *op. cit.,* 126-127. and 215.

Interview with Margie (Mrs. Wade) Swafford and with Alfred Davis.

CBS Evening News, November 13, 1979 in Vanderbilt University Television News Archives

[381] Wheeler and McDonald, *op. cit.,* 173.

Knoxville News-Sentinel, January 9, 1972

[382] Interview with Hiram Hill, August 13, 2004.

Field and Stream Magazine. January, 1964, Volume LXVIII no. 9.

[383] Interview with Hiram Hill, August 13, 2004.

[384] Wheeler and McDonald, *op. cit.,* 196.

Chattanooga Free-Press, February 26, 1976.

[385] Interviews with Hiram Hill, Zygmunt Plater, Peter Alliman.

[386] *Ibid.*

Wheeler and McDonald, *op. cit.,* 208.

[387] *Ibid.*

Interview with Hiram Hill, August 13, 2004.

[388] Wheeler and McDonald. *op. cit.,* 208-209.

Chattanooga Times, Knoxville Journal, and Oak Ridger, October 16, 1978.

[389] *Ibid.*

Wheeler and McDonald, *op. cit.,* 211-212.

[390] Interview with Hiram Hill, August 13, 2004.

[391] *Ibid.*

[392] *Ibid.*

[393] *Ibid.*

[394] Wheeler and McDonald. *op. cit.* 198.

Knoxville News-Sentinel, January 31, 1977, and *Newsweek Magazine,* February 21, 1977.

[395] Interview with Hiram Hill, August 13, 2004.

[396] *Ibid.*

[397] Wheeler and McDonald, *op. cit.,* 212.

[398] *Ibid.*

Interviews with Hiram Hill, Zygmunt Plater, and Peter Alliman.

[399] *Ibid.*

Wheeler and McDonald, *op. cit.,* 213.

[400] *Ibid.* 214.

Interview with Hiram Hill, August 13, 2004.

[401] *Ibid.*

[402] *Ibid.*

[403] Interview with Dr. David Etnier, February, 2004.

[404] *Ibid.*

[405] *Ibid.*

William Bruce Wheeler and Michael J. McDonald. *TVA and the Tellico Dam 1936-1979: A Bureaucratic Crisis in Post-Industrial America.* (Knoxville, Tennessee, University of Tennessee, 1986) 157.

[406] *Ibid.* 192.

Interview with Dr. David Etnier, February, 2004.

[407] *Ibid.*

Beacham's Guide to the Endangered Species of North America. Edited by Walton Beacham, Frank V. Castronova, and Suzanne Sessine. Gale Group, Detroit, 2001. Vol.2, 1086-1088.

[408] *Ibid.*

Interview with Dr. David Etnier, February, 2004.

[409] Etnier, D. A. 1976. *"Percina tanasi, a New Percid Fish from the Little Tennessee River, Tennessee." Proceeds of the Biological Society* 88 (44): 469-645.

Interview with Dr. David Etnier, February, 2004.

[410] *Ibid.*

[411] *Ibid.*

Wheeler, *op cit.,* 188.

[412] *Ibid.* 192-193, and chapter 5 on cost-benefits 87-110.

Knoxville News-Sentinel and the Chattanooga Free-Press, January 8, 1972.

[413] *Knoxville News-Sentinel,* February 4, 1977. *New York Times,* February 25, 1977.

[414] Interview with Dr. David Etnier, February, 2004.

Wheeler, *op. cit.,* 07-208. TVA v. Hill, 437 U.S. 153, 1978. *Knoxville News-Sentinel,* June 15, 1978.

[415] *Ibid.*

[416] *Ibid.* 212.

Knoxville News-Sentinel, June 19, 1979. *Kingsport Times,* June 26, 1979.

[417] Interview with Dr. David Etnier, February, 2004.

[418] Wheeler, *op. cit.,* 188.

Wayne C. Starnes. "The Ecology and Life History of the Endangered Snail Darter." Ph D Dissertation, University of Tennessee, Knoxville. 143

[419] Interview with Dr. David Etnier, February. 2004.

[420] *Ibid.*

[421] *Ibid.*

[422] *Ibid.*

[423] *Ibid.*

[424] *Ibid.*

[425] *Ibid.*

[426] Interview with Jefferson Chapman, J. R. Pugh, Jr., and Richard Lane.

[427] Jefferson Chapman, *Tellico Archaeology 12,000 Years of Native American History.* (Knoxville, Tennessee, Tennessee Valley Authority, 1985), pps. 2, 8, 11, 23, 38, 40-44, 48, 66, 70-72.

Emma Lila Fundaburk and Mary Douglas Foreman, *Sun Circles and Human Hands: Southeastern Indians.* (Luverne, Alabama, E. L. Fundaburk, 1957) 8-9 48.

[428] Chapman, *ob cit.*, 16 56-73, 63, 70-72.

Interview with Dr. Jefferson Chapman, March, 2004.

[429] *Ibid.*

Chapman, *op. cit.*, iii, 121, and Hopewell culture, 70-72.

[430] *Ibid.* 38-47

Alberta and Carson Brewer. *Valley So Wild: A Folk History.* (Knoxville, Tennessee, East Tennessee Historical Society, 1975) 10.

[431] Chapman, *op. cit,.* 40-43, 70-72.

Brewer, *op. cit.,* 91.

[432] *Bowater World*, April 1961.

The *Chattanooga Times*, October 6, 1960.

[433] Interviews with Jefferson Chapman and Bill Keithley.

[434] Interviews with Jefferson Chapman, Lib Kirkland, Bill Keithley.

[435] *Ibid.*

Brewer, *op. cit.,* 88-89, 212, 271, 273-274, 277, 283.

[436] Chapman, *op. cit.,* 2, 3, 11, 23, 37, 100, 102, 110.

Observation at museum and interview with Dr. Chapman, March, 2004.

[437] Chapman, *op. cit.,* iv.

Brewer, *op, cit.,* 93-97.

[438] Interview with Dr. Jefferson Chapman, March, 2004.

William Bruce Wheeler and Michael J. McDonald. *TVA and the Tellico Project 1936-1979: A Bureaucratic Crisis in Post-Industrial America.* (Knoxville, Tennessee, Tennessee Valley Authority, 1986) 200-201.

[439] *Ibid.* 191, 215 177.

Chapman, *op. cit.,* 106.

[440] *Lenoir City News Banner*, April 25, 1963.

Monroe Citizen Democrat, January 6, 1965.

[441] Interview with Melvin Sheets, May 20, 2003

[442] Interview with Beuna Frank Black February 15, 2006

[443] Interview with Lib and Homer Kirkland, September 11, 2003.

[444] Interview with Bea Duncan Bivins, September, 2005

Epigram: Holy Bible. New Internationl Version. Grand Rapids, Michigan. Zondervan Bible Publlishers. 1978. 576. Psalm 127:3

445   Interview with John R. Hall of Sweetwater-Vonore Road, also called Oak Grove Road and Old Lakeside Community. September 17, 2003.

446   William Bruce Wheeler and Michael J. McDonald. *TVA and the Tellico Dam 1936-1979: A Bureaucratic Crisis in Post-Industrial America.* (Knoxville, Tennessee, The University of Tennessee Press. 1986) 222.

      TVA Land Branch Records, Chattanooga, Tennessee.

447   Interview with Don Keeble, October 10, 2003.

448   *Ibid.*

449   *Ibid.*

450   *Ibid.*

451   *Ibid.*

      Alberta and Carson Brown, *River So Wild*, East Tennessee Historical Society, (Knoxville, Tennessee, 1977) 3-25

452   *Ibid.*

      William Bruce Wheeler and Michael J McDonald. *TVA and Tellico Dam 1936-1979: A Bureaucratic Crisis in Post Industrial America.* (Knoxville, Tennessee, University of Tennessee Press. 1986) ix

453   Warren J Morehead. *Prehistoric Implements.* Robert L Clarke Co. (Cincinnati Ohio, 1900) 135; 126-162.

      Jefferson Chapman, *Tellico Archaeology 12,000 Years of Native American History.* (Knoxville, Tennessee, Tennessee Valley Authority, 1985) 2, 8, 1, 23, 38, 40-44, 48, 66, 70-72.

454   Interview with Don Keeble, October 10, 2003

455   *Ibid.*

      William Bruce Wheeler and Michael J McDonald. *TVA and Tellico Dam 1936-1979: A Bureaucratic Crisis in Post Industrial America.* (Knoxville, Tennessee, University of Tennessee Press, 1986) 158-183.

456   *Maryville-Alcoa Daily Times*, Feb 11 1999. *Chattanooga Times*, Feb 8, 2004. *Atlanta Journal-Constitution*, Oct 19, 2003.

457   Interview with Don Keeble, October 10, 2003.

458   *Atlanta Journal-Constitution*, October 19 2003.

      Wheeler and McDonald, *op. cit., 89*-110.

459   *Maryville Daily Times*, February 11, 1999.

460   Interview with Don Keeble, October 10, 2003.

461   William Bruce Wheeler and Michael J McDonald. *TVA and Tellico Dam 1936-1979: A Bureaucratic Crisis in Post Industrial America.* (Knoxville, Tennessee: University of Tennessee Press, 1986) 218.

462   *The Chattanooga Times Free Press*, February 8 2004.

      Interviews with Alfred Davis and Don Keeble.

[463] Interview with Don Keeble, October 10, 2003.

William Bruce Wheeler and Michael J McDonald. *TVA and Tellico Dam 1936-1979: A Bureaucratic Crisis in Post-Industrial America.* (Knoxville, Tennessee. University of Tennessee Press. 1986. 219)

[464] Interview with Don Keeble, October 10, 2003.

[465] *The Chattanooga News Free Press*, August 6 1964 by Bob Birch.

William Bruce Wheeler and Michael J McDonald. *TVA and Tellico Dam 1936-1979: A Bureaucratic Crisis in Post- Industrial America.* (Knoxville, Tennessee, University of Tennessee Press. 1986) 64-86.

[466] *Ibid.* 72-73, 212.

Interview with Don Keeble, October 10, 2003.

[467] *Maryville Times,* October 14 1964. *Knoxville Journal,* October 17, 1964.

[468] Interview with Don Keeble, October 10, 2003.

[469] Interview with Bill Keithley, March, 2003.

[470] *Ibid.*

Letter to the editor, *Knoxville Journal,* February 18, 1965.

[471] *Maryville-Alcoa Times,* September 24, 1964

Madisonville Democrat, September 24, 1964.

[472] Interview with Bill Keithley, March, 2003.

[473] *Ibid.*

[474] *Ibid.*

[475] *Ibid.*

Bowater World Magazine, April 1961, by Bill Diehl

[476] Interview with Bill Keithley, March, 2003.

[477] *Ibid.*

[478] *Ibid.*

[479] *Ibid.*

Bowater World, April 1961.

[480] *Ibid.*

Interview with Bill Keithley, March, 2003.

[481] *Ibid.*

[482] *Ibid.*

[483] *Ibid.*

[484] *Ibid.*

[485] *Ibid.*

[486] *Ibid.*

[487] *Ibid.*

[488] *Ibid.*

[489] *Ibid.*

490   *Ibid.*

491   *Ibid.*

492   Interview with Louis Camisa, November, 2004.

493   Jim Thompson and Cynthia Brooks. *Tellico Dam and the Snail Darter.* (Tellico Plains, Tennessee, Tellico Publications, 1991), 115-116.

      Interview with Charles Hall, March, 2005.

494   Interview with Charles Hall, March, 2005

495   *Ibid.*

496   Magneto-a machine for producing electricity in an engine. Used before dial tone installed.

      Webster's Elementary *Dictionary.* (New York, Merriam-Webster, 1959), 372.

497   Louise Brown, Robert Clemons, Mike Hicks. *Telephones for Tennessee.* (Nashville, Tennessee, Tennessee Telephone Association, 1995) 204-296.

      Interview with Charles Hall, March, 2005.

498   *The Knoxville News-Sentinel,* January 1, 1961.

      The Maryville-Alcoa Daily Times, January 1, 1961.

499   *The Knoxville News-Sentinel,* February 7, 1965. by Mike Miller.

      Interview with Charles Hall, March, 2005.

500   *Lenoir City Newspaper,* February 25, 1965.

      Knoxville News-Sentinel, May 19, 1965.

501   Thompson and Brooks, *op. cit., 112.*

      Interview with Charles Hall, March, 2005.

502   *Ibid.*

503   *Ibid.*

504   *Ibid.*

505   *Ibid.*

506   Interview with Dr Samuel N. Luoma, U.S. Geological Survey, Senior Research Scientist, Menlo Park, California.

      William Bruce Wheeler and Michael J. McDonald. *TVA and the Tellico Dam 1936-1979: A Bureaucractic Crisis in Post-Industrial America.* (Knoxville, Tennessee. University of Tennessee Press. 1986). 124-157.

507   Interview with Charles Hall, March, 2005.

      Thompson and Brooks, *op. cit.,* 125.

508   *Ibid.* 61.

      Ibid. 68.

509   Interview with Charles Hall, March, 2005.

510   William Bruce Wheeler and Michael J. McDonald. *TVA and the Tellico Dam 1936-1979: A Bureaucratic Crisis in Post-Industrial America.* (Knoxville, Tennessee, The University of Tennessee Press. 1986) 222.

TVA Land Branch Records, Chattanooga, Tennessee.

Interview with Violet K. Wolfe, October 24, 2007

[511] Interview with Betty Griffith Wolfe, October 24, 2007

[512] Wilma Dykeman. *Tennessee: A History*. (Newport, Tennessee. Wakestone Books, 1984 and 1975) 26.

Duane H. King, editor. *The Cherokee Indian Nation: A Troubled History*. (Knoxville, Tennessee. University of Tennessee Press, 1979) 66.

The name Matoy also appears as Moyatoy, Matayi, and Unatoy.

[513] Interviews with Mrs. Elder Matoy, Earl Melson, Mildred Lane, and Don Keeble, Bill Land, and Lydia Borden Salvador.

[514] Interview with Bill Land, White Buck, April 26, 2006.

[515] *Ibid.*

[516] Jefferson Chapman, *Tellico Archaeology: 12,000 Years of Native American History*. (Knoxville, Tennessee, The Tennessee Valley Authority, 1985) 1-3.

Warren K. Moorehead. *Prehistoric Implements*. (Cincinnati, Ohio, Robert Company, 1900). 165.

[517] Interview with Bill Land, White Buck, April 26, 2006.

[518] *Ibid.*

[519] *Ibid.*

[520] *Ibid.*

[521] *Ibid.*

[522] *Ibid.*

[523] *Ibid.*

[524] *Ibid.*

[525] *Ibid.*

[526] *Ibid.*

[527] Interview with Lydia Borden Salvador, April 24, 2006

[528] *Ibid.*

[529] Note: A guess is Jarrett Williams, a trader and spy. J. G. M. Ramsey, *Annals of Tennessee to the End of the Eighteenth Century*. (originally published Charleston, South Carolina, Walker and James, 1853, reprinted Kingsport, Tennessee, Kingsport Press, 1926) 148.

Ibid. for Smith-A guess from *Ramsey's Annals* is James Smith, clerk in Land Office at Watauga, 107, 120,121,138,147.

[530] Interview with Lydia Borden Salvador, April 24 and 26, 2006.

[531] *Ibid.* Research suggests that Mentor Freeman was a private in the infantry. M.C. Freeman was listed as from Bakers, Tennessee. Other similar names are MM, MO. *Confederate Veteran Magazine*. Volume XVII, 1909, 487. Several M.

Freeman are listed in the *Prisoner of War Volumes* at Fisher Library, Athens, and on the *Rooster Lists* at the Vonore Library, Vonore, Tennessee.

[532] Interview with Lydia Borden Salvador, April 24, 2006.

[533] *Ibid.*

[534] *Ibid.*

[535] Travis Kavulla, *Jamestown in the American Eye*, *National Review*, June 11, 2007, *22*.

[536] Jefferson Chapman, *Tellico Archaeology: 12,000 Years of Native American History*. (Knoxville, Tennessee, The Tennessee Valley Authority. 1985)

   Alberta and Carson Brewer, *Valley So Wild:* A Folk *History*. (Knoxville, Tennessee, East Tennessee Historical society, 1975) 21-22, 42, 346-347.

[537] Interview with Maynard and Linda Thompson, June 16, 2007

[538] *Ibid.*

   William Bruce Wheeler and Michael J. McDonald, *TVA and the Tellico Project 1936-1979:* A Bureaucratic *Crisis in Post-Industrial America*. (Knoxville, Tennessee, University of Tennessee Press. 1986) 191-192. Meeting was October 1974.

[539] Interview with Maynard Thompson, June 16, 2007.

[540] *Ibid.*

[541] *Ibid.*

[542] *Ibid*

[543] *Ibid.*

[544] *Ibid.*

[545] *Ibid.*

[546] *Ibid.*

[547] *Ibid.*

   Possibly a goshawk, *Accipiter gentils*. Alexander Wetmore and others, *Water, Prey, and Game Birds of North America*. (National Geographic Society, 1965) 224

[548] Interview with Linda and Maynard Thompson, June 16, 2007.

[549] *Ibid.*

[550] Interview with Linda Kirkland Thompson, June 16, 2007.

[551] *Ibid.*

[552] *Ibid.*

[553] *Ibid.*

[554] *Vonore: Yesterday and Today*. (Vonore Historical Society, 1991 and 1996) Volume 1:A-Mc. Pp. 448-476. John Kirkland 477-480.

   Rand McNally Road Atlas, 1997. 70-71.

[555] Interview with Maynard and Linda Kirkland Thompson, June 16, 2007.

[556] Interview with Linda Kirkland Thompson, June 23, 2007.

[557] *Ibid.*

558 *Ibid.*

Sarah G. Cox Sands. *History of Monroe County, Tennessee. Volumes 1, 2, and 3.* (Baltimore, Maryland. Gateway Press, Inc. 1982).

Monroe County Records 1820-1870. Copied by Reba Bayless Boyer. Volume 1. 1969

559 Interview with Maynard Thompson or White Hawk, June 23, 2007.

560 *Ibid.*

561 *Ibid.*

562 Interview with Linda Kirkland Thompson, June 23, 2007

563 Interview with Maynard Thompson, June 23, 2007

564 Interview with George Smith, March 14, 2007.

565 Interview with Robert Denny Moore, July 18, 2006

566 Interview with James and Bertha Patton, July 12, 2006.

Epigraph The Holy Bible. Philadelphia. The National Bible Press. 1954. Isaiah 64:8 787

567 Millenium Ecosystem Assessment, 2005. *Ecosystems and Human Well-Being Synthesis.* Island Press, Washington, DC

568 Forest Trends, the Katoomba Group and UNEP, 2008. *Payments for Ecosystem Services Getting Started: A Primer.* Forest Trends and the Katoomba Group.

Copyedited by Bejay Villaflores

569 Interview with Bill Sloan, Jr. at his Madisonville store, April, 2006.

570 William Bruce Wheeler and Michael J. McDonald. *TVA and the Tellico Dam 1936-1979: A Bureaucratic Crisis in Post-Industrial America.* (Knoxville, TN, University of Tennessee Press, 1986) 218.

Ibid. 270, Note 11, Division of Reservoir Property Files (DRPF and Contract TV 6000A).

571 *Ibid.* 270.

Interview with Frank Isbill, March, 2007.

572 *Ibid.*

Wheeler and McDonald, *Op. cit.*, 87-110.

573 *Daily Post-Athenian*, November 17, 2006

Knoxville News Sentinel, December 3, 2006, Sam Venable's column

574 *Atlanta Journal-Constitution*, October 19, 2003.

575 Interview with Frank Isbill, March, 2007.

576 *Ibid.*

577 *Ibid.*

578 *Ibid.*

579 *Ibid.*

580 *Ibid.*

581 *Ibid.*

Index

N

LaVergne, TN USA
30 October 2009
162567LV00003B/1/P